HOLY PEOPLE

HOLY THINGS FOR THE HOLY PEOPLE.

ONLY ONE THE HOLY FATHER,
ONLY ONE THE HOLY SON,
ONLY ONE THE HOLY SPIRIT,

IN THE UNITY OF THE HOLY SPIRIT.

—*Liturgy of St. Mark*

HOLY PEOPLE

A LITURGICAL ECCLESIOLOGY

Gordon W. Lathrop

Fortress Press

Minneapolis

For Thomas D. McGonigle, O.P.
preacher of the gospel
dear friend

HOLY PEOPLE
A Liturgical Ecclesiology

First paperback edition 2006

Scripture quotations unless otherwise noted are from the New Revised Standard Version Bible, copyright © 1989 by the Division of Christian Education of the National Council of the Churches of Christ in the United States, and are used by permission.

Cover art: Images from the vaults of Lohjan Kirkko in Lohja, Finland, 16th century. Top: The cloak of Mary enfolding humanity. Bottom: The risen Christ empties the mouth of hell.

Excerpts from the Ditchingham Report are reprinted with the permission of the World Council of Churches. Excerpts from the Nairobi Statement are reprinted with the permission of the Lutheran World Federation.

ISBN-13: 978-0-8006-3840-5
ISBN-10: 0-8006-3840-9

The paper used in this publication meets the minimum requirements for American National Standard for Information Sciences—Permanence of Paper for Printed Library Materials, ANSI Z329.48–1984.

Manufactured in the U.S.A.
10   09   08   07   06   1   2   3   4   5   6   7   8   9   10

CONTENTS

Preface

The following reflections on the meaning of "church" continue the work begun with an earlier volume, *Holy Things: A Liturgical Theology* (Minneapolis: Fortress, 1993). The method of that book, its interest in both the use of strong symbols for the sake of communal orientation in the world and the strong critique of symbols for the sake of the gospel of Jesus Christ, is here extended to the symbol "assembly." Here, as in that book, widely shared patterns of Christian liturgy, not systems of Christian theology, provide the primary context for thought. Some readers—agreeing with the author that liturgical speech about *God* must be prior to a liturgically grounded discussion of the *church* and wishing to pursue a further dialogue with the author on these issues—may find it useful to follow the footnote references to passages in *Holy Things*. Other readers, wishing to see how the method used here might have been developed in close relation to the use of the Bible in Christian liturgy, may find it useful to attend especially to chapter 1 of that book. Nonetheless, readers will not need to have read the earlier work in order to approach this one. The present work may stand on its own.

This book proceeds with a simple outline. After an introductory discussion of the methodology of what is here called "liturgical ecclesiology," three parts, each three chapters long, are set out. The first, foundational part considers what is meant by "assembly" in the practice of Christian worship, how diverse Christian assemblies are related to each other, and what may be learned for the practice of such assemblies from these reflections. Then, the second part turns toward issues of *church unity* and the third part toward issues of *church and culture* in order to ask how reflections based in liturgy and liturgical assembly may be helpful in facing these burning questions of contemporary Christian life. The questions thus addressed are these: What is church? What is church unity? And what is the relationship between church and the cultures of the earth? After reflections that are based in the history and meaning of the central matters of liturgy, each section of the book concludes with an essay on *practice*. The work concludes with two recent statements on worship and unity and worship and culture, statements which were crafted by consultations for which parts of the book were originally written.

As the work proceeds, the reader will note a repeated consideration of Scripture reading and preaching, Baptism and the Eucharist. While the root meanings of these "means of grace" were given greater space in *Holy Things*, here they are considered in another light: as the center of assembly, as the heart and grounds of church unity, and as the original pattern for the church's encounter with culture. The author does not wish to minimize the immense difficulties involved in any of these inquiries about ecclesial identity, unity, and mission. But by attending to ecumenically shared liturgical data, the author hopes to engage in liturgical study itself in such a way as "to increase the understanding of what the church is" (Sven-Erik Brodd, in Oloph Bexell, ed., *Kyrkovetenskapliga forskningslinjer,* Lund: 1996, 114). Underneath and behind the work, there are prayers for the renewal of congregational life and for the visible unity and healthy mission of the churches.

The title of the book, drawn from the ancient communion invitation of the eastern liturgies, which is printed as an inscription to this volume and most fully discussed in chapter 9 below, ought always be read with its response in mind: *only one is holy.* The force of that response—and therefore the nearly ironic force of the title itself—is meant to be visually represented by the artwork of the cover: it is only a needy and sinful people whom the merciful and all-holy God draws into holiness. These images from the remarkable, early-sixteenth-century painted interiors of the parish churches of Lohja and Hattula, Finland, are most fully discussed in chapter 3.

This further writing arose out of invitations and assignments that have come to me since the publication of *Holy Things*. My deepest thanks are therefore expressed to Anita Stauffer and the Lutheran World Federation Study Team on Worship and Culture; to Thomas Best and Dagmar Heller of the World Council of Churches; to the participants in the consultations at Ditchingham, Bossey, and Faverges; to Paul Bradshaw and the Council of Societas Liturgica; to Nils-Henrik Nilsson and the participants in the

Swedish ecumenical consultation in Sigtuna; to the participants in the Uniting Church of Australia's workshop on worship in Brisbane; to Oystein Bjordal of the Liturgical Center of the Church of Norway; to Bishop Julius Filo and the participants in the theological conference in Liptovsky Mikulas, Slovakia; and to Sven-Erik Brodd, Oloph Bexell, and the graduate seminar in *kyrkovetenskap*, or ecclesiology, at the University of Uppsala, Sweden.

Because of these kind invitations, parts of the work have been published in earlier, substantially different forms: a section of chapter 2 in S. Anita Stauffer, ed., *Christian Worship: Unity in Cultural Diversity* (Geneva: Lutheran World Federation, 1996); chapter 4 in Thomas F. Best and Dagmar Heller, eds., *So We Believe, So We Pray: Towards Koinonia in Worship* (Geneva: World Council of Churches, 1995); chapter 5 in *Studia Liturgica* 26, no. 1 (1996) and *La Maison Dieu* 204 (1995); a section of chapter 6 in *The Ecumenical Review* 48, no. 1 (1996); chapter 7 in *Worship* 68, no. 6 (1994); chapters 7 and 8 in S. Anita Stauffer, ed., *Worship and Culture in Dialogue* (Geneva: Lutheran World Federation, 1994), and part of chapter 9 in *Australian Journal of Liturgy* 6, no. 3 (1998).

In addition to the editors of these publications and the persons and groups named above, I am also deeply grateful to many other partners in conversation over these last years. Only a few of them may be named here: my colleagues and students at the Lutheran Theological Seminary at Philadelphia, and the Board of that Seminary, which has so generously supported the leave in which I was able to complete the work; Timothy Wengert, Mark Mummert, and Tricia Jaskiewicz, without whose practical understanding of *assembly* as it occurs in the Seminary's chapel I would not have been able to take the leave at all; Anscar Chupungco, O.S.B., my partner and teacher in so many conversations about liturgy and culture; the professors of liturgy at the seminaries of the Evangelical Lutheran Church in America; Paul Nelson and the Task Force on Sacramental Practices of the same church; the seminar on liturgical theology of the North American Academy of Liturgy; Samuel Torvend, whose encouragement and wisdom helped bring the work to completion; Marshall Johnson, Frank Stoldt, J. Michael West, Beth Wright, and David Lott of Fortress Press; Nathaniel Lathrop, Vyshnavi Suntharalingam, Anthony Lathrop, Miriam Schmidt, and Monica Rosemary Schmidt, who always call me to honest speech; Thomas McGonigle, who said that images could be found; and Gail Ramshaw, *sine qua nihil.*

Introduction:
Liturgical Ecclesiology and Its Importance

W hat do you need in order to have *church*?[1]
Some will say, simply, you need to have a certain kind of
building. You need a steepled structure on a gentle rise in the
countryside, a medieval stone building in a European village, a massive cathe-
dral in the heart of a city. Or you need to have stained-glass windows and an
organ. You need pews. You need a bell. You need, at least, a cross on the front
wall of a space where people gather. Or burning candles. Or, somewhere in
or near the room, a tabernacle, a container for the holy bread left from the
Holy Supper. Or, in another sort of community, you need a pulpit and a
washing pool. Or you need an icon-screen and the prescribed icons. Such
answers often demonstrate nostalgia for church as it may have once been
experienced but that now seems threatened or absent. In any case, these
answers are quite concrete, reflecting both local custom and popular
experience.

This way of talking is not necessarily silly and shallow. Such responses
turn strikingly and directly to material matters of Christian worship. Those
who wish to speak of church at all would do well to speak so concretely.
Furthermore, church is sometimes threatened or absent. Anyone who cares
about community in Christ can usefully hear these very particular answers,
can usefully reflect upon this strong longing for an idealized holy place of
assembly. Yet the very particularity of the answers makes them difficult to
apply to us all. Their tendency to nostalgia may turn such longings into a
refusal to see what is actually currently present. And the absence of people

---

1. For another discussion of this question, see Gordon W. Lathrop, *Holy Things: A Liturgical Theology* (Minneapolis: Fortress, 1993), 87ff.

1

in these descriptions—or the presence of people only as an assumption or an implication—makes these responses difficult to square with the New Testament commonplace that *church* is a society, an assembly, of human beings.

Other voices answer the question conceptually, theologically. They make assertions about what a gathering or organization of people must include in order to be faithfully related to the Christian God, in order to be authentic church. You need leaders acting in a certain tradition, appointed in a certain way, a way that indicates a personal linkage to each other and to the origins of the Christian movement. Or you need teaching, texts, songs, sermons that accord with a certain confession of faith, with certain central teachings. Or you need certain holy, grace-giving actions—*sacraments* or *mysteries* or *ordinances,* the Christian tradition has called them—living at the heart of the organization. Or you need each member of the group to be marked by personal faith and by some ethical response to that faith, especially love. Or you need all of these characteristics, established in ways that accord with the practice of the faithful churches of earlier times. You thus need a practice that can be regarded as marked by the so-called "notes of the church":[2] Christian unity, holiness, catholicity, and a linkage to the apostles. Such answers are often marked by an undercurrent of reform, an intention to commend better practice or deeper understanding to one's own community of Christians.

These are not necessarily narrow answers, disconnected from ordinary life, imagining ideal communities of a yet older time. In fact, all of us continue urgently to need reform, deeper understanding, and connection to the intellectual traditions of Christians. Furthermore, theological assertions have quite concrete ways of being powerfully present in our actual communities, shaping our common life, whether or not we pay attention to them. We will do better to pay attention. We will do better to see what conceptions of God and humanity and God's church are running through our practice. Still, one problem is that these conceptual answers are sometimes mutually exclusive. Indeed, they are sometimes specifically intended to exclude other communities than one's own. Then we reach an ancient question: how are the churches of Jesus Christ one church? And a further question: how can the theologies of Christians serve the unity and the renewal of that one church?

---

2. The Nicene Creed confesses: "We believe in one holy catholic and apostolic church." These adjectives have been called the *notae ecclesiae*, the "notes" or marks of the church. For a further discussion of such marks, see chapter 2.

Other voices answer our question about the conditions needed for *church* in a way that seems to be a refusal of both theology and tradition. All you need are witness to Jesus and people who want to be there, where the witness is being made. You need an open door to the stranger and smart ways to draw that stranger in. One such smart way may be the "seeker service," using recognizable marketing techniques to draw people to a meeting that makes few demands but communicates through entertainment. Such an answer, of course, is marked by its own theology and is rooted in its own tradition, one that flourished especially on the nineteenth-century American frontier.[3] The answer is often focused on serious interest in the growth of the church.

Such answers are not necessarily simply American sales techniques applied to religion.[4] Those who wish to speak about the community around Jesus Christ need this passion for the stranger and this straightforward, pragmatic honesty about what works in the service of such passion. But can this response be equally honest about its own theological presuppositions, about what the gatherings marked by such pragmatism actually communicate about who God is and what we are before this God? Perhaps the concern for growth or for "what works" runs the danger of pushing all other values aside, including the value of being church together, in communion with the other churches of all time.

Other voices answer officially, even denominationally. You need authorization and officially designated ministers. You need these creeds or confessions, these liturgical texts, this code of laws. The intention of such answers may be a certain organizational solidarity. These answers themselves often create a new problem: how can we recognize church as existing among those Christians who do not share our official instruments of solidarity? But the official answers also often inspire creative responses to that question, ingenious ways in which the churchly reality of others, outside our group, is acknowledged, if only as an exception.

These official answers are not necessarily power-driven, hierarchical talk. If we wish to speak about how one community of Christians can be church together with other communities, across time and space, we need such concrete concern for organizational solidarity. And—given the limits of all of

3. For the roots of this American evangelical movement, see James F. White, *Protestant Worship: Traditions in Transition* (Louisville: Westminster/John Knox, 1989), 171–91.
4. Nonetheless, for a fine history of the application of commercial techniques in American religion, see R. Laurence Moore, *Selling God: American Religion in the Marketplace of Culture* (New York: Oxford University Press, 1994).

our organizations yet given also the urgent and classic calling to Christian unity—we need the creativity that these organizational responses can evoke in us as we seek to relate to others beyond our bounds. Still, can a universal Christian response to our question be given only by way of exception?

So what *do* you need in order to have church? Many other answers arise. You need a certain kind of experience, a certain kind of spirit, present in the meeting. Then that meeting may be called church: "Now we are having church!" Or you need genuine community and reliable love: "At last, I have found a real church." Or you need social protest, public engagement, and ethical action: "That is what a Christian church should really be doing." None of these answers is wrong. All point to important matters that must be remembered in any discussion about the community gathered around faith in Jesus Christ: experience of the Spirit, community, and social ethics, as well as a concrete place of assembly, unity in doctrine, passion for the stranger, and institutional solidarity. Yet, all of these answers also run some danger of being partial, of being mostly about one's own experience, one's own hopes, perhaps even mostly about oneself.

All of these voices are engaged in ecclesiology, in speech about the church. The list of such respondents could go on. So could our attempts at listening, and our discussion of the strengths and the dangers of each way of answering. Indeed, if you are a Christian, you are engaged in such talk. "Ecclesiology" sounds like an abstract word, but speech about church, about its conditions and its existence, about its well-being and its relationships, is not uncommon. It is as ordinary as a discussion about where to "go to church" next Sunday, as common as the assertion that "I don't need church to be a Christian," as fresh as an attempt to explain to a Hindu friend or a New Age-influenced acquaintance why faith and community go together in Christianity, as basic as inviting a curious but non-Christian inquirer to come to the community and see the faith in action.

Indeed, speech about church can be present in our daily life in ways that are pressing, urgent, with strong images for our longing. John, the seer of the Revelation, saw a great city, coming down out of heaven, with twelve great gates, open to "the glory and honor of the nations" (Rev. 21:26). Martin Luther sang and taught others to sing, remembering the wretchedness and need of Christian communities everywhere, "Protect your poor Christianity, that it may praise you forever."[5] John Donne, the English preacher

5. *"Beschirm' dein' arme Christenheit, dass sie dich lob' in Ewigkeit!"* For the full text of *Erhalt uns, Herr,* see W. G. Polack, *The Handbook to the Lutheran Hymnal* (St. Louis: Concordia, 1958), 191–92.

and poet, speaking amid the painful Christian divisions of the seventeenth century yet using the ancient image of the church as a single people wed to God, cried out, "Show me, deare Christ, thy Spouse, so bright and clear."[6] While we do not use any of these images in our ordinary speech, there is also alive in the searchings of many of our contemporaries the acute longing to find that community which is open to all nations, centered on God and protected by God, genuinely, brightly, here with us. At least there is a search for a community that welcomes one's own self into some association with God, a search for the truth about God in a social form. Perhaps such a longing lives in our own hearts as well. How shall we find that open, bright, faithful community? Or, rather, is the very existence of such a community the object of a deluded, idealistic quest?

This Book: A Liturgical Ecclesiology

This book joins the conversation. The intention here, too, is to speak about the community of Christians, the "people of God" (to use another biblical metaphor), the human social reality that follows from faith in Christ, the church. Here, however, the point of view about the church's conditions and its existence, about its well-being and its relationships, will be liturgical. That is, *church* will be understood here primarily as *assembly*. Church will be seen as a gathering of people to do those central things that identify them as Christian. It will be understood as the concrete meetings-for-worship we do really know. Reflection on the well-being or the fragility of the church will here be reflection on the assembly's worship. Inquiry about the openness of the church will be inquiry about the openness of that assembly. Discussion of the unity of the church will be discussion of the unity of persons within that assembly and of the links between such an assembly and other assemblies in the same town or throughout the world. Consideration of the contemporary relevance of the church will include reflection about the relationships between an assembly's liturgy and the cultural patterns of meaning that surround it. Concreteness in this discussion will be enabled by concrete reference to the actual things that occur in worship. The theology that is present in this kind of speech will be liturgical theology, the search for words adequate to what the actual worship of that assembly says about God.

6. "Holy Sonnet XVIII," in Frank J. Warnke, ed., *John Donne: Poetry and Prose* (New York: Random House, 1967), 275.

Such a way of discussing church is not necessarily an exaggerated ritualism or a romantic idealization of past practices or a reflection intended only for the so-called liturgical churches. Every Christian community has a meeting for worship. It is to that meeting that ordinary English speech refers with such usages as "Do you go to church?" or "Church took a long time today." It may be useful for all Christians to explore the implications of such ordinary speech.

Furthermore, all the other answers to the ecclesiological question have liturgical elements within themselves. The concrete building that some people envision for their answer—this is a building originally built for Christian assembly, for liturgy. The bells, the candles, the organ, the icons, the pulpit, the pool—these are elements of communal worship. So too in the theological answers: The leaders are, primarily, leaders for worship, the texts, liturgical texts. The sacraments or ordinances are the central matters of assembly. The meeting ought to enable faith and to encourage and demonstrate love, and can be criticized on whether or not it does so. Even the "notes of the church" according to the Nicene Creed—unity, holiness, catholicity, apostolicity—can be explored as notes that are first encountered in the church's liturgy.[7]

Indeed, the church-growth passion for the stranger can be seen as a passion for the stranger to be welcomed here, in the assembly for worship. The instruments of solidarity within any denomination are frequently instruments that come to expression in liturgy: approved leaders and approved texts and approved ritual procedures. The Spirit-led meeting that is truly "having church" is a meeting for worship. And authentic community and powerful social action may be expressed in and flow from such a meeting.

The liturgical elements present in these various discussions of church ought to be explored. Perhaps an approach to church by way of the concrete liturgical assembly of Christians will be able to unite certain strengths of these answers, holding the answers together, making them available to each other and to us all. Further, perhaps a liturgical ecclesiology can avoid something of the weaknesses of these answers, the ways in which our own community or an idealized community or my own taste in communities can be put too easily at the heart of a definition of "church."

This is not to say that all other discussions are misled or incomplete. On the contrary. Discussions of the church are in need of all the above men-

---

7. Cf. Geoffrey Wainwright, *Doxology: The Praise of God in Worship, Doctrine and Life* (New York: Oxford University Press, 1980), part 3, 287–434.

tioned perspectives, and more. How could we do without them? Systematic theologians connect us to the critical questions alive in the intellectual tradition of the church. Bishops call us to actual organizational responsibility. Voices passionate for the stranger, for justice, or for the Spirit keep alive New Testament themes that are easily forgotten. And the ordinary voices of those who remember a particular church can keep us concrete.

But this book intends to speak about church as assembly for worship (chapter 1). It means to discuss the linkages that connect the churches as linkages between assemblies for worship (chapter 2) and to discuss images of the church as images for those same assemblies (chapter 3). It then will inquire whether this kind of approach can help us, especially with the current questions of ecumenism (Part Two) and cultural relevance (Part Three).

Having used the liturgy to discuss the meaning of "church," the book will turn to the search for Christian unity and the relationship between Christianity and culture as test cases and clarifying applications for this ecclesiology. In the process, this book will seek to set out what the liturgy says about the church in such a way that dialogue with the many other ways of speaking about church remains open. Still, this book will not be expert in those ways, will not be an exposition of their meanings. What this book will know, what it will discuss, is church as liturgical assembly.

Such discussion on the basis of the data of worship is an instance of liturgical theology. Liturgical theology, of course, focuses its concern primarily on *God,* not on the church. Like all theology, it is "explanation" of God; it is "the search for words appropriate to the nature of God."[8] As *liturgical* theology, however, it finds the materials for such explanation, the sources for such words, in the practice of worship. Furthermore, in current parlance *primary liturgical theology* is what the actual experience of worship—for example, the actual juxtaposition of biblical texts to communal action—says of God.[9] *Secondary liturgical theology,* then, is reflection upon this thing that the liturgy "says." It is "written and spoken discourse that attempts to find words for the experience of the liturgy"[10] as that liturgy speaks of God. Furthermore, what I have elsewhere called *pastoral liturgical theology* is that secondary work as it is turned especially toward the continuing reform

8. Alexander Schmemann, *Introduction to Liturgical Theology* (New York: St. Vladimir's Seminary Press, 1975), 14. See also Lathrop, *Holy Things,* 3.

9. *Cf.* Aidan Kavanagh, *On Liturgical Theology* (New York: Pueblo Publishing, 1984), 74–75, 89.

10. Lathrop, *Holy Things,* 6.

of worship, as it seeks to help make "the liturgical experience of the Church again one of the life-giving sources of the knowledge of God."[11]

But the liturgical theologian hopes that the liturgical experience of the church will already be one of those life-giving sources. While theology speaks most appropriately about God, if it is Christian theology, the church is never far away. The faith in God that Christian theology seeks to elucidate is "the faith of the church." Though that phrase may be understood in differing ways, what is clear, from the New Testament on, is that any Christian's faith in God is held together with other people.[12] Furthermore, the God whom that faith confesses is triune, a community of being. This Trinity, this God-for-us, is also known in a social way: God has created humankind as a race of social beings; Jesus has been at the center of a movement, a meal-fellowship, that still continues; and the Spirit enlivens communities today. From the liturgical point of view, that faith in the triune God comes into existence and comes to expression as the assembly meets, as the church which is the meeting for worship happens. Then, in one sense, "the purpose of worship is to constitute the Church."[13] And "to interpret the meaning of the assembly is to interpret the meaning of 'church' and the church's faith."[14]

It is not that the assembly for worship meets around the theme of ecclesial identity. Only a degenerated church will have its own identity at the heart of the meeting. Only degenerated hymns sing primarily about who we are, using God as an exclamation point to our assertion of ourselves. Such liturgical gestures easily run the danger of the prayers of the publicly pious man of Jesus' parable, "who stood and prayed thus with himself" (Luke 18:11 RSV). As one mid-twentieth-century ditty had it, "Thank you God, for making us us." No. Rather, the meeting is appropriately about God. And the God whom Christians confess comes to expression in the Scriptures—read, preached and prayed—in the meal of Christ, and in the bath that welcomes newcomers to this assembly. These are the "holy things," the great exchanges of the liturgy, that, in the power of the Spirit, proclaim the presence and mercy of God in the face of Jesus Christ. These are the primary symbols of Christian faith communally enacted.

---

11. Schmemann, *Introduction to Liturgical Theology,* 19. *Cf.* Lathrop, *Holy Things,* 7.

12. See, for example, the references to the communal faith in the salutations to the churches at or near the beginning of several Pauline and deutero-Pauline letters: Rom. 1:8,12; 2 Cor. 1:24; Eph. 1:1,15; Phil. 1:25, 27; Col. 1:4; 1 Thess. 1:8; 2 Thess. 1:3-4.

13. Schmemann, *Introduction to Liturgical Theology,* 19.

14. Lathrop, *Holy Things,* 9.

Still, a community, an *assembly,* does these things. An assembly of people, gathered in the name of the triune God around these central things, is also among the primary symbols of Christianity. This assembly's identity is manifest—it is what it is—when it does the central things of Christian faith. If you will, the church begins to know itself not by contemplating its own identity, but by beholding the face of Christ in that word, bath, and table that manifest God's identity.[15] In these things the church is filled with the power of that Spirit to bear witness in the world to the truth about God. The meeting for worship is itself the ground and beginning of such witness. The meeting for worship is the church becoming church.

Liturgical ecclesiology thus appears as a corollary of liturgical theology. Liturgical ecclesiology will be renewed as liturgical theology is renewed.[16] Where liturgical theology tries to speak faithfully and freshly about what Christian worship says of God, there will follow a new attempt to say what Christian worship says of the church. A liturgical ecclesiology will presume and build upon a liturgical theology.

Furthermore, in analogy to liturgical theology, we can speak of the primary liturgical ecclesiology that occurs as people directly experience what church is while they are engaged in doing the liturgy. Such "ecclesiology" is experienced when worship constitutes the assembly to *be* church in God's mercy before the world. Then we can speak of the secondary and pastoral ecclesiology that occurs when spoken and written reflections systematize that liturgical experience and turn its insights toward current reform. This book is such a written reflection. Its work is secondary (especially chapters 1 and 2, 4 and 5, 7 and 8) and pastoral (especially chapters 3, 6, 9). But its

---

15. So the great Swiss Reformed liturgical theologian, Jean-Jacques von Allmen, has written, "Worship is indeed for the Church, while it waits for the Kingdom, the time and place *par excellence* at which it finds its own deep identity; the time and place at which the Church becomes what it is . . . (Yet) worship is not the time and place at which the Church becomes aware of its own identity in the sense that it might be the time and place at which the Church might discover in a purifying mirror its own image cleansed of every spot and wrinkle. It is not by looking at itself, even washed clean, that the Church learns what it is. What makes the Church first glimpse, and then see clearly, its true face is meeting with Christ . . . It is on Christ's face that the Church learns who it is." From "The theological frame of a liturgical renewal," *Church Quarterly* 2 (1969–70): 8–23, quoted in Wainwright, *Doxology,* 122.

16. "The fate of liturgics is not only similar to that of ecclesiology, but is also directly bound up with it . . . The revival of a liturgical consciousness, of a new and in fact theological interest in the liturgical tradition, has therefore accompanied the revival of ecclesiology, that genuine return to the Church which has marked the last few decades." Schmemann, *Introduction to Liturgical Theology,* 11.

invitation intends to point to the primary ecclesiology. Read the book, if you will. But then go into your assembly and be church.

Context: The Public Situation of Liturgical Ecclesiology

The task of liturgical ecclesiology can be defined in another way. Twentieth-century ecumenical thought about the church has been especially interested in asking how the unity of Christians relates to the longing for general, worldwide human unity, how the society of Christians relates to reconciliation in human society. This question presents itself as especially urgent now, at the end of a century marked by nationalism, world wars, genocide, and racism, as well as movements toward global economy and global communication. This question expresses in a global form the longing for authentic local community that we have already noted. Are such local communities, when they occur, help or hindrance to general human reconciliation? How does church fit within this discussion? One cannot fail to remember the roles churches have played in local ethnic violence throughout this century, up to the present time.

To these questions both the World Council of Churches and the Second Vatican Council responded. The church, said the Vatican Council in 1964, is "in Christ like a sacrament or as a sign and instrument both of a very closely knit union with God and of the unity of the whole human race."[17] In a very similar phrase, the World Council of Churches, meeting in Uppsala in 1968, said that the church understands itself to be "a sign of the coming unity" of humankind.[18]

One may ask if this shared assertion is true. Wolfhart Pannenberg, for example, has identified the many ways in which church life is marked by anything but the love and justice required for human reconciliation. "The real expressions of human life in community are found outside the church where people work or play or live their family life. At best the churches express symbolically in their liturgy the community of Christians as the 'sign and instrument of human unity,' as it was so beautifully stated" by the Councils.[19] However, while Pannenberg's assertion may be a counsel of despair, we can take the presence of liturgical symbolization of human

17. *Lumen Gentium*, 1, in *Constitution on the Church*, N.C.W.C. Translation (Boston: Daughters of St. Paul, 1964), 5. This translation into contemporary English remains a more reliable and inclusive text than the authorized translations.

18. "The Holy Spirit and the Catholicity of the Church," 20, in *The Uppsala Report 1968* (Geneva: World Council of Churches, 1968), 17.

19. Wolfhart Pannenberg, *The Church* (Philadelphia: Westminster, 1983), 16–17.

unity, when it does occur, as a sign of hope. The assessment of the truth of the conciliar phrase ought not only to include an honest account of the absence or the presence of Christian communities in historical movements of reconciliation and justice. It also ought to attend to the ways that actual assemblies do symbolize a wider human unity, in the belief that symbols matter in human life. If the role of the church in relationship to human unity is at least partly symbolic, as the councils assert, then it makes sense to look at the place in the church's life where symbols are being exercised. It makes sense to look at the assembly for worship.

Therein we encounter a major reason for the importance of liturgical ecclesiology. If word, bath, and table are for Christians primary reference points of the symbolic universe of faith, if they are a principal source of our "orientation in material and social realities," then the assembly around these things is the community of that orientation.[20] If word, bath, and table are understood as one central Christian response to the human quest for social meaning, a response which Christians believe is God-given, then the community that does these central things may also be seen as one central response to the longing for human unity. Not that the liturgical assembly *is* such unity, but that, at its best, liturgical assembly may be a sign and instrument for unity. The councils were right to set the question of the church within the larger hope for human unity. And the conciliar assertion gives us an agenda for liturgical inquiry: How is the assembly itself now symbolizing human unity? How might it be reformed so that such symbolization may stand forth in greater clarity?

In the present time, however, one discovers that these grand assertions and inquiries lead immediately to many postmodern questions about human unity itself. We will need to set our inquiry about the meaning of church as liturgical assembly next to such questions. Indeed, the urgency for a specifically liturgical ecclesiology, among all the many other ways to discuss church, is increased by these questions.

First, there are the questions about the actual *location of human unity.* Is "human unity" itself an impossible abstraction? Do not people find their "unity" in their own, self-selected groups, in families, in resurgent localism, in national and racial identities? Is not the press for neighborhood unity or city-wide unity enough? Ought not the city or the nation be good enough symbols for human unity? Why do we need the church? On the other hand,

20. See Lathrop, *Holy Things,* 3–4, 204–17.

what are the bonds that are formed by the global economy and global electronic communication and global music? Are national and racial identities
not massive fictions? What is "church" amid these questions?

We will need to ask if the idea of church as assembly for worship can
help us to negotiate this current minefield. The assembly for worship, at its
best, can be a truly local group, with an intense symbolic center but with a
wide open door. The linkages between assemblies together with their liturgical remembrance of the needs of the world can mean that a community
may be concretely here, in one place, while strongly bound also to many
others in other places, away from here.

But then there are the questions put to the Christian assembly by
renascent *individualism*. Why do you need church at all? Jesus or God may
be interesting, even compelling, but cannot faith in them be carried on by
oneself? Is not such religion essentially a private matter? If one really needs
to talk about it, cannot one join a seminar or an electronic forum? If Jesus
or God or the Bible have anything to do with human unity or human fulfillment, should they not simply enter the marketplace of ideas like all other
intellectual proposals?

We will need to ask if the idea of church as assembly for liturgy can
help us respond to these very current forms of individualism. At their best,
the shared symbols of the meeting can help us to a fresh and concrete discussion of the social character of Christian faith. If such faith has a social
meaning, then the Jesus or God of private thought or the electronic forum
must relate to the Jesus or God who is known in the communal reading of
Scriptures or the communal Eucharist or in Baptism into the community.
Indeed, one cannot have the former without the latter, if one is thinking of
the biblical God and not simply a projection of one's own self. The remarkable discovery, however, still waiting to be made in many quarters, is that it
is possible to have a religious tradition that is both communal and personal,
both symbolically strong and democratic. The assembly for worship can
help us see what that might be like.

Then there are the questions about the meaning of *unity* itself. Even if
it is true that something of the Jesus tradition or of the Christian conception of God would be lost without some kind of church, why must that
lead to an accent on unity? How can the churches be "one" without the
domination of one group or person and the submission of others? What is
"visible unity," so alive in contemporary ecumenical rhetoric, and why is it
important? How do you not wind up saying that some people, who have
certain characteristics, are more "church" than others? How do you not

accentuate one culture's ideas of what matters in human life over those of other cultures?

We will need to ask if the idea of church as assembly can assist us in refocusing discussions of unity. On the model of the best liturgical celebrations, unity might be understood as mutual participation in the signs of the presence and mercy of God, mutual reception and recognition and honor, mutual exhortation and encouragement, not uniform organization nor hierarchical structure. The recovery of biblical and liturgical images of community could help us rethink even the human unity of which the church is to be "sign and instrument." The very history of the ways Christian liturgy has been celebrated in diverse cultures could help us toward new and healthy patterns for affirming and criticizing cultures.

But then there are the questions about *religious particularity* or, in Christian theological language, "election." If we speak so strongly about the identity of this one group, called church, how can we really care about the well-being of the world? If we call this group "the people of God," even "the chosen people," what does that idea have to do with all humanity? And how does a conception of a people chosen and singled out by God relate to the care of the earth? Do we think that only these particular humans matter? Furthermore, what is meant by *mission*? How does it relate to the dignity and importance of other peoples and all the earth?

We will need to ask if the idea of church as assembly assists us to reconceive our mission and re-imagine our situation in the earth. Part of our mission, in fact, may well be to maintain strong and healthy communal symbols of the truth about God and to do so for the sake of the well-being of the world. At its best, the way that the meeting for worship shares food and stories and remembers the poor can be a helpful model for being together in the earth.

For an honest contemporary ecclesiology to be worked out, these and similar contemporary questions must be taken seriously as part of the context for this work. Why does it matter what the church is? It matters, among other reasons, because if we let the church be simply another small interest group or a universal, ideological interest group or a new chosen people or a seminar of the like-minded or a name for what I do alone—according each to our own postmodern taste—we will be ignoring the ways in which our conceptions and our practice merely mirror the fragmentations of our time. We will be ignoring the Christian hope that God's transforming power is not just another name for our own status quo.

A liturgical ecclesiology will not be a guaranteed panacea. But focus on the liturgical assembly will require us to face these current questions using the concrete data of worship practice. In worship, issues of the balance between the welcome and the rejection of culture, between the local and the universal, between the personal and the communal, are not abstract. They are matters of practical decision, of actual planning for the next Sunday liturgy. And in worship, at least in worship that has any fidelity at all to the Christian tradition, the trust in God's ability to transform our actual and often poor materials remains at the center of attention, a primary characteristic of the primary theology of the liturgy.

Method: Reflections according to the Eucharist

But while such public questions provide a context for doing liturgical ecclesiology, they do not provide its sources and its method. Those sources are, rather, the very central activities of the assemblies themselves. They are the Scriptures and the sacramental actions that arise from and bear witness to the life, death, and resurrection of Jesus. They are these things done, as the center of worship, in the heart of a participating community. The method of liturgical ecclesiology is the method of the liturgy itself: meaning occurs as one thing is put next to another in such a way that the community is called to faith in the triune God.

In the late second century, Irenaeus of Lyons, perhaps the first great, post-biblical theologian of the church, created a remarkable, brief summary of liturgical theology. He was arguing against those gnostics who belittled "the things around us" and regarded the flesh as evil, when he wrote: "But our judgment is consonant with the Eucharist, and, in turn, the Eucharist establishes our judgment."[21] For Irenaeus, the very bread and cup of the thanksgiving meal, which are the body and blood of the Lord and which nourish our own flesh and blood, proclaim the truth of the God who created the world and redeemed it in Jesus Christ. Encounter with the Eucharist and its practice forms faith in the Creator of all things and gratitude for the creation. If this is so, how could gnostics celebrate Eucharist unless they ignored its very meaning? On the contrary, Irenaeus asserts that there is an impossible contradiction in a celebration of the Eucharist that

---

21. "Nostra autem consonans est sententia Eucharistiae, et Eucharistia rursus confirmat sententiam nostram." Adv. haer. 4:18:5. For the Latin and a reconstructed Greek text see A. Rousseau, ed., Irénée de Lyon, Contre Les Hérésies, Livre IV, 2, Sources Chrétiennes 100 (Paris: Cerf, 1965), 610.

also proclaims alienation from the earth, from "the things around us," conceived as unredeemably evil. No. The Eucharist itself says something else.

These "judgments" of Irenaeus are, in the first place, *theological* judgments. They are about God. They propose that the God of the gnostics is not the God of the Eucharist. At the same time, however, they are assertions about the church, about the community that celebrates the Eucharist and about its relationship with the world.

Like Irenaeus's liturgical theology, a liturgical ecclesiology needs to be "consonant with the Eucharist." This is so, in the first place, for reasons very close to the intention of Irenaeus. Ecclesiology must not be about getting out of God's good world to retreat into a community of the saved. It must not forget its context, must not be used to reinforce "us" against "them." The Eucharist of the church—the thanksgiving for all things at the meal of trinitarian faith; the table of Jesus Christ, which welcomes outsiders and sinners; real food of this world that becomes the presence of Christ's body and blood in the power of the Spirit so that "the many" eat and drink before the face of God now in this world; the universal banquet which is astonishingly personal—says otherwise. The conciliar assertions about the church as sign and instrument of human unity can be seen as consonant with and confirmed by the Eucharist. An ecclesiology according to the Eucharist is exactly what is needed for reflection upon church in the context of our list of postmodern questions. The Eucharist enables a particular people to be here, in touch with other places. The Eucharist turns us toward the world of our time and gives us resources to newly understand the church in response. Most especially, the Eucharist confesses the triune God and so conceives of the church as participant in God's life and witness to God's love in the world.

But liturgical ecclesiology can be seen to accord with the Eucharist in two larger senses. First, let "Eucharist"—Christian thanksgiving for the action of God—stand as a name for all the worship practices from which a liturgical ecclesiology arises. Obviously, a liturgical ecclesiology must accord with those practices. But what liturgy helps us think of church? Some discussions of ecumenical ecclesiology today stumble over the richly diverse worship practices that mark all the various churches. How can one discuss a common conception of church amid this diversity, especially if one intends to draw from liturgical sources? While not denying the diversity— indeed, while treasuring it—our presupposition here is that Irenaeus's Eucharist is the inheritance of all the churches. What is meant by "Eucharist," then—probably in Irenaeus, certainly here—is not just the

Lord's Supper, isolated and considered as one illustration of the Christian message. Rather, Eucharist is the whole economy of word set next to meal, texts set next to preaching, thanksgiving set next to eating and drinking, which makes up the deepest ecumenical pattern for celebration. Eucharist is the every-Sunday assembly for doing this word and meal event set next to the recurring human experience of the week. But Eucharist, in this sense, is also baptism as the way that leads people into this assembly, and it is mission in the world and response to the poor as ways in which the community flows out from the assembly. Eucharist is the assembly itself and its leadership, a leadership best understood as appointed for the sake of that assembly. This economy of meaning is, as one ecumenical consultation put it, "the inheritance of all the churches, founded in the New Testament, locally practiced today, and attested to in the ancient sources of both the Christian East and the Christian West."[22] While this last assertion will need to be tested, reflection on the ecumenical liturgical inheritance as source for church will be the undertaking of this book. A liturgical ecclesiology will need to accord with Eucharist, that is, with the entire economy of word and sacrament, of proclamation and thanksgiving, as that economy is present in all the churches.

Second, Eucharist brings us to humility. A liturgical ecclesiology will need to accord with that humility. Just as we are beggars at the Supper, hands out for the gift of Christ, so also we cannot even begin to be church except by participation in God's gift. The most important thing that the liturgy says about the church may well be a matter that at first sounds negative. We cannot be the church. On one level, that is the message of the ancient liturgical text that provides the title for this volume. "Holy things for the holy people," sings out the presider in an Eastern Church liturgy, standing before the people and holding out the bread and cup of the communion. While this text is ostensibly an invitation to participate in the Eucharist, it is also a warning. Holy things are only for the holy people. Let those who are holy draw near. Let those who are not, repent. "Do not give what is holy to dogs," as the *Didache* of the second century had it. We examine ourselves, telling the truth. We are not the holy people.

But the sung response to this ancient invitation and warning establishes one of the greatest moments of meaning in all Christian liturgy, one of

---

22. "Towards Koinonia in Worship," 4, in Thomas F. Best and Dagmar Heller, eds., *So We Believe, So We Pray*, Faith and Order Paper 171 (Geneva: World Council of Churches, 1995), 6–7.

liturgy's greatest juxtapositions.[23] "Only one the holy Father, only one the holy Son, only one the holy Spirit, in the unity of the Holy Spirit," sings the assembly, in the form known in the ancient Liturgy of St. Mark and in other Syriac and Coptic sources. This meal is not about our holiness, say the people, but about God's. God, who in Christ welcomes sinners and forgives sinners, welcomes us. We eat holiness, drink holiness in the meal of Christ's gift. Participating, we are made a holy people. Gathered in this assembly and in its eucharistic economy, we are formed in the very unity of the Holy Spirit which is the unity of the holiness of God. God makes this assembly to be church.

While the dialogue largely survives only in eastern liturgies, it may rightly be seen as a treasure belonging to all Christians. In every Christian community there exist tensions and linkages between human need and God's holiness, between invitation and warning, between the local ritual and God, between the presence and the absence of holiness in the assembled people and the things they gather around. Such linkages are especially clear in the celebration of the Eucharist, but they belong to all Christian speech. Indeed, these very tensions and linkages are central to the ways Christians experience who God is. The holy-things dialogue, then, may be understood as bringing a universal Christian experience to classic expression. It is rightly a source for liturgical theology. To think with this dialogue is to think "according to the eucharist."

But the dialogue also does something else. It defines the *church*. Around the presider holding the bread and cup there stands an assembly of people. This, too, belongs to all the churches. It is to this people that the warning and the invitation are given. It is this assembly which is or is to become or symbolizes or fails to be or cannot be the "holy people." Then, it is they who respond, taking refuge in the Trinity, taking refuge in the holiness of God-for-us. It is they who are, in this very assembly, in this very meal, in touch with the "unity of the Holy Spirit." Their hope is not invested in a nostalgia for a lost time in the church, for some ideal moment. It is certainly not invested in themselves. Their hope is in the triune God. And if this assembly, which cannot of itself be church, is welcomed here, then it symbolizes a welcome and a meaning that matters for all the world.

23. For a discussion of the dialogue itself and its history since its first recorded appearance in the fourth-century liturgy of Jerusalem, see Robert Taft, "'Holy Things for the Saints': The Ancient Call to Communion and its Response," in G. Austin, ed., *The Fountain of Life* (Washington: Pastoral, 1991), 87–102. The dialogue reflects the much older material found in *Didache* 9:5; 10:6. See further below, chapter 9.

The church is that assembly. It is the people who cannot be the holy people and yet, because of Christ, *are*.

This book must be about that assembly. Only so will the book be marked by reflection that accords with the Eucharist. For such paradoxes and tensions—between no and yes, between our need and God's grace, between the untransformed world and a God who acts to transform—must characterize a liturgical ecclesiology that is consonant with the Eucharist.

PART ONE

A People
Church in Liturgical Perspective

I SING THE ASSEMBLIES,
IN WHICH I PRAY THERE MAY BE UNITY.
—*Ignatius of Antioch*
To the Magnesians, 1:2

1

Assembly

Assembly, a gathering together of participating persons, constitutes the most basic symbol of Christian worship. All the other symbols and symbolic actions of liturgy depend upon this gathering being there in the first place. No texts are read, no preaching occurs, no hymns are sung, no Eucharist is held without an assembly, however small or large this gathering of persons may be. The event we call Baptism brings a person into this assembly.

These primary, assembly-centering events, events that make up the heart of Christian worship, are supported by further, secondary events, which also are assembly based. One may say it this way: Sunday is the day of assembly, the liturgical year a calendar for the work of the assembly. Daily prayer reflects and anticipates the meeting of the Sunday assembly. Confession and forgiveness—acts of reconciliation in the life of the churches—recapitulate baptism, reorienting the individual once again to the purposes of the assembly. Creeds are the faith-confessions of the assembly: "*We* believe in one God, . . ." the Nicene Creed begins.

The basic building blocks of liturgical structure—biblical texts, preaching and sacraments, hymns, prayers, calendars, and creeds—are all essentially communal in nature. In themselves, they presume an assembly. So the texts of the New Testament are addressed to a plural "you,"[1] and they presume that they are to be passed on to yet other assemblies, other gatherings of the

---

1. Even Philemon, which seems at first to be a letter to one individual, includes other names as well as "the church in your house" (Phlmn. 2) in its address. Its opening and closing greetings (verses 3 and 25), echoing a communal liturgical setting, are addressed to a plural *you*. The letter presumes a public reading and a community that will assist and witness the response of the individual.

21

plural "you."[2] The reading of these texts in Christian worship has continued this characteristic of their origin into present practice. In the same pattern, the communal reading of the Hebrew Scriptures, where the sense of
the plural address of the texts to the congregation of Israel is, if anything,
even stronger, has also been adopted by Christians.[3] Furthermore, Eucharist
is a communal meal; preaching and singing and praying are communal acts.
If one assumes that Scripture and meal, prayers and the baptismal bath are
the central matters of Christian worship, then the simple fact of assembly
stands as the first principle.

In contemporary thought about the liturgy, assertions about this centrality of assembly are found everywhere. Writers from many different confessions—and documents of councils and synods[4]—reiterate a conviction that
has become an ecumenical treasure: "The 'coming together' of the Christians
is the distinguishing feature of Christian worship."[5] And "we do all this
together because we *are* a 'together,' and not just individuals. Christian salvation is by its very nature 'church,' a 'gathering.'"[6] And "worship in the sense
of the assembly of the Christian congregation in the name of Jesus is virtu-
ally the dominant mode of the manifestation of the church on earth."[7] And

2. *Cf.* 1 Thess. 5:27; Col. 4:16.

3. It is probably the public reading of the Old Testament books which is indicated by
the *anagnosis,* "reading aloud," of 1 Tim. 4:13; *cf.* Acts 13:15; 2 Cor. 3:14. In any case, if Luke
24:13-33 mirrors the Sunday practice in the assemblies known to the evangelist, then they
also read, "beginning with Moses and all the prophets" (24:27).

4. For example, see the assertions about the manifestation of the whole church in the
local eucharistic assembly found in the documents of the Second Vatican Council: *Constitution on the Sacred Liturgy,* 41; *Dogmatic Constitution on the Church,* 26.

5. So the Lutheran, Ferdinand Hahn (in *Der urchristliche Gottesdienst* [Stuttgart: 1970],
34), quoted in the work of the Roman Catholic, Louis-Marie Chauvet, (*Symbol and Sacrament* [Collegeville: Liturgical, 1995], 185). For a slightly different translation, see F. Hahn, *The
Worship of the Early Church* (Philadelphia: Fortress, 1973), 36. Chauvet continues: "In short, the
coming together in the name of the Lord Jesus was perceived as the chief mark of Christians, the fundamental sacrament of the risen Christ. Christians are people who get together."

6. So the Roman Catholic Robert Taft (*The Liturgy of the Hours in East and West*, [Col-
legeville: Liturgical Press, 1986], 342), quoted in the work of the Anglican, J. Neil Alexander, (*Time and Community* [Washington: Pastoral, 1990], 299).

7. So the Lutheran, Peter Brunner (*Worship in the Name of Jesus* [St Louis: Concordia,
1968], 18–19), quoted in the work of the Swiss Reformed J.-J. von Allmen (*Worship: Its Theology and Practice* [New York: Oxford, 1965], 43). Brunner, loc. cit., also writes: "Among the
New Testament terms, 'to be assembled in the name of Jesus' or 'to convene in the *ekklesia*
or as *ekklesia*' reproduces the common meaning of our word 'worship' most aptly." *Cf.* also
the work of the Orthodox Alexander Schmemann, *Introduction to Liturgical Theology* (New
York: St. Vladimir's Seminary Press, 1975), 19–20.

"among the symbols with which liturgy deals, none is more important than this assembly of believers."[8]

The "assembly" extolled in this ecumenical consensus has some clear characteristics, many of which are quite unusual among current conceptions of public meetings. This assembly should meet regularly, every Sunday at least. It should be of life-and-death importance to its participants. This assembly should be marked by participation and by an honored place for every participant. It should have its strong and cherished center in the things in which the community participates, the things we have called the heart or the basic building blocks of the gathering. Leadership in the meeting should serve the assembly's participation in these central things, the dignity of each of its members, and the openness of its door to the world. Indeed, the assembly should have an open door, a permeable outer boundary, an accessibility to the surrounding world, a marked hospitality. Its practice should have lines of meaning that extend from the meeting into the re-description and re-imagination of all ordinary life.

Such may not be the place where you ordinarily "go to church." But something like this description is the hope that hovers behind all of our liturgical books. Such assembly is the shared vision of all of our best liturgical planning. It is also the memory alive in our oldest descriptions of Christianity. Still, even in the most idealized of those old descriptions, the hope was by no means always realized. Ordinary, quarrelsome, nonexemplary, needy, sinful people met and still meet. But Christian faith finds God active in the meeting, finds in the very fact of meeting a deep ground for thanksgiving. Against the spirit of the age, Christians still gather together, and that simple fact remains symbolically powerful.

According to the classic description of this basic symbol, then, this meeting is not—or ought not be—a crowd, a cheering section, a gathering to hear a lecture or a sales pitch, an audience. It is not a collection of consumers come to an expert, a gathering of the uninvolved come to be entertained. Another kind of assembly—a gathering together of persons in which each of those gathered has a participatory role, in which the central matters of worship are at the heart of this shared participation—constitutes the most basic symbol of Christian worship.

---

8. *Environment and Art in Catholic Worship* (Washington: National Conference of Catholic Bishops, 1978), 18.

Personal Worship and Communal Liturgy

The assertion of the symbolic importance of assembly, an assertion which would have been self-evident in primitive Christianity, needs to be made clearly in the present time. For us, the modern understanding that religion is largely the private concern of an individual has been strengthened by the postmodern availability of spiritualities in individually determined and individually exercised media. A book of prayers held in my own hands or an electronic forum about private rituals consulted on my own time can reinforce in me the sense that my religion is largely my own individual affair.

Of course, for Christians, this sense of the importance of the personal is not entirely wrong. Worship may indeed take place when one is alone. The Sermon on the Mount itself counsels prayer in one's own room, behind the shut door (Matt. 6:6). Especially in the modern age of the hand-held, privately owned book, the Bible can be read alone. But such reading is more than a modern phenomenon. None other than the great Augustine of Hippo, for example, reports that he found his way to Baptism partly by picking up the "book of the apostle" in his solitude and by himself reading Rom. 13:13-14.[9]

But these central matters of Christian worship are misunderstood if, even in this solitary use, their essentially communal context is not recalled. The very prayer that the Matthean Jesus proposes to the one who prays "in secret" is a prayer to *our* Father, for *our* daily bread, for the forgiveness of *our* sins and for *our* rescue (Matt. 6:7-13). The God encountered here is the God of the community. Furthermore, mutual forgiveness within the community is the constant context of prayer (Matt. 6:14-15; *cf.* Mark 11:25). When one prays in secret, that "room" becomes crowded with many other people: all the people one is called upon to forgive as well as all the people with whom one shares God's gift of bread and the hope of God's rescue.

Similarly, the Bible is none other than *ta biblia,* "the books," collected together under one cover. The list of these books, the canon, can best be understood as the list of books accepted for public reading in the church.[10]

9. Augustine, *Confessions* Book 8:12 (29).

10. Important here is the rejection by the "Muratorian canon" (third century?) of the *Shepherd of Hermas:* "it ought indeed be read, but it cannot be read publicly in the church to the people either among the prophets, whose number is settled, or among the apostles to the end of time." R. McL. Wilson, *New Testament Apocrypha* (London: Lutterworth, 1963) 1:45. This rejection makes clear what purpose this list of books serves: public reading in the church.

When I take a Bible in my hands, even when I am alone, I take up the whole community of voices that addresses me there as well as all the people with whom I read these books in a continuing community of interpretation. The very fact of the books being gathered together as one book is a *liturgical* fact. The Bible is a set of books written by, collected by, and intended for assemblies.

Certainly, there is also a sense in which the Scriptures are prior to our communities. Many of the voices of the Bible are individual voices, prophets and apostles speaking to the community in the name and with the authority of God. The story of Jesus told in the New Testament Scriptures is the story of events that precede anything called "the church." Furthermore, an individual may hear in the Scriptures matters that the community has forgotten or distorted. For all these reasons and more, the Christian assembly believes that God speaks in the Scriptures and that this Word of God is prior to our assemblies.

But the prophets and apostles *were* speaking to assemblies. Christians dare to let their current gatherings listen as if they were in continuity with those ancient assemblies. What is more, the Jesus of the New Testament stories was already gathering a collection of people around him in his ministry, and the present assembly for worship does intend to continue the religiously revolutionary business of those old gatherings around him. In fact, the only stories of Jesus that we have are stories that were collected and told in *churches,* for the purposes of the faith alive in those churches. Furthermore, if an individual hears the Scripture freshly, what he or she hears does need to be told to the assembly. Finally Christians believe that the Word of God calls us into assembly. "Assembly" is found throughout the pages of the Scriptures, and assembly continues to be the context in which we receive the Scriptures today.

Even Augustine, in his solitude with the Bible, had a small community about him. He heard the voice of another, of a child, inviting him to "pick up and read." He did so, in that Milanese garden, and heard the voice of Paul, the apostle. His friend Alypius was nearby, and Alypius, hearing about this reading from Augustine, immediately took the book, read it further himself and then discussed with Augustine the next passage of the text as well.[11] And these juxtaposed texts—"put on the Lord Jesus Christ" and "welcome those who are weak in faith"—eventually brought both Augustine and Alypius to Bishop Ambrose and to Baptism and to the assembly. Such is the way with the Scripture.

11. Augustine, *Confessions* Book 8:12 (30).

Similar things can be said of hymnody or of the Eucharist or of Baptism. One can sing a hymn alone, but the "we" of the assembly always keeps appearing in the text of the hymn, and the other voices—those of the hymnwriter and of all the hymn's singers through the ages—sing along in inaudible harmony. A solitary priest might celebrate the Eucharist alone, but even in the hermit's chapel, the "you" of "my body and blood, given and shed for you," is unchangeably plural. And Christian Baptism simply cannot be done alone. One does not baptize oneself. With the baptized there must be at least a baptizer, and with the baptizer comes the opening to the whole assembly. The best practice today always has that whole assembly there.

Christian ritual, therefore, cannot be essentially the exercise of a solitary priest or a lonely worshipper. When pieces of that ritual reach into the life of an individual, the echoes of the assembly always come along. Thus Christians have prayed Psalm 42, thinking of the relationship between their own private hope for the face of God and the communal liturgy: "These things I remember as I pour out my soul: how I went with the throng, and led them in procession to the house of God, with glad shouts and songs of thanksgiving, a multitude keeping festival" (Psalm 42:4). The prayer of the voluntary hermit or the forced exile must be understood in just this sense: such prayer is Christian as it is full of the presence of other Christians, full of the needs of concrete people in the world, full of the longing to see God's salvation together. John, the seer of the Apocalypse, provides the primary example. John is an exile on Patmos, presumably alone as a Christian. "[I]n the Spirit, on the Lord's day" (Rev. 1:10), the day of Christian assembly, this exile encounters the risen one. But this encounter is not a lonely engagement with the divine. It is also, from the outset, full of the presence of the churches—the churches in the midst of which the risen one stands, the churches held in his hand, the churches to which the letters are then addressed (Rev. 1:10-20). Solitary Christian worship always participates in something like this encounter of John. Being "in the Spirit," encountering the risen Christ, means contact with the assembly, direction toward the assembly, evocation of the presence of the assembly.

Meanings of Assembly

So "assembly" constitutes the most basic symbol of Christian worship. But why is this so? What does it mean? If assembly is a symbol, then, like any symbol, it invites, enables, persuades to participation in the thing or things it symbolizes.[12] But what are those things? If we are to use the data of worship as a way to reflect upon church, then we must inquire about the meanings of this basic symbol in liturgical tradition and in actual experience.

Begin with actual experience. Any living symbol will evoke and resonate with current analogous cultural material, even if it seeks to transcend that material. Such evocations will also be true of our "assembly."[13] For example, using only the symbolic references many North Americans (and other participants in the increasingly global consumer culture) know from their own times, we may understand our gathering for worship "simply" as something like a Christian club, or like a lecture, a concert, a drama, a variety show, even somewhat like the throng of a shopping mall, in any case, as *a choosing, consuming audience.* Such an understanding, however, is far from simple, since it involves a complex if sometimes unreflective process: the uncritical adoption of a current cultural model; the reduction of Christianity to a "content" that can be poured into or communicated through this model without further transforming the model itself; the reinforcement of the conception of religion as an essentially individual matter; and the abandonment of any idea of the form of the meeting as itself part of the "content." Many Christian gatherings explicitly designed for the "seeker" have consciously adopted one or other of these conceptions of assembly out of the belief that people unfamiliar with Christianity will at least be comfortable with such a way of meeting. For other Christians, these cultural models may be the only available analogues to the assembly for worship, and even if one of these models does not take over the whole mode of the meeting, their influence will emerge in concrete planning choices that are made: the shape of the building as theater, the manner of the presider as entertainer, the use of electric amplification or projection, the understanding of the "program."

On the other hand, as if in mirror image, North Americans may turn to the dreaming, longing side of our cultural imagination. We may intentionally be resistant to modern paradigms of clubs, concerts, and crowds. To the extent that our gathering for worship awakens in us longings for larger meanings than current forms can hold, we may be imagining ourselves here, in the assembly, as participants or observers at our own versions of a

12. See Stephen Happel, "Symbol," in *The New Dictionary of Sacramental Worship,* P. Fink, ed. (Collegeville: Liturgical, 1990), 1238.

13. On the symbolic meanings that assembly evokes, the symbolic dangers it runs, and the "breaking" of this symbol to Christian purpose, see Gordon Lathrop, *Holy Things: A Liturgical Theology* (Minneapolis: Fortress, 1993), 113–15.

medieval pageant, a royal convocation, an ancient mystery play—in any case, *an archaic, imagination-bearing event.* Some patterns of ceremonial practice especially foster this form of cultural imagination: processions, archaic vesture, hierarchically organized and candlelit space.

Elsewhere in the world and in parts of North America more marginal to mainstream culture, other models and memories of meetings may dominate our consciousness as we practice the Christian assembly: the secret society; the gathering in the "brush arbor" for communication and solidarity in the face of oppression; the extended family or the tribe at a festival; the collection of people seeking healing, direction, and ritual leadership from the shaman—*survival forms of nondominant communities.* These models also bring along contributions to the manner of practice and the shape of the space that Christians use: a powerful role for the central speaker, for example, or significant barriers to the outside world or very specific ideas about the roles men and women are to play.

In some parts of North America and in other places in the world where a long tradition of Christian assembly has been present, the conceptions underlying the gathering may have become linked to the identity of the nation or the "folk." We may understand going to church as a way to enable the nation or the local community to be visible, a way to express our belonging to this *local or national or ethnic group.* Our assemblies may be a modern version of the old Nordic *thing* or an ethnic festival or a kind of Christian town meeting—in any case, a visible expression of communal identity. Such a conception also has its influence on the actual conduct of the meeting. Persons who are powerful in the daily community may also be powerful in the assembly, with special seating or important functions. The archaic national costume or a national flag may play important symbolic roles.

Most likely of all, however, we may make use of a cultural idea that is practically universal at the present time. We may hope that this gathering will be that sacred thing so many of us, throughout the world, desperately long for: *genuine community.* Lacking any experience of public assemblies as reliable communities, we will imagine that "genuine" community must mean intimate community, a collection of friends and lovers. Such an understanding of assembly can also be found to be shaping much current liturgical practice. Intimate, familial speech and narratives of the self, for example, often replace formal and stylized expression in the work of preachers.

Still, "audience" or "mysterious pageant" or "brush arbor" or "family festival" or "ethnic club" or even "community" are not themselves adequate descriptions of the thing symbolized by Christian assembly. In one or another way, they certainly hover behind the practice of assembly in many congregations. They certainly have affected the mode of assembly. Sometimes, when the Christian meaning of assembly is forgotten, they certainly run the danger of so overwhelming all other meanings that, when we go to church, we meet there only ourselves, our own times and preconceptions, only the patterns we started with. Some of the values these conceptions of assembly may bring along—non-participation, the dominant leader, dreaming of another world, rigid gender roles, barriers to outsiders—can themselves be actively anti-Christian.

But even where the mode of assembly has been overwhelmingly determined by one of these cultural models, an excess of symbolic meaning usually remains, larger than this cultural projection of ourselves. "Seeker services," for example, are rarely entirely without classic liturgical content. Something from the Scriptures is read; a speaker arises; there may be prayers, even communal singing. Most especially, the meeting still takes place on Sunday morning, as if the planners knew that the "seeker" has a memory of some important meeting on Sunday that had to do with God.

The question remains, what does this assembly or any of our assemblies have to do with God? Or, to ask the same thing differently, what does assembly itself mean to Christian faith? We need to inquire how the models of meeting we use or evoke can be so practiced as to serve and celebrate this meaning. Our models of meeting are not automatically Christian. To what Christian meaning can these various cultural models, with their symbolic resonances, be bent by the actual liturgical use of assembly? At root, our question is this: Why does assembly constitute the most basic symbol of Christian worship?

These questions are not new. At the very outset of the idea of "church," in the first centuries of the faith, culturally available ideas of assembly were also employed by Christians. The Roman governor Pliny, writing from Asia Minor to Emperor Trajan in the early second century, was not entirely wrong when he assumed that the Christian meetings he sought to suppress were among the various *hetaeriae*,[14] "associations" or "clubs," in the society he was seeking to manage; albeit, for him, the Christian versions of this wider phenomenon were pernicious clubs, infected by a superstition. He

14. Pliny, *Letters,* 10:96. The Latin text with an English translation is found in the Loeb edition, W. Melmoth and W. M. L. Hutchinson, eds. (Cambridge: Harvard University Press, 1963), 2:400–405. The Latin word *hetaeria* reproduces the Greek *hetaireia*, "association" or "club," from *hetairos*, "companion."

29

wrote his description of Christian meetings for prayer, song, and a shared meal, using available cultural analogies.

The Christians met, using the same analogies. Contemporary biblical study has, with increasing clarity, established that as the Christian movement spread, it did so using the models of extended households, voluntary associations, *collegia, hetaeriae,* or philosophical societies that already existed in late Hellenistic culture.[15] The Jewish assembly, the *synagogue,* had already done that in some places, before the spread of Christianity. It, too, like pagan cults or beneficial societies before it, could meet under the patronage of a wealthy benefactor, could make use of someone's house or transform a house for its use, could be marked by patterns and loyalties that belonged to the extended family around its *paterfamilias.* The Christian community adopted these very models as well. The "church in the house of Prisca and Aquila" (Rom. 16:5; *cf.* 1 Cor. 16:19; Col. 4:15; Phlmn. 2), a phrase echoed and supported by many other New Testament references to household communities and house-based benefactors, was not unlike the more general Greek and Latin usage found, for example, in the inscription that speaks of "the *collegium* in the house of Sergia Paulina."[16] Christianity followed then current cultural patterns. Of course. These patterns were the available materials of human life.

But, more interestingly for our purposes, Christianity widely called itself not "club" or *collegium,* but "the meeting" or "the assembly"—*ekklesia,* in Greek. Admittedly, this was a word that also had a specific Greek resonance. *Ekklesia* was especially the name of the assembly of all the free, male citizens of a Greek city-republic, gathered to decide matters in the city. Certainly, in late Hellenistic times, under the rule of first Greek and then Roman emperors, this city assembly was an archaic and largely powerless institution. But its presence and its name continued to be a powerful symbol, evoking memory and hope. Other groups, besides the Christians, modeled their club-organizations on the larger patterns of the city and could use the word *ekklesia* to name their gathering to make decisions.[17] Christians, too, may

15. One central work, in an extensive literature, is Wayne A. Meeks, *The First Urban Christians* (New Haven: Yale University Press, 1983), 74–110. See also L. Michael White, "Christianity: Early Social Life and Organization," *Anchor Bible Dictionary* (New York: Doubleday, 1992), 1:931–33. For an ecclesiological application of these insights, see especially Edward Schillebeeckx, *The Church with a Human Face* (New York: Crossroad, 1985), 42ff. and *Church: The Human Story of God* (New York: Crossroad, 1990), 146f.

16. L. Michael White, *Building God's House in the Roman World* (Baltimore: Johns Hopkins University Press, 1990), 141.

17. Meeks, *The First Urban Christians,* 222 n. 24.

have been playing upon the symbolic power of the remembered, but now perhaps nostalgic, importance of the free city, gathered in *ekklesia*.

But Christians did not just use the word for their own voters' gathering. This Greek word—*ekklesia*—is the one we customarily translate in English, and in other Germanic and Slavic languages, as "church" (or *kirche, kyrka, kerk, cirkev*) and customarily transliterate in the Romance languages as *église, iglesia*. But we need to see its original resonances: read "assembly" wherever our languages say "church" or *iglesia*. Unlike the clubs, the Christians were "the assembly," "the meeting," all of the time. They took this word as the name of their group. They were the assembly in small gatherings, say "in the house of Nympha" (Col. 4:16). They were men and women, slaves and free in assembly (1 Cor. 12:13; Gal. 3:28), not just free males. They were also some sort of massive assembly in all the known world. They were "all the assemblies of the nations" (Rom. 16:4). They were even, in the singular, the whole "assembly of God" (Gal. 1:13; 1 Cor. 10:32; 15:9). These larger references, these names for the whole group of Christians, were drawn from the name for a local, convoked, participatory gathering. The Christians were, all together and in each of their local groups, "the assembly." Here there was surely an excess symbolic meaning, beyond the voters meeting of the Greek city, more than could be indicated by Hellenistic social vocabulary. We must inquire how this name contrasted with the ordinary names of the clubs and how it intended to transform expectations of the purpose for the Christian gathering. We must ask what this name symbolized.

The Biblical Assembly

It appears that Christians were calling their meetings—and the groups that so met—by an ancient, biblical name. However Hellenistic the group may have been in its structure and its place in current society, whatever Hellenistic resonance its name may have had, that name—*ekklesia*—also spoke of an ancient Hebrew hope. Christians understood themselves as living that hope. They were not simply another *collegium* in the marketplace of possible club memberships. Their meeting was more than the town meeting of their city.

Throughout the Hebrew Scriptures, the account of God's saving action repeatedly told of an "assembly." The paradigmatic case occurs in the exodus-story, the central narrative of the Old Testament. According to Exodus, when the people were delivered from slavery in Egypt, they were brought into Sinai, before the holy mountain, and constituted as a consecrated "assembly" before God, to be "a priestly kingdom and a holy nation" (Exodus 19; *cf.* Deut. 18:16; 23:1-4). They were, first of all, that assembly in the person of their elders (Ex. 19:7). Then, on the third day, the whole people met God as a holy people, receiving their common vocation in the world and hearing God's law (19:16ff.) Finally, having heard the law and being gathered as the twelve tribes, sprinkled with the "blood of the covenant," the people, again in the person of their elders, beheld God and ate and drank (24:3-11). The actor in these passive verbs—delivered, brought, constituted, consecrated, gathered—was God.

This powerful narrative symbol of holy assembly recurs repeatedly elsewhere in the Hebrew Scriptures. Each occurrence of the symbol, linked together with the earlier uses like a chain of flowers or gems, intensifies the meaning. In the claiming of the land, according to the promise of God, the whole nation could be said once again to be constituted as the assembly (for example, Judges 20:1-2; *cf.* Josh. 4; 23-24), though here only the men seem to be envisioned, as a holy army. In the return from exile, in the rebuilding of Jerusalem, the people—now explicitly both men and women—are once again an assembly, now for the reading and interpretation of the Word of God, the law, and for the sharing of food, echoing and recapitulating the events of Sinai (Neh. 8:1-12; *cf.* 2 Kings 23:1-3, 21). And at the end, on the day of the Lord, God will act openly again, gathering people from all the nations to come to Mt. Zion, to the One who speaks the living word, that they all may come into a life-giving feast and assembly before the holy presence (Isa. 2:2-4; 25:6-9). Three narrative uses of the symbol "assembly" are thus especially important in the symbolic chain: the assemblies at Sinai, at the return from exile, and at the end.

Frequently, in these accounts, the Hebrew word used for "assembly" is *qahal*, "a convoked gathering." In the Septuagint, the Greek version of the ancient Scriptures most widely used among the earliest churches, the most common translation of *qahal* is *ekklesia*.[18] And in these accounts, especially at Sinai and at the end, God's is the voice, the Word, sounding in the vocation to be assembly, the summons to be *qahal*, the *klesis* to be *ekklesia*. Since the word was used especially in these symbolically significant places in the narratives, *ekklesia* as "the assembly of God" or "the assembly of the people of God" or, simply, "the assembly," came to stand for the hope that God would once again convoke the people,[19] perhaps as a "downpayment" on

18. See especially Deut. 18:16, summarizing the Sinai assembly as *yom haqahal,* in the LXX, *hemera tes ekklesias.* See also Judges 20:2; Neh. 8:2; 13:1.

19. The Qumran scrolls demonstrate that such an eschatological application of the old image of the assembly was quite possible in the time of Christian origins. There, the com-

the life-giving, final convocation of all the nations. The power of the stories could awaken such a hope: hope for God to come; hope for God's Word to be spoken directly or read clearly from the treasured book; hope for the people to be gathered into one as a holy assembly with a clear vocation; hope for a holy meal to seal this covenant with God; hope for such an assembly to be set against all evil—slavery, idolatry, ignorance, finally, as in Isaiah, the "veil" of death itself; hope for an end to violence and death as all peoples begin to be called into such an assembly before God.

Most likely, it is this hope that was being symbolized in the primitive Christian use of the word "assembly." If this is so, then the name of the community of Christians and the meaning of their assemblies belonged to their "eschatology," their belief about the events in the end time of the world. Against all appearances, Christians believed, God's final times have dawned in Jesus Christ, in his cross, his resurrection, and the faith which is through him. Because of Jesus Christ, surprisingly, sinners and outsiders and Gentiles have been called into the assembly of God, joined to the royal, priestly people whose task is to declare the truth of God in the world. Through Jesus Christ, as a sign of these last times, the Spirit of God has been poured out upon all the assembly—not just the leaders and elders and prophets—to enable them in this task. The local meetings of Christians, then, actually are the beginning of "the assembly" of biblical hope.

Primitive liturgical data that points to such an eschatological understanding of the actual gathering of Christians includes the Lord's Prayer itself. The prayer breathes a sense of eschatology. It is filled with petitions for the coming of the Day of God, together with some fear for the terrors expected in the last times. "Make your name holy, we beg you," we may paraphrase the prayer of the community. "Let your reign come; do your will on earth as you do it in the universe." Yet the community also prays, "Do not bring us to the test," for we fear we will fail; in any case, we beg, "deliver us from the evil one." But in the midst of these petitions are also two strong indications that the expected, longed-for Day has already dawned in the life of the community itself. "Give us today the bread of the

---

munity itself, especially in its purity and readiness for the day of God, can be called *qahal* (1QSa 1:25; 2:4; *cf.* CD 7:17; 11:22; 12:6). Similarly, the messianic army in the "war of the sons of light with the sons of darkness" is to carry, among its eight identifying banners when it sets out for battle, the words *qahal el,* "assembly of God" (1QM 4:10). The other seven names for the holy army in this set of banners, all recalling the exodus-story, are "congregation of God," "camps of God," "tribes of God," "clans of God," "divisions of God," "called of God," and "hosts of God" (1QM 4:9-11).

feast before your face," one petition might be translated, indicating the trust of the community that its meal in Christ is already a beginning of the life-giving feast of the end times. And when we remember that forgiveness was primarily a thing to hope for from God at the end, the other petition is equally stunning, equally celebrative of the actual presence of the end: "Forgive us now with your final forgiveness, just as we are turning to each other, ministers of your reconciliation." According to this prayer, the community of Christians is just like everyone else—longing for God, in need of mercy and life, hopeful, fearful, likely to fail. Yet in two characteristics of its real assemblies—in shared bread and in mutual forgiveness—it is already the assembly of Isaiah 25.[20]

Such an eschatological significance of *ekklesia* comes to clear expression in that passage of the letter to the Hebrews in which the Christian assembly is understood to be a new but inverted, revolutionary presence of the ancient Sinai assembly (Heb. 12:18-24):

> You have not come to something that can be touched, a blazing fire,
> and darkness, and gloom, and a tempest, and the sound of a trumpet,
> and a voice whose words made the hearers beg that not another word
> be spoken to them. (For they could not endure the order that was
> given, "If even an animal touches the mountain, it shall be stoned to
> death." Indeed, so terrifying was the sight that Moses said, "I tremble
> with fear.") But you have come to Mount Zion and to the city of the
> living God, the heavenly Jerusalem, and to innumerable angels in fes-
> tal gathering, and to the assembly *(ekklesia)* of the first born who are
> enrolled in heaven, and to God the judge of all, and to the spirits of
> the righteous made perfect, and to Jesus, the mediator of a new
> covenant, and to the sprinkled blood that speaks a better word than
> the blood of Abel.

In this text many characteristics of primitive Christian eschatology come to expression: strong biblical imagery, often connected in chains, yet marked by surprising inversions to accentuate God's grace which includes the outsiders; the presence of the future already now, yet the idea of that presence being "first fruits" or "downpayment" for the full manifestation of all of God's promises; the importance of community; and, in all of this, the centrality of Jesus Christ.

20. For the classic exegetical study of the eschatological spirit of the Lord's Prayer, see Joachim Jeremias, *Das Vater-Unser im Lichte der neueren Forschung* (Stuttgart: Calwer, 1967) and *The Prayers of Jesus* (Philadelphia: Fortress, 1978).

So for the writer to the Hebrews, these "last times" are to be understood as the living presence of the ancient biblical text from Exodus. *Assembly* before a *mountain* in the presence of *God* to be constituted as *a people* with a *vocation*—these old things of the text characterize the actual present gathering. The phrase "you have come" points to people actually coming into the meeting, as well as to people, more generally, joining the Christian community. Only now the mountain to which they have come is the Zion that Isaiah promised would be the place toward which all the nations, not just the Israelites, would stream. Now the mountain of this assembly is present wherever Jesus Christ is present in the Spirit,[21] wherever the new city of God is being formed around him, as in this present assembly. Now the holiness of the people is possible, not because of rigid purity laws and rigid exclusions (*contra* Deut. 23:1-4), but because of Jesus' "blood of the covenant," which does not accuse but rather welcomes in all sinners and outsiders, all the Cains of the world. This assembly, surrounded by the eschatological presence of God's angels, is before the face of God, gathered into the very life of God, but now the one God in that richness—the judge of all, the hope and life of the spirits, the new-covenant mediator—which later Christians would call the holy Trinity. This assembly holds a promise for all the world: it is made up of the "firstborn." All the world may follow in this new birth to mercy, this utterly new sense of the meaning of the world before God.

For the writer of the letter to the Hebrews, now is that "day of assembly" (Deut. 18:16), promised by the succession of biblical assemblies, in which the voice of the Lord can be heard, the people of God can be constituted, the final day of God can be anticipated. "Encourage one another" to meet together, says the author of the letter, "all the more as you see the Day approaching" (Heb. 10:25).

Of course, Hebrews does not necessarily give voice to all of the primitive Christian communities which called themselves the *ekklesia,* "the assembly." But it does provide us with one access to a significant field of meaning in which many other New Testament passages resonate. For important examples, take the letters attributed to both Peter and Paul. The First Letter of Peter makes an explicit application of the royal priesthood imagery of Exodus 19 to the Christian community (1 Pet. 2:9-10), seeing that community as receiving the same vocation as did the Sinai *qahal.* This application occurs in a passage that may be describing the eucharistic assem-

21. *Cf.* John 4:19-24.

bly (2:2-8) constituted through baptism (1:22—2:1). That eucharistic gathering, then, can be described in terms belonging both to the Sinai assembly and to the temple at Zion. Similarly, Paul's epistolary address to the assemblies, the *ekklesiai*, of certain cities is often paired with the idea that these are the holy, the consecrated ones, not unlike the holy assembly at Sinai (Rom. 1:7; 1 Cor. 1:2; 2 Cor. 1:1; *cf.* Phil. 1:1). This same Paul compares the identity-giving Baptism and Eucharist of the Christian assembly to the passage through the sea of the ancient people of the exodus and to their eating and drinking in the wilderness (1 Cor. 10:1-22). It may be that here Paul is seeking explicitly to reintroduce sobering content from the biblical assembly tradition to a community where the idea of eschatological gathering has been cut loose from its biblical origins and anchors, just as he also seeks to reintroduce the proclamation of the cross to an eschatological banquet that has become simply pleasure for the insiders, with no self-critical awareness of limits (1 Cor. 11).

Several other important and early New Testament ideas have an origin that is hidden from us, but a meaning that also can be seen as involving the application of the biblical assembly tradition. The appointment of the "twelve" (Mark 3:16; *cf.* 1 Cor. 15:5) recalls the twelve tribes at Sinai and the setting up of the memorial pillars (Ex. 24:4; Josh. 4:1-7). The appointment, mission and return of the "seventy" (Luke 10:1, 17) recalls the seventy elders of Israel who came up upon the mountain with Moses (Ex. 24:1,9). The proclamation of the cup of the Eucharist to be "my blood of the covenant" (Mark 14:24; Matt. 26:28) recalls the blood of the covenant thrown upon the people at Sinai (Ex. 24:8). The names for Christian proclamation *(kerygma)* and for the "calling" *(klesis)* to be a Christian may even echo the biblical idea, present in all of the old stories, of God's summoning of the people to the holy assembly.[22] The Markan tradition of the "crowd" around Jesus (for example, Mark 6:34), of the hundred-fold brothers, sisters, mothers, and children (10:30; *cf.* 3:34) and of the community in the "house" (for example, 2:1-2) may need to be seen against the same background, as an image that the holy assembly is coming to be in his presence. Something similar might be said of the Matthean and Lukan Jesus who "gathers" (Matt. 12:30; Luke 11:23) and the Johannine Jesus who "draws all" (John 12:32). That Mary Magdalene is "the apostle to the apostles" in John (20:18), inviting their fearful assembly to the transformation of resurrection faith, and

---

22. Louis Bouyer, *Liturgical Piety* (Notre Dame: University of Notre Dame Press, 1955), 24.

that the Mary and Martha of the Johannine narrative, unlike the Lukan figures,[23] have an assembly in their house in which women are capable of strong confessions of faith, in word and sign, and of presiding at table, may echo an eschatological interpretation of the assembly in Nehemiah 8, in which women participated fully, or a serious reading of the promise of Joel 2:28. Furthermore, the "third day" of the Sinai assembly may hover behind the "third day" of the various resurrection accounts as part of its rich field of meaning: the Risen One pulls all people out of death into the holy assembly.

Later Christian voices continued this eschatological understanding of the meeting. Ignatius of Antioch, for example, thought that the gathering for Eucharist—for the Word of God, for praise to God, and for the holy meal—held the very forces of evil themselves at bay. While the biblical references to the Sinai assembly are not present in his assertion, his conception of the assembly breathes the same eschatological spirit: "Make every effort, then, to gather together more frequently for the eucharist of God and for God's glory. For when you are often together in unity, the powers of Satan are pulled down and the destruction Satan brings is destroyed through your concord in faith."[24] In the meeting, in its concord of faith, in its shared meal and in its acts of praise, God's final victory over evil is beginning to be enacted.

Liturgical Assembly as Church

All of these diverse voices can help us to understand the excess of meaning present when ancient Christians called their communities by the name "assembly." We do not know to what extent this primitive Christian identification of their meetings with the end-time "assembly of God" was rooted in the preaching of Jesus himself and the eschatology of the "Jesus-movement."[25] We do know that understandings of "church" in these or in

---

23. John 11:1—12:8; Luke 10:38-42; cf. Jane Schaberg, "Luke," in Carol A. Newsom and Sharon H. Ringe, eds., The Women's Bible Commentary (London: SPCK, 1992), 288–89.

24. Ignatius, To the Ephesians, 13:1. Greek text in Kirsopp Lake, ed., The Apostolic Fathers (New York: Harvard University Press, 1959), 1:186.

25. For example, if the historical Jesus is the source of the idea that the sinners and outsiders who are gathered around him are "wedding guests," an idea present in several parts of the gospel tradition (cf. Mark 2:19; Matt. 22:2ff.), then his eschatology is strongly similar to the later Christian eschatology of ekklesia. The prophetic hope was that the redeemed people should ultimately be sanctified and "wed" to God (cf. Isa. 62:4-5), an expectation pro-

similar biblical terms did have everything to do with the faith that, by the power of the Spirit, the crucified and risen Christ was now gathering a people into the day of God. "The assembly" was the name of that people.

Again, the gathering that was so named may well have been understandable first in one of the available cultural patterns: philosophical association, extended household, club. When Pliny looked at one of these assemblies, he called it *hetaeria*. If we want to make some sociological account of these old meetings, we rightly join Pliny—or other exterior estimators of the Christian movement—in making use of the available categories. Such categories will help us to see that these were real people, with real problems, meeting in the actual circumstances of our world. These categories will allow us to see the continuity between Christian communities and the available human structures.

But we will also need to see how those structures were transformed. For Pliny is no help in understanding what the Christians themselves thought they were doing, what their meetings meant. He had only a confused picture of what the Christians did when they met[26]—confused partly because of his ignorance of Christianity and partly because the information he did have was secured by the threat of violent execution and by actual torture. Indeed, his acts of torture, like his fawning relationship to the emperor and his exaggerated opinion of himself, are despicable and unhelpful things, not illumination of any sort. Nonetheless, he rightly saw that the content of the meeting was the issue. Many other clubs had their rituals, but it was the content of the specifically Christian rituals that Pliny found opprobrious.

Still, in order to understand the Christians, we need to pay attention to what they called themselves and what they believed they should do at their meetings. For the members of the movement itself, their meeting, their group, was *ekklesia*, inheritor of the biblical promise of assembly. And this "assembly" was not just a name. The principal way that the biblical promise was exercised, the principal means for juxtaposing the ancient biblical hope to a current means of meeting, was *liturgical*.

This Christian assembly met for a purpose, met to do something. It had a definite center. It had a different way of gathering. We are shown this by Ignatius with his Eucharist, but also by Paul with his baptism like crossing

foundly parallel to the hope for the holy assembly. In the ministry of Jesus, this expectation is inverted, made available to the sinners and impure, and celebrated as actually present.

26. Pliny, *Letters* 10:96. The Christians meet early on a "fixed day," they sing in alternation a hymn "to Christ as to a god," they bind themselves to each other in certain "oaths" (*sacramenta*), and they disperse, gathering together again in the evening for a shared meal.

the sea and his Eucharist like drinking from the rock (1 Cor. 10:1-4), and by Peter with his "new birth" (1 Pet. 1:3, 23) and his tasting "that the Lord is good" (2:3). We are shown that center by the ancient Lord's Prayer: the meeting is marked by a meal and by mutual forgiveness. And we are shown it by Paul's pairing of his appeal for mutual peace and love in the local assembly and his sending of greetings from other assemblies, from "all the holy people" (2 Cor. 13:13; *cf.* 1 Cor. 16:19), with an appeal for the exercise of the "holy kiss" and with a formal, liturgical trinitarian greeting (2 Cor. 13:11-13). This is a meeting, an association, that is transformed in its mode and its content by being gathered into the very life of the triune God. This is a meeting transformed by the Word of God which calls the assembly together, gives a center to the meeting, and criticizes and transforms the mode of mutual relationship.

For the Christians, then, the *ekklesia* met to gather around the same thing the ancient biblical assemblies had at their heart: the presence of the Word of God. The biblical Word gave their assemblies a name. It gave them a chain of images with which to interpret their own meetings, to give a history and a future to what was being done with them. It also gave them an actual practice—Scriptures to be read and interpreted,[27] psalms and hymns to be sung, prayers to be prayed, the biblical meal to be held, a pattern of consecration to be followed by those who came to join them, a faith to be taught. Only now many Christians had a sense that these were the final times (*cf.* 1 Cor. 10:11). This was the actual voice and presence of God reverberating in the assembly. Because of the resurrection of Jesus Christ, because of his gift and the Spirit of his rising, the assembly met in the presence of the triune God.

From our vantage point, we might say this all in the imagery of Exodus 19-24. If the ancient Sinai assembly had gathered to hear the law of God and to eat and drink before God's face, this gathering in Jesus Christ assembled to hear the Scriptures and preaching and to share the bread and cup of the Eucharist. If that ancient people had been "consecrated" for the meeting with God, this assembly was constituted by the great washing called Baptism. And if that people had been made a priestly people, this community was established as witness to God's truth among the nations. However the *ordo* of Christian worship, the great outline of its actions, came into

27. On the reading of Scripture in the first-century churches, see Luke 24:27, 32; 1 Thess. 5:27; Col. 4:16. For the second century, see Justin, *1 Apology* 67; Ignatius, *To the Philadelphians* 8:2.

existence, we can note its correspondence to the pattern of events at Sinai. And we can see that the *ordo* evokes the great assembly of the return from exile (Nehemiah 8) and anticipates the gathering of all nations to Zion (Isaiah 25).

Such a sense of the presence of the end times in the practices of the assembly was alive in the Lukan community, for example. Its gospel-book images the Sunday assembly as gathered around the risen Christ in Scripture and table (Luke 24:13-34; *cf.* Acts 2:41-42; 20:7-11), as marked by the poured-out Spirit of God, and as sent out in mission to gather the world (Luke 24:36-49). Even without the Sinai imagery, the parallel *ordo* is striking. Similarly, the Johannine gospel imaged the Sunday assembly as gathered around the presence of the risen Christ, as using the book that enables them to believe in him, as seeing his wounds in faith, as being marked by the Spirit, as being forgiven, as being sent with forgiveness, just as the Father had sent the Son, and as thereby participating in the life of God (John 20:19-31).[28] These are practices shaped by an eschatological faith, ways in which Christian faith reshaped the biblical idea of assembly as a thing that could be practiced now. They accord with a further text, from the Matthean community, also about mutual and eschatological forgiveness in the *ekklesia*: "For where two or three are gathered together in my name, I am there among them" (Matt. 18:20). These practices accord with the Markan sense that the crowd around Jesus hears his teaching and comes to his miraculous meal served by the twelve or the seven (Mark 6:30-44; 8:1-9). And they accord with Ignatius of Antioch: "Wherever Jesus Christ is, there is the catholic *ekklesia.*"[29] Christian assemblies can be called *ekklesia,* their practices can be understood as practices of the "holy people" in "holy assembly," because of the presence of Jesus Christ.

A biblical name, a chain of biblical images, biblical practices, a biblical faith—these were juxtaposed to something that, to outsiders and probably many insiders, too, looked like a Hellenistic club, a ritual interest group, a philosophical society, a meeting in somebody's house, under someone's patronage. By that essentially liturgical juxtaposition a new thing was proposed: the presence of the biblical promise in a transformed local meeting. A current but transformed social pattern was made the bearer of an ancient biblical hope, just as the bread of the Eucharist was current bread conjoined

28. On these passages as images of the ongoing practice of the Lukan and Johannine *assemblies,* see Lathrop, *Holy Things,* 48–49.

29. Ignatius, *To the Smyrnaeans* 8:2.

with the lively biblical Word. The *ekklesia* was marked by both continuity and transformation.

Ancient Christians themselves knew about this double character of their communities. One anonymous second- or third-century Christian wrote about his or her co-religionists: "Living in Greek and barbarian cities ... and following the local customs, in clothing and dwelling places and the rest of life, they demonstrate the amazing and confessedly unexpected *(paradoxon)* character of the make up of their own citizenship. They are at home in their own countries, but as sojourners. They participate in all things as citizens and they endure all things as foreigners. Every foreign country is their homeland and every homeland is a foreign country."[30]

The transformation of an ordinary meeting to become "amazing" and "unexpected" can be seen in yet another biblical image. The story of the healing of the paralyzed man (Mark 2:1-12) begins with Jesus being "in the house" or "at home" *(en oiko)*. This "house," of course, evokes the house of the church which the Markan readers know and which the Gospel itself seems to repeatedly evoke (1:29; 3:20; 7:17; 9:28; 14:3), a place for the speaking of the Word (2:2) and the forgiveness of sins. The crowd of the story evokes our biblical idea of the eschatological gathering. But in order for the story to proceed, the house itself—and the meeting of which it is a concrete symbol—must be transformed: its roof must be removed. A human being who would not ordinarily be included in any "meeting"—a human being who is marginal and ordinarily out of sight—must be included. The ongoing history of the transformation of houses and basilicas to become places for the assembly indicates one trajectory forward from this story. The continuing struggle for the church to see how the Word and the forgiveness of sins in the heart of the meeting—the presence of the Risen One—necessarily imply an open door to all the marginalized—the chronically ill, the disabled, the poor, the women, the people other than us—is another trajectory forward.[31] But the story itself represents the deep Christian faith in the God who transforms both "crowd" and "house" to be "assembly" and "house of the assembly."

Did people get it? We may rightly ask if the biblical name and the ritual content that corresponded to the name made any difference, if the "club," the "meeting," the "crowd," was really transformed into something else. Sometimes yes and sometimes no. The local Christian community was

---

30. *Epistle to Diognetus* 5:4–5. Greek text in Lake, *The Apostolic Fathers,* 2:358–60.

31. Stephen Weisser of Philadelphia, in an as yet unpublished paper, has helpfully pursued the ecclesiological and pastoral trajectories from this pericope.

inevitably marked by the real difficulties and misuses that came along with those various contemporary models. Paul's exhortation against the insiders' dining group (1 Cor. 11:17ff.) or against over-identification with a benefactor through baptism (1:12), Jude's rage against the misuse of the symposium, the drinking society (Jude 12), and Ignatius's famous appeals for unity (for example, *To the Philadelphians,* 4) suggest as much. These are complaints about the actual misuse of rituals in these communities. Here is evidence that the ideals of equality and mutual forgiveness in the assembly were by no means always achieved.[32] The ideal churches of Acts are just that: *ideals,* themselves evidence of the existence of their polar opposites. As at Corinth, a local community may even have been misunderstanding its own eschatology, calling a party of like-minded friends from the same social group by the name "assembly." The biblical name, images, practices, faith were in tension with the available assembly patterns.[33]

But the tension was alive, and often transformative. The very exhortations of Paul and Ignatius are evidences of the creative tension present in these communities. The juxtaposition of the name and the biblical tradition to these local Hellenistic groups acknowledged the faith that something more was occurring here than the agenda of a *collegium.* Indeed, the name *ekklesia* helped to create the pressure that these groups might be that thing that they were called. For the word *ekklesia* was more than a mere name. It carried with itself the expectation that the content of the meeting would be claiming the entire life of its participants, radically reinterpreting their world. Further, the Word of God that convoked this gathering, the gospel of Jesus Christ alive in preaching, in his inclusion and forgiveness of sinners, in his meal, was making this meeting something more than any conventional meeting could be. As the lector Emeritus, who allowed the Christian Sunday assembly to gather for Eucharist in his early-fourth-century North African house, was to say at his trial: "They are my brothers and sisters and I am not able to stop them . . . for we cannot be without the supper of the

32. Nonetheless, Pliny does indicate that the accused members of the local Christian *ekklesia* included many "persons of all ranks and ages, and of both sexes" ("multi enim omnis aetatis, omnis ordinis, utriusque sexus etiam"). Melmoth and Hutchinson, 405. Meeks also quotes a remarkable fourth-century pagan text in which the author accuses those of his own class who had become Christians with receiving their doctrines from "your mother, your wife, your housekeeper, your cook." *First Urban Christians,* 214 n. 4.

33. On this tension, see Wayne A. Meeks, *The Origins of Christian Morality* (New Haven: Yale University Press, 1993), 49–50, and Erik M. Heen, *Saturnalicius Princeps:The Enthronement of Jesus in Early Christian Discourse,* Ph.D. diss., Columbia University (Ann Arbor: UMI, 1997), 238–41.

Lord."[34] This gathering for which Emeritus was willing to die was what we call "church."

Our Liturgical Assemblies

We ought not to overstate the case. There is much we do not know about the origins of the ancient Christian churches. We do not, for example, know if the chain of biblical assembly-images was always behind the Christian use of the word *ekklesia*. But we do know enough to note that this word, which also denoted the worldwide body of Christians, first meant a local, actual assembly. We do know enough to be ourselves moved by the resonances of biblical meaning we can now see around that assembly, resonances which are sometimes explicitly present in early Christian sources as both gift and task for the local Christian group. We can claim for ourselves the tradition of biblical images. In the transformative juxtaposition of the biblical tradition of assembly to the gatherings of early Christianity, we can find resources for our own re-estimation of our current meetings.

What might this re-estimation mean for our own experience of "assembly" as the most basic liturgical symbol of Christians?

At the outset, we can experience the liturgical assembly as *church*, as the primary meaning of that important Christian word. Of course, we will need to recall other meanings of the word. We will need to ask how this local assembly is united with all the other assemblies and how it participates in that worldwide "assembly" that the earliest sources also envision. But in the first place, *church* has a quite concrete, local, accessible meaning. It is a real assembly of people, gathered in a real place, face-to-face, to carry out the agenda of the *ekklesia*.

We can even assent to using the later English (and German, Norse, and Slavic) word "church" for this assembly. Drawn from a transliteration of the Greek *kyriakon*, "belonging to the Lord," the word was first used in those languages as the name for a Christian building and only later for the people who assembled in the building. But its northern European development rightly reverted to its original Greek sense. In Greek, the word pointed to the house of the Lord as the house of the assembly around the Risen One. The distance was not great from the New Testament names for the

34. "Quoniam fratres mei sunt, et non poteram illos prohibere . . . quoniam sine dominico non possumus." Latin text in J.-P. Migne, ed., *Patrilogiae Cursus Completus, Series Prima* 8 (Paris:1844), 695. The volumes of Migne will henceforth be cited as *PL* and, in the case of *Patrologiae Graece, PG*.

Eucharist and for Sunday—*ton kyriakon deipnon,* "the Lord's supper," (1 Cor. 11:20); *he kyriake hemera,* "the Lord's day," (Rev. 1:10)—to the sense of the risen Lord's presence in the assembly and in the house of that assembly.[35] Of course, we will need to refresh our sense that it is precisely this eschatological presence of the Risen One in the midst of the assembly that is being underlined by the use of the word *church:* "the risen Lord's place," "the Risen One's gathering."

For the *ekklesia* tradition also invites us to see that participation in this assembly is participation in Christian eschatology. This means not that we will all be able to come to discursive, cognitive agreement about what talk about the "last things" means, but that for us to be in the assembly will mean that we are immersed in the characteristics of Christian eschatology. The texts and the actions of our liturgies, if they are faithful to the great tradition of liturgy, will show us that we are here as before God's own face. Those texts and actions will also seek to tell the truth about us and our world. The sense will be that there must be more to time and to life, since, to tell the truth, the world is both so beautiful and so full of evil, death, and sorrow. But for Christians, the truth includes this: Jesus Christ, the crucified and risen one, is the beginning of God's "more." He is the meaning of the world itself, before God. In the power of the Spirit of God, this assembly will then be made a community around him, as he is present in Scripture and in the breaking of bread.

The resurrection of Jesus Christ, which Christians believe is the "first fruits" of the last things of God and is present to us in the power of the Spirit, changes everything, including our assemblies. Because of the resurrection, biblical texts will be read as of present events, but they will be read in chains, with surprising, mercy-centered reversals, welcoming the outsiders. Because of the resurrection, the meal that is held here will be a small community, eating the feast of the end of death, a feast that, like the food that is to be spread on the "mountain of the Lord" (Isa. 25:6-7), is ultimately meant for everyone. Because of the resurrection, those who enter this assembly will be washed into the witnessing life of the community, as if they were being awakened from sleep, born anew to life, raised from the

---

35. The first clear use of the word *kyriakon* to mean a church building—in the fourth century of our era—is found quite clearly in the context of assembly and liturgy: "But gather together each day, morning and evening, singing and praying in the churches (in the places of the Lord, *en tois kyriakois*), saying Psalm 63 in the morning and Psalm 141 in the evening." *Apostolic Constitutions* 2:59:2. Greek text in F. X. Funk, ed., *Didascalia et Constitutiones Apostolorum* (Paderborn: Schoeningh, 1905), 1:171.

dead. And because of the resurrection, this gathering will understand itself as raised up, together with Christ, to be a holy assembly, to hear God's truth about the world, in the name and for the sake of all the others, to pray for the others, to send signs of God's truth to places of need, to forgive and be forgiven, to taste the downpayment of God's intention for all the world, and to be a communal witness to what they have heard and seen and tasted. "Assembly" is the rich biblical image for this understanding of the purpose of our meetings.

The ancient image of *ekklesia* will also help us to see the contents of our liturgies more clearly. We do not gather as individual consumers come to a priestly distributor of religious goods. We come to do a communal thing, to be a people, to receive a common vocation, to be a tangible representation of the biblical image "assembly." Churches that keep one of the classic rites as the source for the core words of their present celebration will be assisted in this, since those words are so filled with the ancient sense of a holy people gathered before the holy God: the "we" of *gloria in excelsis,* the creed, and the eucharistic prayer, for example, or the prayers for the unity of all the churches of God as well as for the unity of the people here present, or the greeting of peace, or the mutuality of the repeated *dominus vobiscum* greeting combined with its sense of the presence of the Risen One in this plural gathering.

But whether or not the old liturgical words are present, the communal meaning of the great outline of the *ordo,* that heritage of all Christians, must be clear. From the initial remembrance of the baptism that joined us to this assembly, to the common singing of the assembly, to the opening greeting that intends to surround us all verbally with the life of the triune God, to the book opened as our communal book, to the meal as our communal meal, to the common dismissal—all will be a shared action. This must be a community that treasures the persons who make up the gathering, that honors the mystery of their individuality, but that constantly calls them into the common work. The presider here will preside for the sake of the assembly, honoring the assembly and each of its constituents, serving the purposes of the assembly. The assisting ministers or deacons will assist the assembly, will serve the table of the assembly, will help connect the assembly to the world. In all of this, *ekklesia* will be a principal interpretive key for understanding the interaction of text and action in creating the meaning of the meeting. This symbol will be available to interpret our liturgy because of the faith that God is acting here.

After all, at a basic level, any assembly we call "church" is just us. Local people are here. If we come, what we encounter will be our words, our music, our bread and wine, our water, our meeting place, our cultural conceptions of what it is to meet at all. But by the mercy of God, it also will be those things "broken" to serve a new purpose.[36] The use of the biblical assembly tradition in the early history of the church helps us to see this. A *collegium* or a Romano-Hellenistic household is called the *ekklesia* and given those central things to do, that Scripture and bath and meal, which correspond to the Christian reception of this name. The *collegium* thereby is called to a larger and different agenda; the household is given new lines of relationship; the philosophical society is given an open door to people who are not philosophers. As the churches came to own houses outright in the third century, they found that the houses had to be remodeled to accord with the purposes of the assembly around Christ. The old domestic architecture, with its conception of society, did not provide a space fit for *ekklesia*. As the churches began, in the fourth century, to build large public buildings on the plan of the buildings used for imperial business, those buildings also needed a new organizing center: not so much a throne for a royal magistrate as an *ambo* for the word and a table for a community.[37]

In exactly the same way, whatever conceptions we bring to the meeting, whatever ideas of assembly we have, need to undergo transformation. Ours is not a sacred assembly just by saying so. Or, rather, the "god" of our sacred assemblies can simply be our own projection of ourselves. But the biblical Word in its liturgical forms can be the principal tool of a remodeling, house-changing transformation. Take what may seem, at first glance, to be our chosen place to consume religious goods, our religious club, our audience, our pageant, our secret society, our folk festival, our town meeting, our attempt at genuine community. These are models found in all of our churches. Then heighten the sources of the symbolic excess for this meeting, the ways this meeting is called to be more than it is. Set out the Scriptures and the table in the midst of our preconceptions. Set out the bread and the mutual forgiveness of the Lord's Prayer. In song and preaching and prayer, make it clear that these things are central because they gather us all into the very triune life of God. Make these central symbols large. Encourage participation. Open the door. Ask about the accessibility of the meeting to people who are ordinarily marginalized. Pray for the world. Encourage each to turn to the other in

---

36. On the "breaking" of symbols, see below, chapters 2 and 7–9.
37. On the public liturgies of magistrates, see Heen, *Saturnalicius Princeps,* 63–68.

mutual forgiveness and love, according dignity and respect. Discourage individual displays of power. Send signs of God's mercy to places in need. By these things the meaning of the meeting will be changed, with different lines of relationship, different connections to our times.

Our conceptions of assembly may still come to the meeting, but they will not dominate, not be foundational. They will instead be inverted, bringing their insights and strengths paradoxically: this is an audience that participates, a pageant that is truth telling and not romantic, a secret society or an ethnic gathering where everyone ought to be welcome, a collection of people choosing to be here who find themselves being chosen (John 15:16). This is genuine community not by immediate access to each other's souls but by shared participation in the signs of God's great mercy. These inversions and transformations will not be perfect in any of our assemblies. The social material out of which the assembly is made will constantly be reasserting itself, just as the basilica has been frequently reclaimed as an imperial throne room instead of an assembly hall. But if our preconceptions of "meeting" are not brought under considerable tension, if the critique of our preconceptions is not becoming part of the meaning of the meeting itself, we may ask if the central matters of the liturgy have been set out with sufficient clarity and strength or if they have, rather, been tamed to our own purposes.

In fact, the liturgy and its *ordo* are remnants of a long history of the fruitful and tension-laden juxtaposition of the biblical Word to a human history of meetings. This history may help to give us some distance from our cultural moment and its power. Those remnants will be our best tools for the conversion and transformation of our meetings. Indeed, Christian faith will say that this is so not because we have done this or that to transform "our" meeting, but because God acts in the central matters of those "remnants," in the word and sacraments that claim the meeting as God's own. God acts, just as the incognito risen Christ, come as a guest, became the host and the meaning of the table at Emmaus (Luke 24:29-30).

But then we will see that the possibility of calling our gatherings "the assembly," the *ekklesia*, is a merciful gift of God. The church, as some Roman Catholic theologians have argued, is not only a church of sinners; it is a sinful church. The church, as Lutherans and other Protestants have maintained, belongs to the structures of this world, not, in the first place, to the structures of grace. We are not, in ourselves, the holy assembly. But in the mercy of God, this sinful gathering, this structure of our world, is called *ekklesia*. As the Orthodox theologian Alexander Schmemann argues, "the purpose of worship is to constitute the church,"[38] as the holy assembly of God, set out in the world.

If we are to let these initial reflections on assembly and the liturgy go on to become a liturgical ecclesiology, we will need to ask a number of questions. How are such liturgical assemblies connected to a wider sense of "church"? What insights follow for the actual practice of assembly? Can the liturgy, conceived as the shared inheritance of the assemblies, indeed contribute to ecumenical unity? When we speak of "holy assembly," what do we actually mean by "holiness"? And if *ekklesia* always involves a crisis in our cultural conceptions of meeting, what insights can be drawn for the relationships between Christian worship and the cultures of the world?

But here is a beginning: Assembly, a gathering together of participating persons, constitutes the most basic symbol of Christian worship. The symbol means something in the practice of assembly, in the exercise of those central things that belong to assembly, in the experience of juxtaposing word, table, bath, prayer, and song to our conceptions of meeting. Those things invite, persuade, enable our gatherings to be understood as gatherings around the resurrection of Jesus Christ, in the power of the Spirit, before the face of God, for the sake of the world. And these gatherings are called "church."

---

38. Schmemann, *Introduction to Liturgical Theology,* 19.

2

With All, in Every Place

The church is an assembly. The church is a gathering of people in a particular place who are, together, through concrete means, participating in the mystery of Christ and so are being formed into the holy assembly. The church is not a collection of consuming individuals, choosing religious goods according to their own self-perceived needs or desires. It is not a club supporting a particular ideology. It is not the audience for a speaker's eloquence, a choir's concert, or a priest's rituals. The local church-assembly is itself, as gathering, the primary symbol. By its participation, by its communal mode of song and prayer around Scripture reading, meal keeping, and bathing, it is being transformed into a primary witness to the identity of God and the identity of the world before God. These assertions can be taken to summarize the deepest insights of the twentieth-century liturgical movement.

But in what way does one assembly, in one place, relate to other assemblies, in other places? How are they found to be bearing witness together? Can a liturgical ecclesiology cast any light on this relationship?

The New Testament uses its term—"the assembly"—primarily for a group that has its local gathering in a local place. But that is not the word's only usage. The New Testament also occasionally speaks of all Christians, in every place, as *ekklesia,* church, assembly, using the singular noun.[1] Indeed, for Paul, his own early zeal for hurting Christians of several different communities could be called, simply, a persecution of the *ekklesia,* of "the assembly" (Phil. 3:6). Similarly, using body and building metaphors for

1. So Matt. 16:18; Gal. 1:13; 1 Cor. 10:32; 15:9; Phil. 3:6; Eph. 1:22; 3:10; 5:23-32; Col. 1:18, 24. See Wayne A. Meeks, *The First Urban Christians* (New Haven: Yale University Press, 1983), 109.

49

the whole of the Christian movement, the deutero-Pauline letters could call Christ the "head of the body, the assembly" (Col. 1:18; *cf.* Eph. 1:22) and the Matthean Jesus could say, "On this rock I will build my assembly" (Matt. 16:18). Again, the nouns are singular. If we translate these familiar passages with "assembly," instead of "church," we see the remarkable point more clearly.

Later Christian speech could express something of the same idea with the word "catholic." The mid-second-century book, the *Martyrdom of Polycarp,* was sent from "the assembly of God which sojourns in Smyrna to the assembly of God which sojourns in Philomelium and to all the sojournings in every place of the holy and catholic assembly."[2] The singular term—the church, the assembly—could be used both of the local gathering and of the universal body, too, as if it were also a gathering. Indeed, this same book calls its subject, Polycarp, "a bishop of the catholic assembly in Smyrna," and reports both that he prayed night and day "for the assemblies in the whole inhabited world" and that he prayed at length "for all the catholic assembly in the whole inhabited world."[3] Singular and plural seem oddly interchangeable.

Here, in this one second-century book, is a comprehensive vocabulary for later ecclesiology. Here is the term *ekklesia* we have been considering, now used for both local and more-than-local realities. But here also are "holy" assembly, "catholic" or "universal" assembly, the *paroikia* or "sojourning" of the assembly, and the assembly in the *oikoumene* or "whole inhabited world." "Assembly" or "church" is used for the local gathering but also for the more-than-local, "ecumenical" reality of the Christian movement, as also for that more-than-local reality understood as "dwelling" here, locally. How can we make sense of this use of terms? How is the church in Smyrna also the holy and universal church sojourning in Smyrna? And how is the whole Christian movement an "assembly?"

2. *Martyrdom of Polycarp,* inscr. Greek text in Kirsopp Lake, ed., *The Apostolic Fathers* (New York: Harvard University Press, 1959), 2:310. With the term "sojourning," *paroikia,* here one should compare the description of Christians as both sojourners and citizens in *Diognetus* 5:5. See above, chapter 1, note 30, and below, note 5. The term is the origin of the later Christian word for a local assembly and its place: "parish."

3. *Martyrdom of Polycarp* 16:2; 5:1; 8:1. Greek text in Lake, *The Apostolic Fathers,* 2:334, 318, 322. The term for "the whole inhabited world" is *oikumene,* the current Christian "ecumene," source of such words as "ecumenical" and "ecumenism." Polycarp's intercessions, reflecting the list of prayers we can find in later Christian liturgical patterns, are actually for both world and church, "for all and for the assemblies in the *oikoumene*" (5:1), "for all he had ever met, both little and great, eminent and disreputable, and for all the catholic assembly in the *oikoumene*" (8:1).

The Catholic Church, the Catholic Churches

The temptation may be to answer these questions with a kind of platonism. In such a way of thinking, "church" is an idea in the mind of God, a universal ideal that is largely invisible and can only be represented, perhaps, by certain leaders—say, the pope, understood as a "universal" pastor, together with the pope's court or *curia*—or certain doctrines, say, *election,* understood as the idea that there is an invisible list in the mind of God of all the people included among the "saved." Then the local "church" is a lesser emanation of the universal church, a descent of the idea into messy, unworthy, local matter, at some distance from the ideal. By this conception, the local assembly may always be trying to become the pure idea of church, but will never be quite able to do so. The local assembly may represent the church, but the church itself remains invisible, or, in any case, somewhere else. Even at its mystical best, this platonism suggests that the reality of church may, in the local experience, only be intuited, and then only by the spiritually sensitive. Unlike the word usage of the New Testament, "local church" then circles around and depends upon "universal church" as a greater idea.

There have been other temptations. For some practical, Protestant Christians, the question of a universal church is simply refused. The only church is the local assembly. Ignoring the linguistic uses of the New Testament and the early centuries, they will speak of connections among churches, but not *the church,* when speaking of the more-than-local. Or they will use the singular term for the wider reality only analogically, by way of extension from the local.

If another, medieval temptation was to regard the church as a kind of universal empire, with the clergy as local magistrates or satraps, there is also a more recent form of the same model. The current temptation may be to answer inquiry about local relationship to the more-than-local by pointing to sales organizations. A multinational corporation may have a local representative agent or agents. To encounter and deal with these agents is to deal with the corporation, though the corporation itself is far larger. But though the local agents may be "authorized" to act on behalf of the corporation, they can also always be overruled or even fired. Again unlike the New Testament or the church in Smyrna, authority is finally never local. In the sales-corporation analogy, the local church is only "authorized" to act on behalf of a larger body. Christianity is an international entity with local and regional representation. And in this analogy just as in its medieval form, a great deal of accent comes to fall on clergy, on local pastors as "authorized representatives," and on more-than-local officials as the authorizers.

None of these models adequately represents the fascinating language of the *Martyrdom of Polycarp* nor that of Paul. For Paul as for the Smyrnaean Christians, the *assembly* really exists, both locally and more-than-locally. Neither is a lesser or analogical or representative form of the other, though each local assembly is somehow the whole catholic church "sojourning here."

It seems better to turn to the Bible and early Christian eschatology, the sources of the term *ekklesia,* to understand what may be meant. If the assembly of the last days, the gathering before God's face, is beginning to take place now, it is taking place concretely where the Word that goes out from God is being read and proclaimed and the meal before the face of God is being eaten and our actual gatherings are being transformed. Those things happen locally, in many different places. But Christian faith says that there is one dawning day, one word from God, one risen Lord who opens that Word, one Spirit that enlivens the communion in that Word, one triune God into whose life all are drawn. Indeed, because there is one God acting, there is one assembly of the last times, from all over the earth, beginning to appear before God. Wherever the Word of God is appearing, wherever the meal in Christ is being held, the entire possibility for assembly is open, the whole assembly is coming to be there.

It is as if we all, from the whole world, were gathered at that square before the gate in Jerusalem where Ezra is beginning to read from the book (Neh. 8:1-3). Then, as expression of the whole assembly and participation in its meaning, smaller circles of us turn to a nearby Levite who is interpreting the reading, giving us the sense (Neh. 8:7-8). And it is as if, at the counsel of Ezra and the Levites and because this is a holy day, we eat and drink the holy meal, and together with all the assembly, as a sign of the truth of the God proclaimed here, a sign of our having understood what has been read, we send portions to those for whom nothing is prepared (Neh. 8:10-12).

Only we are not at Jerusalem. We are in our own towns and cities. We are not physically side by side with the all the others in other places. And it is not a Levite, but our own presider who stands to interpret in our midst.

Still, our meeting to read the book can occur at all only because of the resurrection. We are in the company of the risen Christ, who is at the heart of the reading of the book and the interpretation of its meaning, whose risen presence is at the center of the meal. With Christ come all those who are drawn to him (John 12:32), who are in him, who live with his life.

Where Jesus Christ is, they are. Indeed, wherever the Risen One is, in the truth of the Spirit, there is the new mountain of meeting with God, the new city, the new temple, the new assembly (John 4:20-26). So "wherever Jesus Christ is, there is the catholic *ekklesia*,"[4] also here, in our particular place. And because of the outpoured Spirit, the entire assembly may declare the sense of the reading, each of us turning to our neighbor with the word of peace, our presider gifted to preside at and articulate this opening of the Scriptures, keeping of the meal, sending of the portions.

Because of God's presence, our local meeting becomes the whole catholic church dwelling here. Because of God's acting, not because of our ability at intuiting the universal in the particular, each local meeting becomes a sign of the dawning of the day of God. Anyone who comes into this meeting encounters the whole assembly of God. Such a meeting is not authorized by some other official headquarters, elsewhere. If the word and sacrament of God's acting are here, the whole powerful, world-transform-ing mystery is here. Local church, an actual gathering of people always being made into holy assembly, is the primary form of church.

And yet, the whole assembly is also present in all the other local churches. The whole assembly, therefore, gathers each local place into its meaning. Coming into the assembly is not about going away to distant Jerusalem, nor to a distant God. The meaning of the assembly is declared to the whole beloved earth by local gatherings of those who are both local cit-izens and sojourners. Indeed, because of the assembly, they are citizens also of all the other particular places, lovers of the well-being of all the earth.[5] The network of assemblies is beginning to hold the whole earth before God, as if the earth itself were Jerusalem, the place of assembly to hear the life-giving Word. And when assemblies begin to gather on Mars or Jupiter's moons, the wider resonance of that same truth will be shown forth: the beloved universe itself is the place for hearing that Word.

"Network," we say. One rightly asks how these assemblies show signs of communion with each other, signs that they recognize those they know in the risen Christ, signs that they belong to each other. Through such signs of communion, all the meetings, together, can be shown to be the assembly

---

4. Ignatius, *To the Smyrnaeans* 8:2; cf. *Martyrdom of Polycarp* 19:2: "our Lord Jesus Christ, the savior of our lives, guide of our bodies, and shepherd of the catholic assembly in the whole inhabited world."

5. "They are at home in their own countries, but as sojourners. They participate in all things as citizens and they endure all things as foreigners. Every foreign country is their homeland and every homeland is a foreign country." *Epistle to Diognetus* 5:5. See above, chap-ter 1, n. 30.

God is creating in the earth as a serving and witnessing people. All the assemblies together, in communion with each other, can also be called by the singular noun: the catholic church, the universal assembly. Indeed, the presence of signs of communion among local churches may be taken as a mark that what we are encountering in any given assembly is truly the assembly of God.

But then the linkage between local and more-than-local, between the assembly of God in this city and the whole catholic assembly in all the inhabited earth, is neither mystical nor hierarchical nor merely organizational nor invisible. It is theological and concretely liturgical. This linkage exists because of the action of the one triune God for the sake of the life of all the world. The churches visibly participate in the linkage by tangible signs of communion.

The Marks of the Church

But what are those signs? Throughout the ages theologians have variously catalogued the instruments of communion among the churches, sometimes calling them "notes of the church" or "marks of the church." The notes that describe the church in the Nicene Creed—that the church is one, holy, catholic, and apostolic—came especially to function significantly in controversial writing at the time of the Reformation and again in the nineteenth century. Theologians sought to use various interpretations of these marks to identify the true church, to include their own churches and to argue against other churches.

Such an undertaking was not, however, an innovation of the sixteenth century. Against the very real dangers of heresy, theologians of the patristic period also inquired, though somewhat less systematically, if certain traits— namely, apostolic Scriptures, apostolic doctrine, and apostolic ministry— were present in a supposed Christian assembly. The presence of these traits would enable that assembly to be acknowledged as a *catholic* church. Such a use of the adjective "catholic" may already be present in the *Martyrdom of Polycarp* itself: it may be that "the catholic assembly in Smyrna" (16:2) of which Polycarp had been the bishop is being distinguished from some other assembly or assemblies, also in Smyrna. In any case, the word "catholic" was certainly used in the later history of the church to indicate communities where Scripture, doctrine, and ministry united those communities with all other Christian churches, across space and time, in which the practice in these regards was "always and everywhere" *(semper et ubique)* the same. Such "catholic unity" inherited the early Christian eschatological sense that God was convoking one worldwide assembly to be a faithful witness to the world.

More recently, certain "notes" have been used to propose ways in which the unity of the churches could be re-established in the face of generations of disunity. The famous Lambeth Quadrilateral of the Anglicans—that Christian unity could be sought on the sufficient basis of these four things: the Scriptures, the creeds, the sacraments of Baptism and Holy Communion, and the historic episcopate as it may be locally adapted[6]—was one such proposal. The exploration of Baptism, Eucharist, and ministry by the Lima Document could be conceived as another.

Martin Luther, too, had his entry into the discussion, an entry born in the age of controversy, but marked with a pastoral concern. In an essay in which he sought to help "a poor confused person tell where such a Christian holy people are to be found in this world,"[7] he articulated seven outward and tangible marks of the church. They are the preached Word of God, the sacrament of Baptism, the sacrament of the altar, the use of absolution or the forgiveness of sins, the calling and consecrating of ministers, the public use of thanksgiving and prayer, and "the holy possession of the cross," that is, the presence of suffering as a mark of the communal life. Where one finds these signs, there "you may know that the church, or the holy Christian people, must surely be present."[8]

One does not have to choose between the lists. Rather, one can take all these discussions as indicating a deep conviction that the local assemblies, if they are indeed "catholic," are in communion with each other, sending and receiving signs of their unity, their catholic singleness in the life of the triune God.

For our purposes, it is important to note that many of the proposed marks would be especially evident in liturgical life. Both the Lambeth Quadrilateral and Luther's marks are largely liturgical lists, especially if one remembers that the Scriptures are intended for assembly reading, the creeds are summaries of teaching in the baptismal process, and bishops are the

---

6. See Stephen Sykes and John Booty, eds., *The Study of Anglicanism* (Philadelphia: Fortress, 1988), 40.

7. *Luther's Works* (Philadelphia: Fortress, 1966), 41:148. This American translation is henceforth cited as *LW.* The essay is *Von den Conziliis und Kirchen,* in *D. Martin Luthers Werke* (Weimar: 1914), 50:509–653. This German edition from Weimar is henceforth cited as *WA.* The English translation of this essay is "On the Councils and the Church," in *LW,* 41:9–178.

8. *LW,* 41:151; *cf.* 148–66.

principal presiders in a local church.[9] Even Luther's "holy possession of the cross" can at least come to expression liturgically, in prayer for the suffering, in collections for the wretched, in the confessed truth about our own need, and in an absence of triumphalism in worship. Furthermore, the ancient patristic interest in "apostolic" practice was an interest especially expressed in the liturgy: by the canon of Scripture to be read in the assembly, by a creed to be handed over to those coming for baptism, by a recognized *ordo* for the celebration of the liturgy, by patterns of praying, especially for use at the eucharistic table, and by a regularizing of the ways that ministers who are specifically appointed in one local community should also be recognized in all the churches, the ways that ministry itself could be a sign of communion among the churches. Further, even the classic creedal *notae ecclesiae* have been interpreted as present in the church at least partly through its worshipping life.[10]

What might result for our understanding of *church* if we were to resolutely interpret the signs of communion among local churches as liturgical gifts? The results are significant: The assemblies in many different places are *one* because they are gathered into the life of the one triune God by the use of one Baptism, the hearing of one Word, the celebration of one table. Those same assemblies are *holy* because they are being called as the holy assembly of scriptural promise by that Word of God they are hearing and because, in their nakedness and need, in their union with all the needy people of the earth, they are eating and drinking and speaking to each other the very forgiveness of God. The assemblies are the *catholic* church because they do these things in ever new cultural situations, according to the dignity of each local place, bringing the gifts of lands and peoples into the unity that links all the assemblies across time and space. And the assemblies are *apostolic* because there reverberates, as the assembly's central meaning in the midst of all these marks of their life, the apostolic witness, made with apostolic, God-sent, authority, that Christ is risen and that in his resurrection all things are becoming new.

9. On bishops as presiders, see Gordon W. Lathrop, *Holy Things: A Liturgical Theology* (Minneapolis: Fortress, 1993), 185–87, 200.

10. Geoffrey Wainwright, *Doxology: The Praise of God in Worship, Doctrine and Life* (New York: Oxford University Press, 1980), 7–8, 122–38, 287–434. For an example of Luther's marks of the church interpreted in nineteenth-century Sweden both as signs of the assembly and ecclesial sources of personal spirituality, see Oloph Bexell, "Notae ecclesiae under 1800-talets kyrkokritik," in Alf Härdelin, ed., *Svensk spiritualitet, Tro och Tanke* 1994:1–2, 175–216.

That these assemblies send and receive gifts as signs of their unity is not a new idea. Already in the New Testament, the local churches send greetings to each other, to be received in the assembly with the exchange of the kiss (Rom. 16:16; 1 Cor. 16:19-20; 2 Cor. 13:12). They pray for each other, in assembly (2 Cor. 9:14).[11] They exchange letters that are to be read in the assembly (Col. 4:16).[12] They even take up collections on the Lord's day, presumably in the assembly, and send them on to another church in its need (1 Cor. 16:1-3). The gospel books themselves can be taken as catechetical patterns that come to be sent among the churches as patterns for the formation in faith which was part of baptism.[13] The exhortations of Paul and the deutero-Paulines remind the churches that "we all were made to drink of one Spirit" (1 Cor. 12:13) and that there is "one Lord, one faith, one baptism" (Ephesians 4:4). Moreover, in the second century, Ignatius begged for the churches to send *persons* to the assembly in Antioch from which he had been separated, persons who in their presence would be a sign of encouragement, recognition, and communion.[14] These mutual marks of communion have been liturgical gifts, manifest in the practice of the assembly itself. In the liturgy, the signs of communion among the churches came to tangible, visible expression.

The Marks in Liturgical Practice

Is this exchange of gifts still present? The assemblies in each local place are still sending and receiving quite concrete signs of communion, signs that are especially manifest in the liturgy. The sending and receiving communities include assemblies of the past, sending us fragments from their patterns of liturgical life and their local interpretations of the gospel, but also, in a way, still receiving our present reinterpretations of their life and sometimes our admonishing of their mistakes. But the present local churches are also engaged in the exchange with each other. In present liturgical practice, we begin to see the visible unity for which many of us pray. What is sent and received includes the following list, familiar partly from the New Testament itself, partly from the old *notae ecclesiae,* especially Luther's list:

11. *Cf.* Ignatius, *To the Magnesians* 14:1.

12. 1 Peter, which may be modelled on the shared pattern of Baptism (see below, chapter 7), seems to have been intended to be passed around in the several communities of Asia Minor (1:1).

13. Marianne Sawicki, *Seeing the Lord: Resurrection and Early Christian Practice* (Minneapolis: Fortress, 1994).

14. Ignatius, *To the Philadelphians* 10:1–2.

—the order of the celebration of the *Eucharist* and examples of ways that order has been locally and faithfully unfolded;

—the books of the *Scriptures,* the list or canon of those books that are to be read in the assembly, and the mutual and ongoing evaluation of what is of central importance in those books;

—patterns and examples of faithful *preaching;*

—prayers for each other and the pattern of urgent *intercession* for all the world;

—patterns and examples for the *eucharistic prayer* at the assembly's table;

—sometimes, as there is need, *collections* of money or food for each other and each other's localities and, in any case, the challenge to "send portions" in each local place as a sign of God's truth;

—the ancient traditions of *Sunday assembly and paschal observance* and ideas for other celebrations and commemorations;

—traditions of *daily prayer* to mark morning and evening, noon and night, and examples of faithful local unfolding of these traditions;

—the patterns of *Baptism:* teaching, bathing, and welcoming into the assembly;

—*creeds and catechisms* that summarize this process and its content;

—patterns of the *forgiveness of sins* as a remembrance of baptism and a reconciliation to the assembly's vocation;

—patterns of serving *leadership* in the midst of the assembly and a growing mutual recognition of such ministries;

—songs, hymns, and other *music* as a mode for all the gatherings of the assembly;

—the challenge for *localization* of these gifts and the sharing of local wisdom;

—the idea that *rites of passage* are celebrated by the Christian assembly with the juxtaposition of the word of God and baptismal remembrance to local cultural patterns for birth, adoption, marriage, reconciliation, sickness, bereavement, and death;

—sometimes, as travel makes possible, the bodily presence of *each other's members;*

—and, as an especially important gift to each other, the truth about our own local *neediness.*

These things are actually being sent and received, their exchange being encouraged not least by the ecumenical liturgical movement. The means for this exchange has included lively local study of the tradition and of current practice elsewhere in the world and the influence of shared biblical and liturgical study on the development of new denominational worship materials. It has also included conferences, personal encounters, and a whole range of scholarly books and articles. These things do flow across national boundaries and denominational lines. Although the churches may be formally disunited, by the sharing of many of these gifts they are engaged in a greater mutual and visible communion than they have yet been able to openly acknowledge. Now, however, as we look for a catholic assembly sojourning in any particular place, we may rightly look for indications that these signs are being received and being sent there.

Among some of the assemblies, these things may take on an even more concrete form. The list of books that may be read in the assembly can become a shared lectionary. The central tradition of Sunday and *Pascha* can become a shared calendar and a shared list of commemorations. The liturgy of one city—for example, Rome or Byzantium, or in the sixteenth century, Wittenberg or Geneva—can become a shared "rite," determinative for many other assemblies outside of that city. This rite can encompass shared liturgical books or become the basis of "church orders" that share essential traits.

Because of the catholic character of the churches, however, because of their vocation to do the central things in ways responsive to diverse cultural situations, these things—lectionary, calendar, rite, church order—probably ought never be fully universal. Liturgical calendars, for example, partly reflect a Christian response to the local experience of the cycles of the year. In any case, these things certainly ought never be imposed as conditions of unity or communion.[15] For the most part, the signs of communion among churches are patterns, principles, and mutual challenges, not fixed texts, certainly not full liturgies. Actual liturgies are always done locally. They have no non-local, platonic, universal existence.

But we cannot do without lectionaries, calendars, and the wide use of specific rites. Both the western and the various eastern rites, with their differing yet similar patterns of juxtapositions between traditional texts and

15. In this regard, there is a danger in regarding too literally the Roman "typical editions" of liturgical books that are supposed to be translated into local language and practice everywhere in the Roman Catholic churches. Such a literalism indicates a disregard for the dignity of local churches and acts as if the church of the city of Rome were the only or universal church. It is far better to regard the typical editions as authoritative witnesses to the *ordo* of the western rite and to some traditional texts, witnesses that are then to be unfolded according to the gifts and dignity of each local place. "Translation," then, will be much more a local application of the *ordo* to which the typical editions bear witness, not so much a literal rendering of the Latin in the local vernacular, word for word.

actions, contain wisdom that should not be lost and is not easily supplanted. The existence of such rites, together with their calendars and lectionaries, shared among a large number of churches as a central discipline, can be an important witness to the wider unity.[16] This witness will be most clear when the rite is experienced as primarily an *ordo* unfolded with some traditional texts and when the calendar and its related lectionary make sense locally, in dialogue with the seasons of the year in the several different places. Indeed, the idea of a shared calendar and lectionary, based in a dialogue between Christian faith and the human experience of time and based also in the sense of the givenness of the texts, is larger than any specific calendar. The idea itself is a gift shared among all the churches. Both the resonances and reversals between differing lectionaries can themselves point toward a richness in unity, without uniformity.[17] Indeed, the creation of the current, widely observed "Christmas cycle," made out of the mutual exchange of the gifts of the Roman Christmas and the eastern and Gallican Epiphany, is an example of richness in unity, in which a diversity of accent is still maintained.

Sometimes actual texts, not just patterns and outlines, are shared. When a hymn arises in one place, expressing the truth of the gospel in a very particular, local way, its genuine contribution to the whole body of Christian hymnody may be seen, and the hymn text itself become a sign of catholic communion. Similarly, classic eucharistic prayers arose in one of the centers of the ancient church and then spread, partly by the wider recognition of their very particular eloquence. A new explosion of euchology is likewise beginning to spread. It is wise for those communions of churches that share a book or books of such texts as a sign of their unity (hymnals or liturgy books: one thinks of the *Roman Sacramentary* or the *Book of Common Prayer* or the *Lutheran Book of Worship* or the *United Methodist Hymnal* or the Church of Sweden *Psalmbok*) to bear in mind that such books are not the liturgy, but a deeply important gift from other churches, past and present, bringing patterns and resources for doing the liturgy in the local place now. It is also important for those churches to see this uniting book as only partial—part of a wider network of books that carry the uniting *ordo* into local places. Understood in such a way, such books are a treasure, a participation in the giving and receiving of signs of communion.

16. *The Revised Common Lectionary*, with its calendar, is a most important example.

17. The use of the pericopes of the woman at the well (John 4:5-42) and of the man born blind (John 9:1-38) on the Sundays of Easter in the Byzantine lectionary and on the Sundays in Lent in the western lectionary, is one such rich example.

Sometimes these gifts come in the form of exhortation. The churches do not only send greetings and prayers; they also admonish each other to fidelity. If, in our local assembly, there is no seriousness about localization and no passion for Christian unity, if the prayers are only for ourselves here, if there is no collection for the poor and no open door to the marginalized, if music functions as concert, if leadership does not serve the assembly, or if the *ordo* of the Eucharist has so decayed that the Supper is celebrated infrequently or preaching is absent or has become only local story-telling, indeed if the whole celebration has nothing to do with the action of the triune God for the life of the world, then the other churches address us with admonition. Then a local response to the gifts of communion is rightly repentance. The critical function of the marks of the church continues to be useful in their liturgical interpretation.

The understanding of these things as gifts, flowing among local assemblies and expressing the communion of assemblies, the participation in the one catholic assembly, is immensely important. Each local assembly cannot be the others, but because it knows the others in Christ and belongs to the others in communion, it can turn to the others in profound respect, in mutual recognition and encouragement, in mutual challenge and admonition.

Locality in Universality

This local church, the actual liturgical assembly, takes all kinds of forms. It is especially found in the groups that some Christians call "congregations" and others call "parishes," both words translating important terminology from the ancient history of the assembly: *ekklesia* and *paroikia*. These are always groups that gather at least every Lord's day in a particular place, also bearing responsibility for the baptismal process of those who join their assembly and also for the regular flow of the witness of the assembly into daily life. But local church is also found in larger and smaller gatherings, both regular and infrequent: a gathering around the Eucharist celebrated in schools, monasteries, and committed communities; a celebration in a hospital room or in a prison; the extension of the parish gathering by communion ministers bearing the word and the holy meal into the places of those who are necessarily separated from the assembly; the synod of churches come together at worship; the diocese gathered, with the bishop presiding. All of these are church.

This last reality—the diocese, as that term has been understood in the West to be those Christians in a city or region among whom a bishop presides[18]—has especially and helpfully been regarded as "the local church" in some recent ecclesiological discussions.[19] For that conception of diocese as local church to have any reality or weight, however, it must be brought to liturgical expression. One ancient Roman form of this expression was the use of the *fermentum,* a fragment of the eucharistic bread sent from the assembly where the bishop presided with the intention that it be added to the eucharistic cup in all the other assemblies of the city as a sign of unity. But other forms of *diocese* exist: the bishop as a frequent visitor (in the classic sense of *visitation* for supervision and instruction, but also in the modern sense of one who comes humbly to listen, and is received hospitably) and a frequent presider in all of the assemblies; the encouragement of all the local presiders to understand themselves as a presbytery, a council of elders, for the local church; the celebration of central liturgies—say, the baptisms at the *Pascha*—in a shared way, with all of the diocesan assemblies contributing and the bishop presiding; the intentional sending and receiving between the assemblies of the diocese of the gifts enumerated in the lists above. Still, if the idea of the "universal church" ought not to diminish the dignity of each diocese, conceived as itself fully *church,* so also the idea of diocese ought not to diminish the dignity of an actual, weekly, baptizing, eucharistic assembly. Wherever the word and the sacraments are set out amid a participating assembly, that assembly is to be and be seen as the whole catholic church dwelling in this place.

But this problem is not new. It is very likely that the very "catholic assembly in Smyrna," not to mention the church in Rome or Antioch, was already meeting in diverse separate houses in the second century. The same may be true of the assemblies addressed in the New Testament letters, "the church of God that is in Corinth" (1 Cor. 1:2), for example. But then the call for these assemblies to manifest signs of communion with each other, to show the way that God is convoking one eschatological assembly to bear

18. In the East, *diocese* has usually meant a larger administrative region, what some in the West now call a "province," and has thereby continued the original Roman use of the term. In keeping with what we have seen in the *Martyrdom of Polycarp,* in the East that collection of Christians in a place, among which a bishop presides, is called a *paroikia,* a "sojourning," a "parish." As is appropriate in reflections on assembly after the end of "Christendom," the tendency of this book will be to use "diocese" or "parish" to refer to groups of people, not to territory, though such a group of people is intimately related to the land on which they gather.

19. See, most helpfully and with rich ecumenical implications, the work of Jean-Marie Roger Tillard, *Église d'Églises* (Paris: Cerf, 1987); English translation as *Church of Churches: The Ecclesiology of Communion* (Collegeville: Liturgical, 1992).

witness in the world, is very ancient. Indeed, the call to send and receive gifts of liturgical communion, to send and receive recognition and admonition, comes to all liturgical assemblies, small or large, if they are Christian. That call to concrete signs of unity comes as part of the fundamental vocation: to be the holy assembly of God in this place.

If the vocation of any Christian assembly is thus to strong and concrete liturgical *locality* in vigorous communion with *universality,* two major problems are immediately apparent. The first is the most obvious: the Christian communities are deeply divided. It is not only that we let a worldwide *denominational* communion substitute for a wider catholic unity, that we primarily send and receive gifts between assemblies along a denominational or even ethnic-denominational network. It is also that even the search for signs of unity in a given city or region—a "diocese"—is frequently content to ignore all the other Christian assemblies in that city besides "our own." If the assembly exists for the sake of witness to the world, then the question of local liturgical unity is urgent. Not that all assemblies must be one assembly, nor that legitimate differences in doctrine or in gifts are to be overlooked. But new attention must be given to the importance of tangible reality standing behind such phrases as "the church in Philadelphia" or "the church in Nairobi" or, for that matter, "the church in Puerto Rico" or "the church in Alberta." At the same time, the question of the appropriate and faithful forms of communion between that emerging church-in-a-place and all the other churches of Christ, in every place, remains the overarching ecumenical impetus.

The second problem follows and concerns local culture. Our very tendency to accentuate denominational unity and to fail to see all the various assemblies that make up the church-in-a-place distracts us from the major task of attending to the central matters of liturgical assembly in ways that are in accord with the dignity and gifts of each locality. This tendency can be further strengthened by the contemporary interest in consumerism. By appealing to consumerism we may be tacitly saying, here the Roman Catholic sacraments are made available to seeking individuals; here you can "get" the Lutheran word; here the Methodist way; here the Orthodox mystique. Or even here is "church" the way I like it; in the marketplace of religion, I will buy what I need here. But the question remains: how are word and sacraments to be done *in this place,* in participating *assemblies,* even in assemblies that receive the Orthodox or Methodist or Lutheran or Roman Catholic gifts as treasures, especially in assemblies that increasingly draw the post-denominational seekers, so that these assemblies bear witness together to the mercy of God for this particular place? The fascinating and paradoxical truth is that one of the *universal* gifts, shared across time and space by Christian communities, a gift which admonishes us yet today, is the call to *localization*. Of course, such local celebration must also always be marked by the signs that connect with all, in every place. For the phenomenon of religion as sales commodity has had another unhappy effect. There are now local Christian gatherings that have no perceived interest in historic or catholic connection, no interest in being anything but local places for answering individually perceived needs. To the extent that these are indeed Christian gatherings, they are in need of challenge and exhortation.

These two matters, Christian unity and faithful cultural localization, will occupy much of the rest of this book. Asserting that in liturgical renewal the gifts among communities are still flowing, even across considerable boundaries of Christian division, we will ask here if reflection on the liturgical assembly and its central acts of word and sacrament can specifically assist us in the further search for Christian unity as well as in the dialogue with local cultures. Indeed, these very questions form much of the reason for the urgency in a liturgical ecclesiology.

Local Assembly

In order to carry on this inquiry, we need to summarize and extend what we have said about those two ancient poles of ecclesiology, "locality" and "universality." From the point of view of the liturgy, the catholic church is always *local;* it has no other existence. The church is not a centralized, universal, faceless society. It is always a local gathering of people with their leaders, around the Scriptures and the sacraments, knowing Christ risen and *here.* In classic Reformation terms, the church is none other than that local assembly where "the gospel is preached in its purity and the holy sacraments are administered according to the gospel."[20]

But the catholic church is never "merely" local. That is, it is not only a reflection of local attitudes and local reality. And it is not all alone. The communion of this local assembly with the other assemblies around Christ in other places is enabled by certain concrete means—above all, by that very "gospel" and those very "holy sacraments" around which it gathers. Indeed,

20. Augsburg Confession, Article 7, "The Church." In Theodore Tappert, trans. and ed., *The Book of Concord: The Confessions of the Evangelical Lutheran Church* (Philadelphia: Fortress, 1959), 32. For the German and Latin texts, see *Die Bekenntnisschriften der evangelisch-lutherischen Kirche* (Göttingen: Vandenhoeck und Ruprecht, 1986), 61.

these means are needed for this local assembly to be "church" at all, for people to know that this assembly is in communion with all the churches of Christ, in every time and place, and that what it celebrates is a gospel that has universal significance, albeit expressed in local terms. Each of these central things, while done locally, active locally, expresses at the same time a linkage between this assembly and the other assemblies in time and space. Indeed, these very things are always *at the center* of the "catholic church dwelling in this place."

At the center *in this place*. For even in the central matters, the gospel takes on a local form. The people are from here. The leadership is for here. The language of the Word is the local language. The water of Baptism is local water. Even the food of the Eucharist is either local or locally recognizable and is shared in the local "economy" of a meal.[21] A meal is always an intensely local event. Indeed, the transcultural gifts of water, word, and meal may be a parable of the church's task. Christian faith finds it a gift from God that these things—always local gifts in their actual origin, yet always universal in human resonance and recognition—have been made into the bearers of the central Christian meanings and, by the promise of God and the power of the Spirit, of the very presence of Jesus Christ.

Sometimes the minimizing of the local resonance of the central Christian symbols has led to a certain "shrinkage" in their practice.[22] Drops of water for Baptism, brief formulas for the Word, bread wafers for the meal—these things have been seen to have "universal" validity, even though they lack local recognition as bathing waters, meaningful speech, and food that can sustain life. In fact, "universal validity" is not an accurate measuring stick for liturgical celebration. One needs rather to ask about the wholeness and integrity of the signs[23] of water, word, bread, wine, assembly, leadership as these things appropriately correspond to both biblical meaning and local culture.

---

21. It remains a widespread question in Christian liturgical discussion whether the food of the Eucharist is part of the *universal* linkage of the assembly (thus, wheat bread and grape wine) or part of the *local* celebration of the universal pattern of Eucharist (thus, local staple food and festive drink, especially in poor areas where the importing of foreign wine and bread is very difficult). Both practices can be supported from Christology: the incarnation occurred at a specific time and place, in a specific food-culture; the incarnation gathers up all that is human. Both practices may be regarded as "catholic," if accompanied with the gospel.

22. On "shriveled, desiccated symbols," see Robert Hovda, *Strong, Loving and Wise* (Washington: Liturgical Conference, 1976), 80–82.

23. On the "wholeness and integrity of the sign," see Lathrop, *Holy Things,* 165.

For "culture," too, is not a universal abstraction. At least one way of understanding the meaning of that term is to take it as the symbolic and social meanings that a group of people reinforce among themselves and pass on to their children as the wisdom necessary to live in a locality. Culture is the orientation necessary to survive and thrive in a place, the linguistic and symbolic but also the practical tools necessary for a human community to interact with the land and create a local order of meaning. Culture and geography go together. Culture involves human beings in some kind of relationship—healthy or unhealthy—to the local earth, its weather and water and its other forms of life,[24] including its other forms of human life. In fact, sometimes, as in New Testament times, cultures are complex layerings of different ways that groups of people live on the land, in relationship and in conflict with one another. The interpenetration of cultures is closely related—for good or for ill—to the interpenetration of ecosystems and the possibility of living together on the earth.

The ongoing *localization* of the liturgy places the local event of assembly around word and sacrament in dialogue with this local wisdom. It sets the politics of Baptism in dialogue with local politics, the story of the scriptural Word, its judgment and its forgiveness, in dialogue with local memory, the economy of the Eucharist in dialogue with local economy. The liturgy must do this of course, in order to be locally understood. But it must also do this since localization belongs to the gift of God and the nature of the catholic church. Christian worship has engaged in this dialogue from the beginning. And Christians believe that God's creative power is involved both in the natural environment to which local culture responds and in the human response itself. The wisdom about life and the earth as it is found in Jesus Christ has from the beginning been placed in critical dialogue with local wisdoms, beginning at least with the very language of preaching and the very formation of Christian Baptism and the Christian eucharistic meal.[25]

That dialogue between local culture and the transcultural content of Christian faith has sometimes affirmed and celebrated the local wisdom. On the other hand, that dialogue has also involved the transformation, re-orientation, inversion, and rejection of elements of local culture. It must be clear, however, that the purpose of such transformation ought never to be (as it has

24. "The only true and effective 'operator's manual for spaceship earth' is not a book that any human will ever write; it is the hundreds of thousands of local cultures." Wendell Berry, "The Work of Local Culture," in *What are People For?* (San Francisco: North Point, 1990), 166.

25. See below, chapters 7 and 8.

sometimes been) the suppression of a local culture in favor of another, dominant, colonizing one nor in favor of a centralized rejection of all local wisdom. Rather, from the point of view of Christian faith, such transformation must be for the sake of the locality itself coming most truly to expression by being gathered around the one who creates each place in goodness and saves each place in mercy. Christians believe that we are restored to faith and thanksgiving to the Creator—restored to being *creatures*—through Jesus Christ, and that thereby the "made order" of our cultures is given its fitting and holy place within the "given order" of creation.[26]

Indeed, the local character of the catholic church may be one important contribution to the maintenance of local culture in a time of centralization and global mass marketing techniques. In "the age of networks"[27] in communications, information, commerce, and the arts, local cultures are themselves threatened, sometimes only remaining as an expression of nostalgia for a simpler time, or, more positively, as treasured fragments of local skills and local meanings. The assembly can aid that treasuring. At the same time, the catholic character of the church will offer another vision of human connectedness in a critical dialogue with the new international "culture" of consumerism and communication.

This gift of the church to culture can be described quite simply: God has created all things good; each place, in connection with all other places, is held in the hands of the life-giving God. The cultures of each place, the ways people live in the earth, show the signs of God's good creation: food and drink; naming, language, and music; sexuality and child rearing; work, tools, and exchange; rest, thought, festivity, and the arts; even our religious hopes and their expressions are all great goods. But humankind and all the earth are also marked by sin, by a turning from God and from life. The greatest of goods have been fully turned to evil purpose, to the working of death and sorrow and hurt, to ignorance, enslavement, and war. But in Jesus Christ, through his death and resurrection, God has used our very flesh and the stuff of our cultural life in the created earth—our words, our food and drink, our religious hopes—to utterly new purpose: to restore creation even more wonderfully; to draw us into communion; to give us forgiveness and life together, more than our own work and our own cultures could ever do. In each beloved, created place, God is raising up the assembly of faith, gath-

---

26. "The made order must seek the given order, and find its place in it." Wendell Berry, "Healing," in *What are People For?*, 12.

27. Jean-Marie Guéhenno, *The End of the Nation-State* (Minneapolis: University of Minnesota Press, 1995).

ered around the central story of Christ and around his risen and local presence in word and bath and meal, to be the catholic church in this place, enacting the universal means of grace in a local way. There, as in a workshop, as in a foretaste of the feast to come, elements of our cultures are being welcomed and transformed to do their original work: to be creation and the work of creatures, to be the ways we live peacefully together in the land and to be witnesses of God's intention for all the earth.

For the localizing task, for the continuous work of forming a liturgy that is both fully local and fully in communion with the other assemblies, some tools are needed. These tools will include concrete means to keep asking the local Christian assembly whether its liturgy does indeed clearly receive, welcome, and sift the local wisdom. They will also include means to ask whether that liturgy represents the central and transforming faith in Jesus Christ. Our list of marks or signs of communion among the assemblies may represent some of those tools. The *ordo* of the Sunday assembly, passed on as of preeminent importance among those signs, will especially help us with both sides of the task.

Universal Communion

Such local celebration belongs to the universal vision of Christianity. Christian universality is not, therefore, a kind of empire, with a centralized government and local outposts. Christian universality is also not the presence of "the kingdom of God," the final realization of all that God intends for creation. It is rather a communion of local assemblies in each place. These assemblies have the humble yet immensely important vocation simply to bear witness to God's actions for the sake of the life of the world.

One form of that witness is actual resistance. Indeed, one sign of the universal communion among Christian assemblies is found in the mutual encouragement of resistance to local abuses. It is probably not possible to make, out of context, an abstract list of cultural matters that require such resistance and critique. But if culture involves the symbolic tools whereby a society survives on the land, we can identify some of the characteristics that will be problematic for Christian faith and thus for the Christian liturgy. If social roles, perhaps originally adopted for the sake of work-specialization on the land, are absolutized and made the basis of an unjust distribution of the food and products of a culture, Christian faith will recoil. There ought to be no place for such absolutized status structures in the Christian assembly. A similar thing can be said if dignity is denied people because they come from those whom one culture formerly conquered or enslaved, or if lower place is accorded to people on the basis of their sex or age or disability or chronic illness. This is where the politics of Baptism and the economy of the Eucharist will critically engage the local practice and the local status system.

But this politics and economy will also engage a culture that idolizes the free individual self at the expense of a wider humanity, or that protects and idealizes only the local group or tribe at the cost of openness to others, or that gives central place to the acquisition and holding of wealth at the expense of the care of the earth and its poor. Religious cultures that make the purity of the insiders or the power of the adept into the central themes will need to be engaged. So will those cultural systems in which human identity is disconnected from the earth itself, as if the human being floated free of responsibility for the care of the earth. Cultural conceptions of hierarchy, of purity, of tribal or sexual identity, of self-realization cannot be ignored by Christian liturgy. But neither can they be left untouched.

Let it be said clearly: it is not the Lord's Supper we celebrate—or it is the Lord's Supper celebrated in such a way as to make us sick or to kill us—if it is celebrated for men only, for women only, for one tribe or nationality only, for those with caste status only, for the wealthy only, for the able-bodied only. It is simply no defense to say: "But this is my culture." Such a cultural element is wrong and is to be rejected. This is the meaning of Paul's critique of the Corinthian meal practice (1 Cor. 11:20-21), a critique that is of very great importance for the countercultural and transformative power of the liturgy.

Such a transformation, known throughout the Scriptures and in the history of the Christian liturgy, can be called a *breaking of symbols*.[28] In such a "breaking," the symbol is accorded great respect, with sympathetic insight into its wisdom and its meaning in the relationship of peoples to the earth and to their hopes for life. Indeed, the terms of the symbol and its power to evoke our sense of meaning are maintained, but its attempt at coherent and powerful meaning in itself is seen as insufficient and equivocal. The symbol means something for us because of the grace and presence of Jesus Christ, because of its juxtaposition to the promises of God in the Scriptures.

In the task of liturgical localization, hundreds of such transformations and transvaluations go on. They are matters small and large. Sometimes, in

---

28. *Cf.* Paul Tillich, *Dynamics of Faith* (New York: Harper, 1957), 52–54. See also Lathrop, *Holy Things*, 27–31.

Christian worship, local cultural matters will be simply welcomed and celebrated. The clothing and colors people wear, for example, may be a good and beautiful image of human interaction with each other and with the land. There is no "Christian clothing," but brought to the assembly, clothing may signify this local place gathered before God's lavish mercy. In other situations, local symbols will be significantly transformed by the juxtaposition of the scriptural Word. Again, one biblical meaning for clothing, the "wedding garment" for the marriage between God and the earth (*cf.* Isa. 61:10), may invite us to see our ordinary clothing, worn to the liturgy and in our daily lives, as "garments of salvation," carrying out our baptismal "putting on Christ." In other situations, local symbols may be reoriented by the intentional liturgical use of practices that are *not* ordinary, drawn from elsewhere among the churches or in church history but adapted to the local community. Again, the actual clothing given the newly baptized or worn by the leaders in the assembly may be the ancient clean white garments of festivity and the traditional Mediterranean festal and court clothing or some adaptation of these, helping us to imagine the human being in another way.

But in other situations, elements of local practice will need to be largely resisted. Again, if certain colors or clothing may only be used to indicate wealth or rank or caste, to the rejection of others, Christians may have serious question about their use. In any case, such badges of rank ought not be garments for the assembly. In the light of this critique, western clergy need seriously to reconsider their academic garb or their wearing of signs of civil rank when they take part in the gathering around word and sacrament.

This process of sifting and transvaluing will take place most clearly if it can be centered around the strong presence of the Scripture, Baptism, and Eucharist in the heart of a participating congregation as the way the people are gathered around Jesus Christ, crucified, risen, and present. The sifting will take place most clearly if it uses the *ordo* that unites us, exactly at the same time that it asks how that *ordo* is to be done locally. Then the central scriptural Word will be available to give new meaning and new orientation to cultural symbols. Then the central sacramental presence of God's grace in Christ will be available to be juxtaposed to cultural symbols that are now required to refer outside of themselves.

But who decides what local cultural elements are to be rejected or transformed? There is only a "messy" answer, not a neat, authoritarian one. The *church* does. That is, the local church, by faithful life in the gospel, perceives how much God loves this place and how the local cultures bear witness to God. But it also perceives, in its struggle and fidelity and mutual conversation over generations, how much this local place is in need of being saved, what requires reorientation and what requires rejection. Then the local church also needs the mutual conversation with all the other churches, calling it to aspects of the gospel, aspects of local wisdom, and aspects of local need that it may have forgotten or ignored or undervalued. The dynamic of resistance, of the countercultural, is a tool for a liturgy that is authentically local and authentically catholic at once.

The communion of the churches thus calls the local assembly toward authentic and faithful local witness. And the faithful local assembly gives expression to the catholic character of the church. The unity of the church serves the witness of the church in localities. Passion for liturgical ecumenism and passion for a serving mission in the world belong together.

So first we must ask about the actual practice of assembly. Then, we must turn to consider further those paired interests of a liturgical ecclesiology: ecumenism and localization; the search for Christian unity and the dialogue with human cultures.

3

The Practice of Assembly

C an a congregation actually set out to be the assembly we have been describing, in communion with all the other assemblies? If so, then what does the congregation do? Or, given that the description proposes that *God* creates this assembly, is it even possible to do anything?

Christian faith says that this assembly for which the biblical texts have caused us to hope—the *qahal,* the *ekklesia*—is actually taking place. According to that faith, the last-day assembly, in which God promises to begin to gather the nations around the holy Word, is as near as your local church. Or, at least, your local church is coming to be God's meeting as it, in communion with all the other sojournings of the holy assembly throughout the world, participates in the presence of the life-giving Word. The holy assembly, the people who are all together the meeting before God, showing forth God's mercy for the life of the world, has actual existence. It is people you know, a community of which you may be part.

Of course, *coming to be* may be the appropriate form of the verb, given a certain tentativeness in these assertions. There are theologians and canon lawyers in some churches who could even heighten the degree of tentativeness. They have made it their concern to point out how the ministries and the order of other ecclesial communities are "defective," lacking one or more of the marks that would be required of a true church, lacking the validity or reliability that would flow from this character as true church. Such theologians have quite clear ideas about what confession of faith, what re-ordering of ministers, what liturgical practices would be required for such a defective congregation to become authentic church.

From the point of view of our liturgical ecclesiology, however, all of the churches are shaky and unreliable. The whole lot of our assemblies and all of the ministries that serve them are defective. That is so, at least in part, because all of our assemblies engage in a divided church, insufficiently sending and receiving the signs of communion with the other gatherings around Christ. Some humility on our part in dealing with the defectiveness of other churches is always appropriate, given the massive defects of our own. For our churches are defective, even more, because every Christian gathering is perpetually in need of transformation. We are the ones who hold the meeting. Our gatherings are made up by our own social ways of constituting a group, by our tendency to turn toward reliance on ourselves, by our great ability at self-deception. Such unreliable ground marks every one of our church-assemblies. "Nothing could more surely convince me of God's unending mercy," says writer and naturalist Annie Dillard, "than the continued existence on earth of the church"—continued existence, when what we might rather expect is being blasted.[1]

But Christian faith sees the risen Christ standing at the mouth of hell, pulling a whole community of people out of the jaws of death. Christian faith sees the risen Christ doing this work now, forming these people so wrenched out of the sway of death into a living community of witnesses to God's intention of life for all things, into an assembly of the first fruits for all the earth. Every local church may be understood to be the place where this people is being pulled from fear and loss and is being so constituted as assembly.

The church of Laodicea, the seventh and last of the manifestly defective churches addressed in the Revelation (3:14-22)—the only sort of church that occurs in the Revelation—can stand as type for us all. That ancient assembly of Asia Minor, thinking that it was prosperous, did not know that it was "wretched, pitiable, poor, blind and naked" (3:17). "I know your works," said the Risen One (3:15). There followed, for the Laodicean assembly, counsel to buy and use what is actually given away for free, the cross-refined treasure, sight-giving salve, and garments of grace that come from the Risen One, and then counsel to open the door to that Risen One as he comes to keep the feast. Our congregations can hear this text giving us counsel as well: to make lively use of Baptism, the Scriptures, and the Holy Meal at the heart of our meetings; to put these things on our eyes, to clothe ourselves in them, to eat and drink them as at a feast. The Risen One

1. Annie Dillard, *Holy the Firm* (New York: Bantam, 1979), 60.

in the midst of these things is always pulling us into life, into the transformation of our meeting to be God's assembly. The triune life that enfolds and clothes us through these things is our only reliable ground.

Still, we have a thing or two to do. The things recommended to the Laodiceans are all concrete, life-enfolding gifts of utter grace, yet the Laodiceans need to buy them, use them, put them on, open the door. Just so, every church, as the assembly-witness of the last times, is always God's creation. We may trust that it is coming to be, reliably, wherever God's Word is sounding forth, regardless of the worthiness of the congregation or the excellence of the priest. But "therefore I counsel you to buy from me . . ." (Rev. 3:18) calls a congregation to concrete *practices.*

Practices

Understood this way, practices are not inconsistent with God's grace. On the contrary, at their best they are simply our naked bodies presented for the clothing, our eyes open for the salve, our hands out for the supper. Practices respond to and use the things that are in our midst as gifts. They are "things Christian people do together over time in response to and in the light of God's active presence for the life of the world."[2] Thus, one of the major things Christian people do together over time is the assembly for worship. Doing the assembly, maintaining the assembly, gathering with the assembly, keeping the assembly in communion with other assemblies require practices.

Still, those practices do ask of us a certain caution, lest they become the way we think we are climbing up to the top of the pile of humanity. When the liturgical things we do are conceived as our ladder to God, our way to compel God, our marks of excellence distinguishing us from other wretches, they become part of our self-deception. Still, none of the core matters—the practices—of Christian worship can be appropriately used in such a way when they are understood according to their origin and their deepest intention. Their meaning will ultimately explode in the face of such stances of self-righteousness.

---

2. Craig Dykstra and Dorothy C. Bass, "Times of Yearning, Practices of Faith," in Dorothy C. Bass, ed., *Practicing Our Faith* (San Francisco: Jossey-Bass, 1997), 5. One may find an excellent example of the application of thought about "practices" to communal liturgical action in Richard R. Gaillardetz, "Doing Liturgy in a Technological Age," *Worship* 71 (1997): 429–51. Much of what follows in this chapter could be set usefully beside the reflections of Gaillardetz in an "ecclesiology of focal practice."

Take a matter so basic to Christian liturgy as the Lord's Prayer. Both the theological and the ecclesiological bases of the healthy practice of assembly can be clarified by the consideration of the liturgical use of that classic and form-giving prayer. The use of the prayer is itself a practice. As one of the gifts Christians have from their baptism,[3] it is repeated Sunday after Sunday in the Eucharist[4] and every day in the prayers of the church. But we have seen that our communal insertion into this prayer that we have in Jesus Christ does not distinguish us from the rest of needy humanity.[5] Rather, the prayer in our mouths causes us to articulate with honesty the human condition that we share. Borrowing the terms of first-century Jewish eschatology, we cry out our need for the "reign of God," for the day to come when God's life-giving intention for all things is openly enacted. Yet—fearfully, aware that such a "day" will be full of "trials" that we do not think we can pass, thinking that any such goodness must also be attended by great pain—we also beg to be spared, delivered in the midst of the horrors. By such a prayer, Christians stand with all humanity, in its need and in its fear. In such a prayer, the church exercises its priesthood for the world, making the "our" and the "us" of the petitions as broad as it can imagine. This articulation of human need before God makes up a basic Christian practice.

At the same time, in the heart of the prayer, we ask God, with an astonishing confidence, to forgive us now and give us bread now. Again we borrow first-century Jewish apocalyptic language, but here we find that language transformed, reversed. These things are the presence now of expected end-time gifts. Only God forgives, and that at the end. Only God will spread the great, life-giving feast—at the end. Here, in the assembly, in celebration of the actual presence of these things, Christians turn to each other in mutual forgiveness that corresponds to and receives God's forgiveness now, and the community holds a meal that it believes to be already God's meal.[6] More, the assembly is sent into the world to forgive and the

---

3. In liturgical history, the prayer comes to summarize and symbolize the catechetical process whereby catechumens are taught how to pray. The prayer thus belongs to the "catechism," to the symbolic texts handed over to those being baptized. See below, chapter 6.

4. See Robert Taft, "The Lord's Prayer in the Eucharistic Liturgy: When and Why?" *Ecclesia Orans* 2 (1997): 137–55.

5. See above, chapter 1.

6. Taft, op. cit., believes the fourth- and fifth-century evidence shows the prayer being used as an act of mutual forgiveness before coming to the Holy Supper, an act necessary to avoid the judgment present in the Supper for those who come unforgiving, without discerning the whole body of the church.

assembly shares food with the hungry. Its daily meals and its personal interactions are invited to echo and extend the assembly, to become focused signs of the presence of God's life-giving grace.

All these things are practices. They involve us in enacting things we believe God is doing. That enacting is first of all ritual, communal, repetitive: the prayer itself, but also ritual acts of mutual forgiveness and the ritual meal. But then our hearts and lives are invited to follow—in forgiving others, in exercising hospitality at all of our meals, in "sending portions to those for whom nothing is prepared." Such practices are neither distancing nor distinguishing. They still do not separate us from the rest of humanity, whose condition the prayer so eloquently articulates. On the contrary— they connect us, in bread and forgiveness.

So the theology of the prayer is this: God is the one to whom we pray, before whom humanity is full of both longing and fear. Further, God is the one who in Jesus Christ has come to be with humanity, in its longing, need, and death. Since the prayer is regarded as being taught to us by Jesus and as being therefore an extension of his presence, its articulation of that human need is a concrete sign of the incarnation, of God's coming all the way into needy death. Further, God is the one who—in the resurrection of Jesus poured out in the assembly through the presence of the Spirit—has begun to give us both forgiveness and bread as a first taste of the healing of all harms. The uniqueness of the prayer thus does not lie in its use of the word "Father." With that word, the Christian community simply joins the rest of humanity—for example, the ancient Romans who called on *Zeus Pater, Jupiter*—in calling out to the divine. The uniqueness of the prayer is found, rather, in our having the articulation of need from and together with Jesus and in the presence of bread and forgiveness, thus in the *trinitarian* heart of the prayer. For this God is not three gods, but one life-giving God. Such a trinitarian theology can be seen as manifest in the three reference points of the prayer, all enfolded in the divine unity—God who is addressed; Jesus who teaches us the prayer of need; and the presence in this assembly of the fulfillment of the prayer in bread and forgiveness.

The ecclesiology of the prayer is this: The assembly is the community given this prayer, taught it in Baptism, repeating it at Eucharist, invited to stand articulately with humanity—indeed, with all things—where Christ is amid the need and fear. The assembly is the community that is given now— by the power of the Spirit and the presence of the Risen One, as an earnest gift of all that God intends for the world, the bread and forgiveness that the world needs. The assembly is the community, therefore, that confesses the enfolding presence of the triune God and is called to practice the word of forgiveness and the meal of resurrection.

The practices of the Christian assembly are all like those of the Lord's Prayer: praying the prayer, being consciously present to and part of human need, knowing our need of God, waiting for God, yet tasting the forgiveness and bread of God's presence, mutually forgiving each other, holding the meal, finding its echo in all of our meals, bearing witness to God. For our meetings to be transformed into witnesses to the day of God, we *do* need to do something. We do need to set out the word of forgiveness and the bread.

Much the same can be said of Baptism, preaching, and the Eucharist. They each look like—indeed, they *are*—the very practices of the Lord's Prayer, the articulation of human need, the setting out of forgiveness and bread. They each have a theology and an ecclesiology coherent with that of the prayer. Baptism is the washing that unites us with Christ as he is united to all humanity in its need.[7] Its "purity" exactly opposes religious purity. Baptism unites; it does not distinguish. Its church is the assembly of those so united with Christ, who is united with humanity. Preaching always comes as a word to those who need to come to faith or come again to faith or come deeper into faith, as if we all were outsiders. Its speech exactly opposes self-congratulation. Yet its speech is an act of truth-telling praise. Preaching comes describing all human need, speaking of the God "who has imprisoned all in disobedience in order to be merciful to all" (Romans 11:32). Yet preaching gives the very gift of mercy of which it speaks, enabling faith in its hearers to trust that gift. Its church is an assembly with an articulate center and open doors; there are no insiders here. The Eucharist is the meal for the hungry, the meal that always makes its participants hungrier, the meal that unites us to the wretched everywhere, calling us all to life.[8] Its church is the multitude described in the feeding miracles, the invited crowd in the wedding banquet parable: "Go out at once into the streets and lanes of the town and bring in the poor, the crippled, the blind, and the lame" (Luke

7. "It is a question of Christ who is in communion with human misery and in whom God himself is in communion with human misery . . . Entrance into Christ in a state of communion with humanity and entrance into the ecclesial Body coincide." J.-M. R. Tillard, *Church of Churches: The Ecclesiology of Communion* (Collegeville: Liturgical, 1992), 30–31. On baptismal purity as religious purity inverted, see below, chapter 7.

8. Martin Luther, "The Blessed Sacrament of the Holy and True Body of Christ, and the Brotherhoods," in *Luther's Works* (Philadelphia: Fortress, 1966), 35:49–73 (this American translation is henceforth cited as *LW*) and in *D. Martin Luthers Werke* (Weimar: 1914), 2:742–58 (this German edition from Weimar is henceforth cited as *WA*). On the Eucharist as an inclusive meal, see below, chapter 8.

14:21). All of these central matters express the solidarity of the community with human need. All of them are full of God's grace. All of them are to be practiced by the assembly.

The sending and receiving of signs of communion among the churches involve such practices. These signs—the *ordo* of the liturgy, the canon of books for public reading, the patterns of praying, our ministers themselves, and more—come to us as gifts, and yet they need to be put into use. The creedal "marks" of the church may be considered in the same light; they are characteristics of any assembly God is creating around the word and sacraments of Christ's gift, an assembly that is one, holy, catholic, and apostolic. At the same time, these marks are each a summons to be the thing that they describe,[9] to work on *unity* with the other assemblies, on that paradoxical *holiness* of the assembly that is union with humanity's need, on *catholicity* as the localization of the assembly, and on the continual renewal in the assembly of the *apostolic witness* to the resurrection.

In fact, the current ecumenical liturgical movement is full of counsel for practice. Contemporary commentaries on the liturgy have extensive advice for understanding the shape of the liturgy as a thing that needs to be put into action, for understanding the spirit and the rationale for the classic rubrics, for understanding the discipline of practice that needs to characterize each of the assembly's ministers. We need to engage in this counsel in the spirit of the letter to the church at Laodicea, to engage in these practices in the spirit of the practices of the Lord's Prayer. A liturgical ecclesiology that accords with the ecclesiology of the Lord's Prayer—the ecclesiology of Baptism, preaching, and Eucharist—needs to recommend practices marked with the same spirit: awareness of the assembly's linkage to all humanity and encouragement toward the centrality of mutual forgiveness and the holy bread of Christ's gift.

What shall an assembly and its leaders do? They shall do again, more profoundly, the central matters that make them church. Use the *ordo* that they share with the other churches.[10] Juxtapose the parts of that *ordo* to each other and to their manner of meeting so that the meeting itself is broken to the purposes of God. Work on the open door to the meeting and on its powerful center. Set the central matters of the meeting in dialogue with

9. Edward Schillebeeckx, *Church: The Human Story of God* (New York: Crossroad, 1990), 197.

10. For a reflection on the *ordo* as a set of questions to local liturgical practice, see Gordon W. Lathrop, *Holy Things: A Liturgical Theology* (Minneapolis: Fortress, 1993), chapter 7.

local cultures. Read and consider the best and latest rubrical counsel from at least two other "denominations."[11] Consider how other signs of unity are being sent and received. The list might go on. Here we do not need to repeat such liturgical advice as is widely and beautifully articulated elsewhere. Our task has been to think about practice in the light of ecclesiology. But we may usefully attend to three matters that are not so widely discussed, all of which bear on ecclesiology in a central way: the practiced images of the church we meet in the liturgy; the practice of participation in the assembly; and the practice of leadership.

Images of the Church

Of course, what we actually do when we enact our gathering as an assembly will be powerfully influenced by what we *think* we are doing. To imagine that we are the people of the Lord's Prayer, in the manner outlined above, will make a difference in our liturgical practice of both shared bread and mutual forgiveness. It will also affect the ways in which our prayers, our open doors, and our collections—among other liturgical matters—connect our assembly to other people and to the earth itself.

The classic Christian liturgy is full of images of the church that might so affect our practice. These images are found not only in the implied ecclesiology of the Lord's Prayer or of preaching and the sacraments. They are also latent in other secondary texts and actions used in many Christian assemblies. The mutual greeting of presider and people—the *dominus vobiscum* dialogue—that precedes major liturgical events in the classic rites, creates the sense of an assembly empowered by the presence of the risen Lord and marked by the mutual honor and service flowing from that presence. The "kiss of peace," which is gaining renewed acceptance in the churches, turns this same enacted image into a ministry from person to person in the

11. Such a list of books might include especially the following from North American Episcopalian, Lutheran, Methodist, and Roman Catholic sources: Howard Galley, *The Ceremonies of the Eucharist: A Guide to Celebration* (Cambridge: Cowley, 1989); Daniel Stevick, *Crafting the Liturgy* (New York: Church Hymnal Corporation, 1990); Byron Stuhlmann, *Prayer Book Rubrics Expanded* (New York: Church Hymnal Corporation, 1987); *The Use of the Means of Grace: A Statement on the Practice of Word and Sacrament* (Minneapolis: Augsburg Fortress, 1997); Ralph Van Loon and S. Anita Stauffer, *Worship Wordbook: A Practical Guide for Parish Worship* (Minneapolis: Augsburg Fortress, 1995); Hoyt Hickman, *A Primer for Church Worship* (Nashville: Abingdon, 1984); Aidan Kavanagh, *Elements of Rite: A Handbook of Liturgical Style* (New York: Pueblo Publishing, 1982); the publications of Liturgy Training Publications of Chicago, and especially the videotapes of the *Sunday Mass Series*.

assembly, sealing our prayers and remembering our baptism.[12] Furthermore, when one recalls that Paul associated his encouragement of the use of this sign with his sending of greetings from the other assemblies (Rom. 16:16; 1 Cor. 16:19-20; 2 Cor. 13:12), then each personal greeting may also carry in itself the greeting of all those who are "in Christ," and the mutual service of the "peace" can then image the continual reconstitution of local assembly, in communion with all in every place.

There is more. The "we" of liturgical texts—"we worship you, we give you thanks, we praise you for your glory," for example—is the "we" of the church. The very fact of communal singing images a diverse body in harmony around the content and direction of the song. The "entrance song" at the outset of a liturgy is a song giving words and images to the entrance of the entire assembly, not just the ministers or the choir, and the prayer that sums up that entrance—the *collect* of the western rite—gathers together a movement beginning when the least member of the assembly starts to come toward the gathering place. The brief communal responses—*amen* and *kyrie eleison* and "hear our prayer"—with which healthy liturgy is filled, allow a diverse, honored, yet needy community to freely enter into and assent to texts, without compulsion. The songs sung at the other processions—especially, the procession to the font for Baptism or the bringing of the gifts for the Eucharist or the movement to communion—frequently exhibit biblical imagery for the assembly as it does its needy, merciful work. The recovery of the celebration of the Eucharist *versus populum,* with the presider facing the entire assembly across the table or standing all about the table, creates the image of a community of the shared meal. And in those assemblies that conclude the communion rite with the remarkable practice of the Song of Simeon—"Lord, now you let your servant go in peace . . ."—the meal community is shown forth as those who have seen God's light and are called to speak of it, like Anna, to all who are "looking for the redemption of Jerusalem" (Luke 2:38).

None of these gestures, words, and practiced images says much by itself. They are all liable to misunderstanding or neglect. But when they are intentionally gathered together around the central matters of word and sacrament, they can powerfully speak about the transformation of our meeting to be the assembly of God. Were we to attend to these images of the church, allow them to stand forth in our teaching and to influence our prac-

---

12. L. Edward Phillips, *The Ritual Kiss in Early Christian Worship* (Cambridge: Grove Books, 1996).

tice, we would be well on the way toward a needed paradigm shift in our sense of the purpose of the assembly itself. For the Scripture read and preached, Baptism enacted and remembered, and the Holy Supper celebrated are not consumer goods, commodities to be picked up by individuals according to personally perceived need, ministerial goods for distribution by the expert, validity moments controlled by the priest, property owned by any particular group. All these misunderstandings are quite possible and currently practiced, even by churches that suppose they have a most proper "use of the means of grace." Preaching, Baptism, and Eucharist are rather living "words" that create the assembly, calling it to do the assembly's work. The assembly cannot exist without them, but they also cannot occur without calling an assembly into being.[13] Images of the church, practiced in the assembly, can help us reclaim this social character of Christian faith and the full, flowing contours of the communal liturgy.

But, again, the assembly does not exist to image the assembly. We can see this clearly in several interesting places. The programs of painted church building walls—which can be found throughout Christian history, from third-century Dura-Europas in Syria through medieval Europe and the Orthodox East to several modern experiments, in Asia, Africa, and America—can help us get our image use in order. In the Dura house-church, for example, the images painted on the walls of the room used for baptisms were overwhelmingly biblical scenes and characters, now applied to what God was doing in Baptism itself. Here David perpetually conquers Goliath, the paralytic takes up his bed and walks, the Samaritan woman receives the ever-flowing water, and pictured right over the font, the Good Shepherd shoulders the lost sheep, leading the flock, reversing the fall of Adam and Eve. But on the lower north wall of the room, immediately next to the font on the west well and arranged as if they are proceeding toward the font, a group of women carrying torches are painted, approaching a tomb over which the stars that herald the morning are rising. These women are, of course, the women coming to the tomb of Jesus with spices to anoint the body, the women who will discover the resurrection. But they also image the gathered assembly itself and the ritual taking place in the room. The people who are standing in the room face the font and move toward it just as the pictured women do. They probably carry lamps or candles or torches

---

13. *Cf.* the dictum of Luther: "Denn Gottes wort kan nicht on Gottes Volck sein, wiederumb Gottes Volck kan nicht on Gottes wort sein"; "[F]or God's word cannot be without God's people, and conversely, God's people cannot be without God's word." *WA*, 50:629; *LW*, 41:150.

as those women do. And they discover the resurrection itself, the true rising dawn, the presence of the Good Shepherd, in the Baptism that is taking place in their midst.[14]

In the midst of a program full of witness to the action of God in Baptism, these women on the wall give us an image of the church as an assembly of witnesses to and needy beneficiaries of this divine action. The primary place of the church at Dura, of course, was the empty space of the room itself, wherein the movement of Baptism was to be enacted as the living presence of the biblical God. The primary business of this church was to proclaim and enact the presence of that life-giving mercy manifest in the great stories on the wall. But this assembled and acting congregation could also find in the "myrrh-bearing women," among the pictured stories and participating in them, an echo of its own identity, a pattern for its own work.

A similar location for the image of the church is found in the program of painting that surrounds the interior of the late medieval buildings of Holy Cross Church at Hattula, Finland, and St. Lawrence Church at Lohja, Finland. These early sixteenth-century paintings are largely made up of biblical images of creation, the exodus, the stories of Mary, and most especially, the life of Christ and the final judgment. Painted on all the walls that surround the assembled people and all the vaults that cover them, the images entirely enfold the congregation, wrapping around those who stand in the space. On the pillars underneath the biblical narratives of the vaulting—pillars standing among the people of the assembly—there are further images of women and men from the history of the church—"the saints." The whole effect is of the present assembly, in communion with all of every place, wrapped in the life of Christ, which is present in this room by the power of the Spirit, and so facing the God of creation and judgment, who comes from the East and is known at the altar. The room is a eucharistic room, a place for the assembly around the table, and the images on the wall show forth the mercy of God which, the anonymous artist-for-the-community seems to have believed, acts in the Eucharist. Indeed, the central image over the altar and on the east wall is the western medieval "mercy

14. For the program of painting at Dura, see Robert Milburn, *Early Christian Art and Architecture*, (Berkeley: University of California Press, 1988), 10–13; and L. Michael White, *The Social Origins of Christian Architecture* (Valley Forge, Pa.: Trinity, 1997), 2:130–31. The movement of the women may reflect the movement of all the images on the walls toward the font and then, beyond the font, out of the door, and toward the room for assembly. This may be the very flow of the baptismal liturgy celebrated at Dura.

seat," the mysterious Father and the hovering Spirit holding forth the crucified Christ.[15]

In both Hattula and Lohja, the primary place of the church is in the empty space that these images surround. The primary work of the church is the liturgy, the mass, the current proclamation of the life-giving power that the wall paintings interpret. But in two relatively small places on the walls, the assemblies in these old churches might also have found images for their own identity. In each case the image is a painting of a collection of naked people, reminding us of the church at Laodicea. In the first case, in a vault over the south aisle, just over the entryway into the assembly space, Mary opens her cloak, the very mantle of mercy with which she was clothed by the mighty God, and the cloak is seen to enfold all of needy humanity. The grace of God that chose Mary, the grace of the incarnation and of the reversals of her *Magnificat,* is here, available for all who need it. According to medieval faith, what happens in mercy to Mary, happens in mercy to the church, so much so that we may call this image, quite simply, *ecclesia,* "church." In the second case, on the north wall, just above the heads of the assembly and in plain sight, the risen Christ pulls naked humanity out of the mouth of hell. The church is the assembly that knows itself to share the common lot of death, sin, and need and has the gift of articulating that situation for the sake of humanity. It is also the assembly that knows itself as witness to the life-giving power of the resurrection. In the Eucharist, the assembly is hungry with the hungry, taking refuge in the mercy of God. In the Eucharist, the assembly is pulled out of death.

These images—from third-century Syria and sixteenth-century Finland, the very margins of their respective worlds—took their place in the midst of buildings devoted to assemblies around word and sacraments, a baptistery and a room for the Eucharist. They were one small part of a whole program of biblical painting. They were like the relatively inconspicuous "we" of a great song sung in the praise of God, reciting the deeds of God: ". . . we praise you for your glory . . ."

15. The programs at Hattula and Lohja, both dated around 1510, are remarkably similar in style and content and almost identical in arrangement. They are presumed to be the work of the same artist, perhaps someone trained in the workshop of Albertus Pictor of Stockholm. See Olof af Hällström, *Hattula Church* (Hämeenlinna: Hattulan Seurakunta, 1990); and Tove Riska, "Kyrkans inredning, malningsdekor och lösöre," in *Lojo Kyrka* (Tavastehus: Lojo Församling, 1991), 127–96. The images most closely considered here are widely known elsewhere, both East and West, in diverse forms, as *the harrowing of hell,* or *the resurrection,* and *the protective veil of Mary* or *veil of Ecclesia.* The latter image was known, in the West, especially among Cistercians and Dominicans.

But we need that *we*, especially now, in the midst of religious individualism, consumerism, and ethnocentrism. As long as images of the church do not take center stage in worship, as long as they help us to imagine what we are doing when we gather together to do the central matters of the liturgy, they can be immensely important to a recovered practice of assembly. The image of the women coming to the tomb at Dura and the images of needy humanity delivered from death in Finland are especially apt images for us today. They correspond to what we have here called the ecclesiology of the Lord's Prayer and the ecclesiology of preaching, Baptism, and the Eucharist. They interpret the liturgical action going on near them. They give the assembly an imaginative pattern for practice.

But not every image of the church may be so apt. For most of us, the images of the church we encounter in the liturgy will not be painted on a wall near our participation in the action. More likely, they will be verbal images, found especially in the readings of the day, in the preaching, and in the hymnody. And as we teach and practice the liturgy, they will require some sorting and an intentional linking to the practice and the ecclesiology of the central things. These images will need to be verbally "painted on the walls" of a space in which the assembly does word and sacrament, or they may be misunderstood. So when we read from the Hebrew Scriptures, we may join the ancient liturgical practice of hearing references to "Zion" and "Jerusalem," to the city's rebuilding and the city's hope, as references to the church. But then we will need to be careful. It is grace that allows us to borrow this language, to understand our gathering as the city and the temple and the mountain in which God appears. It is not our "right" to do so, not "the fulfillment of prophecy" in which we are the ones prophesied. Such speech is finally not about us, but about God and God's mercy, about what has happened in Jesus Christ. We are the "city" because the Word that goes out from Zion is being proclaimed here, the feast for all nations that will be spread on Mount Zion is beginning to be held here.

Similarly, if we make use of the western three-year lectionary, with its three readings for each Sunday, we may understand the second reading, from the New Testament letters, as always supplying "the horizon of the church."[16] But it will do so not because it is necessarily a reading "about" the church, nor because its counsel is always currently wise, but because we stand with those ancient Christians, evoked in that ancient correspondence,

16. William Skudlarek, *The Word in Worship: Preaching in a Liturgical Context* (Nashville: Abingdon, 1981).

like the people of Hattula stand with the saints on the pillars, around the mystery of risen Christ present in the reading of Hebrew Scriptures and Gospels and present in the preaching of those texts into our *today*.[17] Furthermore, the hymns we sing may be full of vigorous images of the church—as in "built on a rock the church shall stand, even when steeples are falling,"[18] for example—but those images will come especially into their intention when they are sung as part of the flow of the full liturgy, around the central matters that proclaim not the church but God's mercy.

The sorting will go on. Scripture and hymnody are full of yet other metaphors for church: city, nation, camp, army, people of God, holy people, bride, body, family, colony, exiles, vineyard, olive tree, ark, temple, priests, the elect.[19] It is especially important to remember that these are *metaphors*, the application of the wrong name to something in order to reveal a thing that could not otherwise be spoken. The core name for the thing to which these metaphors is applied is *ekklesia*, "assembly," and its core reality is a gathering of people around the triune God in word and sacrament. Assembly is what the church *is*, just as the Eucharist is a *meal* and Baptism is a *bath*.[20] What the metaphors are trying to name in the explosions of their wrong words, what is otherwise unspeakable among us, available only to faith, is the gracious and powerful transformation of our meetings to be not just any assembly, but this assembly of God.

The danger remains that we will take the metaphors literally, forgetting their core reference to liturgical assembly and to the central matters of liturgical assembly. This literal spirit is especially problematic when it brings along practices that do not accord with the root ecclesiology of the liturgy. "Body of Christ" can be used to support a monolithic, closed, and hierarchical organization, where each of us are cells of the whole and the rulers are closer to the "head." The metaphor will be healthier, more authentically related to its origins,[21] if it is genuinely taken as metaphor and not metaphysical reality, and if it is always set next to the Eucharist and always used to name an open, diverse, and centered assembly. Then calling that assembly

17. Luke 4:21 and 24:27 are models for such preaching.
18. "Kirken den er et gammelt hus," by N. F. S. Grundtvig, hymn 365 in the *Lutheran Book of Worship.*
19. An especially useful catalogue may still be found in Paul S. Minear, *Images of the Church in the New Testament* (Philadelphia: Westminster, 1960).
20. Then this assembly is the "temple," for example, like Baptism is a "sacrifice" (so Justin, 1 *Apology* 61) and Eucharist is the application of Isaiah's coal to our lips (so many patristic writers).
21. See 1 Cor. 10:16-17.

"body of Christ" will be stunning. It will connote that this diverse gathering of people, which has been fed by the risen body of Christ, is one shared life. The assembly is becoming the mystery that it eats, intended now to be itself broken and given away in the world. Similarly, "bride of Christ" runs the danger of being used to support late-antique and medieval conceptions of gender roles, rather than to connote the rejoicing assembly before the rejoicing God, who comes "to marry" all the earth, with Baptism and Eucharist as a beginning of the nuptials.[22] And "elect of God" can be taken to support a faith that takes us out of the world, removing us from the side of our neighbor, quite contrary to the deepest conceptions of Baptism or of the Lord's Prayer. Rather, this assembly is "elect" in an utterly new way, chosen to enact the signs of the liturgy itself, called out and chosen in Christ for witness, service, and love in a beloved world. Used with these reversals and this liturgical reference, these metaphors can be powerfully revelatory.

Exactly the same reversals, so characteristic of all Christian eschatological language, need to be applied to the other images as well: this assembly is the army that does no war, the priests that make no sacrifice, the nation that has no boundaries, the exiles who are at home everywhere, the family that has no blood relation and no familial roles, the holy people made up of needy, dying sinners.[23] But such things may only be said in the faith that God is acting here, for eschatological language is always language about the nearness of God, a stuttering of images for an encounter beyond speech.

Indeed, we have seen how *assembly*, the core name for church to which the metaphors and images are applied, is itself dependent upon Christian eschatology for its meaning. This word evokes images of the Sinai assembly of Exodus and the Great Synagogue of Nehemiah as well as the final gathering of the nations of Isaiah. It dares to apply these images to our meetings as a testimony to the faith that God acts here, through word and sacrament, for the sake of the life of the world. And as with all the other metaphors, this one, too, has its reversals: all the people—women and men, children and adults, not just the elders, not just the wise—have the word and the holy meal in their mouths; and sinners are welcome here.

22. See Kim Power, *Veiled Desire: Augustine's Writings on Women* (London: Darton, Longman and Todd, 1995), 237.

23. On the reversals present in the metaphor "holy people," the name for the church in the communion invitation of the East and the title of this book, see especially below, chapter 9.

In order to make this core image available to liturgical practice—indeed, in order to use all of the images well—the assembly will need to have some sense of eschatology. Again, having this sense will not necessarily mean that a member of the assembly must believe that "the world is going to come to an end" anytime soon. Eschatology must also be used with care; it must also be required to serve the purposes of the gospel of Jesus Christ. Christian faith has mostly been agnostic about such assertions of "the end,"[24] being much more interested in using this language to speak about the current meaning of Jesus Christ, about the presence of God's activity now, and about the reliability of God in whatever end we may face. Modern critical thought can see that eschatology itself had a cultural origin, in the agony of an ancient oppressed people, and that this language, like all cultural artifacts, underwent a "breaking" in its New Testament use.[25] This breaking must continue. The force of eschatological language for the church ought not assert knowledge of the end of things and our privileged position, our escape, in relation to that end. It ought rather provide a rich field of images that, unlike many other religious symbol systems, express the seriousness of history, the acuteness of human need, the limits within which we all live, the merciful action of God to transform us within those limits, and the church as an assembly of witness to that action. The images of church, *ekklesia*, assembly, provide us with an imaginative vocabulary, brought through the fire of years of Christian experience, with which to speak of the worldly importance of the practice of liturgy.

The Practice of Participation

From the point of view of practice, the intention of the images is to enable our participation in the assembly-event. They give us a way to imagine what we are doing and so to follow our imagination with our bodies and our "affections" also inserted into the communal event.[26] Of course, Christian faith asserts that God acts here, even without our imagination. God will create the merciful assembly of witness, even failing strong and healthy symbolization. But that is the issue of "practice": "Therefore I coun-

24. *Cf.* Mark 13:32: "But about that day or hour no one knows, neither the angels in heaven, nor the Son."

25. On the "breaking" of the eschatological language associated with the origins of Baptism and the Eucharist, see below, chapters 7 and 8.

26. See Don E. Saliers, *Worship Come to Its Senses* (Nashville: Abingdon Press, 1996). Saliers is the preeminent theologian writing about such involvement of the senses and the affections in Christian worship.

sel you to buy from me . . . white robes to clothe you . . . and salve to anoint your eyes" (Rev. 3:18). Here is no denial of grace, but we have a thing to do. We can make the images stronger, putting them in the right place, seeing that they accord with the ecclesiology of word and sacraments, so that the assembly can see something of itself in the biblical story, reach out for garment and salve, understand the significance of the liturgy for the world, and take joy in doing the church's work.

Such a reflection on images of the church in the liturgy is a call to the leaders of local worship. Preachers need to make strong images available for the community itself—not just for individuals—subjecting those images to the eschatological reversals that witness to God's activity. Leaders of music and crafters of prayers need to put some images of the church—the dawn procession bearing candles, the naked ones covered with the cloak—in the right places: in the flow of other images around word and sacrament for the sake of the world. Presiders need to enact the *dominus vobiscum* and their deep respect and love for the assembly, their sense of the awesome thing it is, in everything they do, verbally and non-verbally. And they all need to do this to enable the participation of a community in the central things.

On first glance, it seems that among the painted images of our consideration, the old Dura fresco—the women coming to the tomb, both echoing and encouraging the baptismal procession in the room—best accords with the goal of participation. We ought to look for images of this sort: the *ekklesia* is Simeon singing and Anna preaching; it is the friends letting down the bed of the paralytic into the house; it is the women coming to the tomb; it is Mary Magdalene running to tell. But we also need the more passive images of the Finnish churches: the *ekklesia* is humanity pulled out of death, humanity cloaked; the assembly, like the Laodiceans, receives garments and salve and a meal. That we have such images in our midst, flowing through our liturgy, accentuates the solidarity of the church with needy humanity, underlines the role of the church in articulating the crises of the world, and makes room in our midst for people in pain to bring into participation their sorrowful selves, not just their successful *personae*. Indeed, even the women pictured at Dura were travelling to the tomb out of sorrow and need. The surprise of resurrection was still to be given by God. Still, leaders will misuse both kinds of images for the church if they do not recall that images invite the assembly to participation in word and sacrament, not to reflection on the church apart from word and sacrament. The women at Dura encourage and interpret the baptismal process in the room. And the Finnish wall paintings echo and explain a community at *Eucharist*.

Indeed, it is primarily the gracious and multivalent character of those central signs, together with the evocative character of the Scripture itself, that grabs up the selves of the people in the room, pulling them into participation. The liturgical virtue of "participation," so widely discussed in the twentieth-century liturgical movement, primarily means that *koinonia* which is a mutual sharing in the *koina,* the "common things" at the heart of the assembly. Thus, in one of the earliest Christian uses of the idea of communal participation or *koinonia,* Paul points to the shared cup and the shared loaf.[27] And in the phrase originated by Pius X, the early-twentieth-century bishop of Rome, a phrase popularized by Lambert Beauduin, the Belgian founder of the twentieth-century liturgical movement, and often repeated in works on pastoral liturgy, the goal of liturgical reform remains "the active participation" of all the faithful "in the most holy and sacred mysteries."[28]

A primary task of local leadership is thus to further that reform by making the central matters large, clear, unobstructed, noble in simplicity, engaging in presentation, powerfully involved with life and death. The minister of communion needs to know, in presenting the holy bread to the communicant, that "Body of Christ" or "The Body of Christ, given for you" only partly means "for you, Susan" or "for you, Peter." Rather, addressed with dignity and love to each person, this word at communion should have communal resonance each time, drawing the communicant into the plural meaning of the biblical words of the Eucharist: "The Body of Christ, given for all of you." Of course, the communion minister addresses each individual need, though the actual details of that need may be revealed only in the reaching hands and hungry eyes. But the minister should yet more powerfully draw each individual into the larger resonance, creating the *ekklesia* anew, sending the body into the world. Each baptism and each sermon should be similarly addressed with care to individuals, but always with the undergirding of an ecclesial imagination, always to form *ekklesia* anew. Preaching, on such a model, will be like the administration of the bread and the cup. So will presiding at baptism. Furthermore, the Sunday intercessions should be a strong sign of the whole body at prayer, not for itself, but doing its work for the world, interceding for peoples and churches, the sick, the war-torn and the dying, throughout the world. And the music should be the whole body in song. The images of *church* that then surround such a presentation of the participated center, informing the imagination of the lead-

27. 1 Cor. 10:15-17. For further discussion of *koinonia,* see below, chapter 5.
28. See Louis Bouyer, *Liturgical Piety* (Notre Dame: University of Notre Dame Press, 1955),60.

ers and appearing in preaching, hymnody, chant, and prayer, will be secondary but important interpretations of the assembly that comes into existence through these central things.

But the call to the practice of assembly does not just go out to the leadership. Since ancient times Christians have heard the exhortation that they should not neglect participation in the meeting. The writer to the Hebrews used an eschatological motivation: "Let us consider how to provoke one another to love and good deeds, not neglecting to meet together, as is the habit of some, but encouraging one another, and all the more as you see the Day approaching" (10:24-25). For Ignatius of Antioch, that motivation had become cosmic: "For when you are often together in unity, the powers of Satan are pulled down" (*To the Ephesians* 3:1). Justin's report of the Sunday assembly repeatedly spoke, probably with at least a little idealization, of what the *community* did: "On the day named after the sun all . . . are gathered together in unity. . . . Then we all stand together and offer prayer. . . . We all hold this meeting together" (1 *Apology* 67). The author of the third-century *Didascalia* urged Christians not to diminish the church by failing to assemble: "[D]o not deprive our Saviour of his members, and do not rend and scatter his body."[29] And, while the early fourth century saw the martyr Emeritus confessing that "we cannot be" without the Sunday Eucharist, in the same period of time the Council of Elvira in Spain ordered that anyone who missed the assembly for three Sundays in a row should be subsequently shut out.[30]

The very existence of these exhortations and conciliar rules demonstrates that the encouragement of participation has long been a Christian concern. It is no less so today. Indeed, our own postmodern, electronic, New Age times, have brought to us all a strong array of individualist religious ideologies and personal religious explorations. These seem to make the "assembling of ourselves together" (as the King James Version translates Heb. 10:25) unattractive and archaic to many people. Ours is the time of "bowling alone," of a decline in any sort of mutually engaged, public group,[31] a decline that has also affected people's enthusiasm for "going to church." This

---

29. *Didascalia*, 2:59 in Sebastian Brock, trans., and Michael Vasey, ed., *The Liturgical Portions of the Didascalia* (Bramcote, Notts.: Grove Books, 1982), 17.

30. For more on Emeritus, see above, chapter 1. For Elvira, see Willy Rordorf, *Sabbat und Sonntag in der Alten Kirche*, (Zürich: Theologischer Verlag, 1972), 176–77.

31. Robert D. Putnam, "Bowling Alone: America's Declining Social Capital," *Journal of Democracy* 6, no.1 (1995): 65–78. Putnam finds the cause of this decline primarily in the increased time spent before the television. Television, like computer networks, provides a "virtual community" without actual, bodily contact.

is the time of "God decentralized," of local, personally controlled experiments in the divine.[32] These experiments can make communal liturgy seem passé—especially if that liturgy appears unresponsive to local reality.

How shall we practice participation, then, in our time? While there may be many ways to respond to this question, two particular responses have drawn a great deal of attention in present-day North America, and these responses have also spread widely in world Christianity. One of them is the marketing response, many characteristics of which have already been examined here. The marketing response essentially seeks to abandon *ekklesia*, in the sense we have been discussing here, on the grounds that what people are capable of today—what they will *buy*—is being an audience. Planners of "seekers services" and "alternative worship" attempt to use the best means of communication that our culture provides and that they can stage in order to pass on to the audience, in a non-threatening and friendly way, the idea of the gospel. "Participation" here means being in the audience. Communal existence as a witnessing assembly, gathered around the centrality of "the means of grace," is not envisioned, except perhaps for an insider, committed group which meets at another time.

The open door of these seeker services, the gracious freedom accorded to anyone who comes through the door—these are characteristics a liturgical ecclesiology can admire in this movement. The absence of word and sacraments and intercessory prayer is not. The questions that liturgical ecclesiology raises to this movement include these: Can Christian faith be reduced to an idea, without the body of the Bible, communally read, sung and preached, and without the body of the sacraments? Will not the very manner of the seeker service, with its studied attempt to make no demands upon the audience, communicate a Christianity without assembly, a Christianity that has become only an individually useful commodity? In fact, can the gospel be authentically presented without the assembly?

But the other widely publicized response is equally problematic. It involves the creation of intentional communities of "resident aliens,"[33] with supposedly clear boundaries between the community and the surrounding culture. Such communities might look to us like serious enactments of the old decision of the bishops at Elvira: those who miss three Sundays in a row are out. The answer of these communities to the quandary of participation

---

32. "God Decentralized," a special issue of *The New York Times Magazine*, December 7, 1997.

33. See Stanley Hauerwas and William H. Willimon, *Resident Aliens* (Nashville: Abingdon, 1989).

would be the closed circle and the closed door. They call for a high degree of commitment, an initiation process that introduces the newcomer to a community marked by strong self-awareness, and the maintenance of a countercultural rhetoric.

Much about this proposal may be appealing to people who have come to treasure the liturgical tradition of the churches and to be schooled by the experience of the liturgy. Its accent on communal identity and on the countercultural character of Christianity may sound, at first, like what we have here been saying about local assemblies, answering North American tendencies to individualism. Its seriousness about initiation may seem to echo ancient conceptions of baptism. Indeed, the widespread movement toward creating parishes that are largely shaped by the catechumenate could become a movement toward such intentional communities. Many teachers of liturgy have repeated, with a wistful longing, reports from the fourth- and fifth-century days of the church when they imagine that the *disciplina arcani* was in full force, when those who were not fully "initiated" were supposedly not allowed to even *see* the mysteries of the Eucharist, yet alone participate.

But the reports of that "discipline of the secret" are surely much exaggerated. If this keeping watch over the doors was ever actually practiced—and was not just a ritual fiction, an elaborate metaphor, a law more notable in the breach than in the enforcement, or even the creation of much later scholars—then we ought to be willing to call it what it was: a cultural artifact, borrowed from the Hellenistic mystery cults and perhaps useful in the early days of the imperial church as a way to encourage baptism. This cultural artifact ran—and still runs—the very real danger of betraying the gospel of Jesus Christ. If it was ever really practiced, then it was good that it died away. It belonged to the mysteries, to ideas of "purity" and of "the elect" unbroken by the Christian reversals, to "church" as insider group. It currently belongs to the "shadow side" of our cultural individualism, the longing for intimate and "true" community, but it is still our own cultural artifact. It does not belong to the ecclesiology of the Lord's Prayer. It does not belong to the deepest spirit of the liturgy.

A practice of participation that accords with the Lord's Prayer—and with Jesus' baptism and Jesus' meals, with Laodicea and Dura and Lohja— will look different from either of these models. It will encourage a strong center and an open door. It will be based not on the vigorous identification of *us* as the in-group, but on a vigorous and engaging, holy and hospitable presentation of Scripture, bath, and meal as full of God's mercy, drawing a community freely into their network of meaning. It will enact these things as "focal practices," casting their light over all of daily life, calling other meals, other conversations and narrations, other communal gatherings, into rich patterns of meaning.[34] It will be profoundly personal, drawing each person's deepest emotions into the common work, respecting and honoring the dignity and freedom of each person present, compelling nothing. It will also be remarkably communal, in a way that involves something different from unmediated participation in each other as the identified group, something deeper than simply being together as an audience to ideas. This *koinonia* will always be participation together, side by side, in the concrete gifts of the mercy of God.

Such an assembly will not be an ideal community. Some of us will come in the procession, doing the ministries, like the Dura women bearing torches to the baptism. Others of us will be more tentatively present, huddling in a corner, physically or spiritually, to see if a cloak to cover our nakedness may be available here. Most of us will be both, active with our mouths and bodies, hanging back, skeptical with part of our hearts. In any case, each will do the office of participation or the office of observation for the other, for all of us are the naked and all of us are to be drawn into the procession. A task for the leaders will be to make the center strong while also continually urging upon the community the preciousness of the open door—for the marginalized and the "mainstream," the able-bodied and the disabled, the homosexual and the heterosexual, the active and the inactive, the "believers" and the skeptics.

Then everyone who comes to the assembly, each of the leaders included, needs to understand herself or himself as together with the outsiders and seekers, representing a seeking earth. Together we will come fresh to the gift of the articulation of our need. Together we will "go deeper" by reminding each other of our baptism or welcoming each other to the way of baptism for the first time. And at the heart of our meeting will be that word and the Supper in which we encounter the resurrection and find the great cloak of God's life-giving mercy. The practice of participation in such an assembly calls us to come to the gathering, as vulnerable to its center as we can be, ready to hear the Word, hungry for the Supper, and glad to have richly diverse company in the room: not just "our kind," not just the insiders, but the *hoi polloi,* the "many" for whom Jesus said that his blood was poured out (Matt. 26:28). We ourselves are part of the many. Of course, our assemblies will be constituted by many other social factors than these char-

34. Gaillardetz, "Doing Liturgy in a Technological Age," 446–47.

acteristics of participation, but word, bath, and meal at the heart of our assemblies—and images of the church that accord with them—will also be constantly transforming our meetings to be such an *ekklesia*, showing forth the truth of the triune God for the world.

The Practice of Leadership

Such a practice of participation brings us again to the leaders. Leaders with a clear conception of the assembly are needed in order to set out the center of the meeting in strength, to attend to the open door, to help all to come in—weak and strong, fearful and courageous, and to set the image of Laodicea or the ecclesiology of the Lord's Prayer in critical dialogue with local congregational practices. Leaders are needed to teach the local Christians what the *Didascalia* called upon the ancient bishop to teach the congregation: "Do not consider your worldly affairs more important than the word of God; but on the Lord's day leave everything and dash eagerly to your church, for it is your glory. . . . [W]hat excuse before God have those who do not assemble on the Lord's day to hear the word of life and to be nourished with the divine food which abides forever?"[35] Indeed, in a time when meeting together at all may be in some trouble, leaders are called upon to teach the nature of the *ekklesia*. Leaders are needed to help the local assembly gather around those things that are worth running toward—not just ourselves or our ideas or our membership procedures, but the Word and food of life.

As we have seen, the practice of leadership will also be shaped by images.[36] The leaders need to carry in themselves a practice that flows from imagining this assembly to be the gathering at the Water Gate (Neh. 8:1) or the dawn procession to the empty tomb. They need to understand that they are holding out—in words and gestures, in water bath, in bread and cup—the cloak of mercy. They need to imagine this assembly activity as set within a needy world, which they know in some specific detail and which they behold as held in the compassion of God. Such an interior way of approaching liturgical ministry will make a visible difference in the ability of leaders to convene rather than obscure the *ekklesia*. Again, God can do

35. *Didascalia,* 2:59 (Brock and Vasey, *Liturgical Portions,* 17–18).
36. William Seth Adams, *Shaped by Images: One Who Presides* (New York: Church Hymnal Corporation, 1995). Adams proposes, in this remarkable and ecumenically accessible book, that the principal leader of the assembly ought to be shaped by certain verbal images: presiding, keeping rituals, handling and embodying symbols, hosting, remembering, offering, speaking, celebrating.

church without worthy leaders. But in the manner of all practices, leaders, too, need to buy with their lives the things that are being given away. They especially need the salve for their eyes, that they may see this ordinary collection of people as God's church, as a sign of the resurrection, against all death.

Leadership—*ministry*—is ordinarily discussed as one of the leading articles in any systematic approach to the doctrine of the church. In a polemical discussion of ecclesiology, the presence or absence of a mutual recognition of ministries is also usually high on the agenda. But in our liturgical ecclesiology, ministry takes its place in the assembly. It understands itself as existing only for the service of the assembly, only to help the assembly gather around the central things.[37] It is best discussed under the rubric "practices."

That does not mean that a liturgical ecclesiology has nothing to say about the controverted issues of ministry. If "assembly" is the primary ecclesial symbol and if ministry is subordinated to this symbol, it follows that the many different Christian groups have critical gifts to give and to take from each other, also in regard to leadership. Catholic and Orthodox Christians who have maintained the episcopacy as well as other ministries can rejoice in that heritage, especially as they find in this tradition how all of the ministries have their basis in the assembly. But they can also acknowledge other legitimate ways, from the earliest days and into the present, in which assemblies have actually been led to gather around the life-giving Word and so be church.[38] It would simply be a lie to act as if these assemblies did not exist or to call them by some name short of *ekklesia*. These catholics can also continue to seek ways to make the bishops genuine local leaders, with their chair in an assembly and their *raison d'être* assembly ministry.[39] The bishop of Rome himself, were he to return to such an assembly chair, rather than continue the abstract, exhausting, and ultimately impossible effort to be a "universal pastor" through travel and centralized organization, would have a better chance of being seen by the diverse churches of the world as exer-

---

37. For a discussion of ministry in this light, see Lathrop, *Holy Things*, 180–203.

38. Even Ignatius of Antioch, who in the second century tirelessly called for the local assemblies and all their ministries to gather around the local bishop, acknowledged that in Antioch, from which he had been taken, there was now no bishop. Only Jesus Christ and the love of other assemblies would now "bishop" the church. *To the Romans* 9:1. Other congregations were now called upon to pray for this assembly, to visit it, to show signs of communion with it, but not to provide it with a bishop. *To the Magnesians* 14:1; *To the Philadelphians* 10:1-2.

39. On this and related proposals, see Lathrop, *Holy Things*, 198–203.

cising something of Peter's role for us all. In the matter of the Petrine office, less would be very, very much more.

Protestants can also strongly reconsider welcoming again or renewing the ministry of bishops. Bishops can be understood as the principal local liturgical presidents, personally representing the historical continuity of liturgical assemblies in any given place and in communion with other places. They can again become helpful symbols of the assembly, especially as a local church in a given place begins to become a communion of several formerly separated congregations and as the ministry of bishops comes to serve that local unity through actual visitation, frequently and liturgically exercised. But Protestants also need to continue to remember to hold out to the churches the critique of all ministries, even the most "protestant" ones: "Whatever does not teach Christ is not yet apostolic, even though St. Peter or St. Paul does the teaching. Again, whatever preaches Christ would be apostolic, even if Judas, Annas, Pilate, and Herod were doing it."[40] This critique is exactly to the purpose of the assembly. The mere presence of an authorized and formal ministry, of any sort, profits nothing if that ministry is not turned to set out Christ in the heart of the meeting. Such a "ministry" may help a meeting occur, but will be obscuring *ekklesia*.

These various proposals to the controversies remain counsels of practice. They arise out of the trust that a renewed clarity about liturgical assembly and the practice of leadership within assembly will cast new light on many historic divisions. They call for ministers to serve the assembly.

Help for such patterns of ministerial service can be found, again, in the earliest full description of the Sunday assembly, in Justin's *Apology*, written in mid-second-century Rome.[41] Justin tells us that an assembly is an event that "we all" do, but that this event is also served by many ministries: a reader, servers of table, those who bring food and money for the hungry, and one who presides. Three clear tasks are attributed to the presider, probably the bishop, in that ancient Roman church: preaching on the texts that have been read by the reader; giving thanks at the table; and overseeing the collection and distribution for the poor. One might add to these a phrase that comes from the beginning of Justin's report: "We continually remind each other of these things"—the things that belong to baptism. The

---

40. Martin Luther, "Preface to the Epistles of St. James and St. Jude," *LW,* 35:396; "Was Christum nicht leret, das ist nicht Apostolisch, wens gleich S. Petrus oder Paulus leret. Widerumb, was Christum prediget, das were Apostolisch, wens gleich Judas, Hannas, Pilatus, und Herodes thet." *Die Deutsche Bibel,* 7, *WA,* 385.

41. 1 *Apology* 67. English translation in Lathrop, *Holy Things,* 45.

presider joins this discussion, helping the assembly both enact and remember the holy bath. These tasks remain the central touchstones of a presiding ministry to this day. They can form the basis of a pastoral spirituality, the heart of the practice of presiding, the central vocation of bishops, priests, elders, or pastors: recalling Baptism, opening the Scriptures, gathering a community in prayer around the table, urging and enabling the connection to the surrounding world. These things are the gold, garments, and salve for the Laodiceans, the merciful cloak for the naked, the bread and forgiveness of the Lord's Prayer. They are the heart of assembly, the focal practice of the church, the beginning of merciful witness in the world.

"I sing the assemblies," wrote the second-century bishop, Ignatius of Antioch, seeking to characterize one major theme in his own rich collection of letters. We have tried to join his song here, especially focussing on imagining the meaning of assembly in order to enable its practice. But the inquiry after practice brings with itself two other major concerns. How does each assembly turn toward the other assemblies in communion and unity? And how shall each assembly be authentically present in the midst of its own local cultures? In order to "sing the assemblies," we turn now to the matters of liturgy and unity and liturgy and culture.

PART TWO

One People
Liturgy and Church Unity

IF I LOOK TO MYSELF ALONE, I AM RIGHT
NOUGHT; BUT IF I LOOK TO ALL TOGETHER,
I AM IN HOPE, IN ONENESS OF CHARITY
WITH ALL MY EVEN-CHRISTIANS
—*Julian of Norwich*
Revelations 9

4

Knowing Something Together

Among the Dene peoples of northern Canada there has been one people, commonly called the "Yellowknife," who have named themselves the *Tetsot'ine,* "those who know something a little."[1] Their name reflects the respectful and careful common life of a people surrounded by a vast and mysterious land marked by powerful natural forces: no one knows everything about such a land. But their name also reflects a community that treasures the life-giving, survival-enabling skills of the things they do know together. "Know" here, of course, means something more profound than "be able to think about." It reflects rather experienced hands and eyes and lives, in concert with each other and with the fearful and beautiful rhythms of the land. Their name can serve as a gentle rebuke to the usual attitudes of dominant cultures toward minority cultures and toward the land. But borrowed here, hovering behind our reflections, such a name might be used to invite Christians to enter into reflections on worship and ecumenism with both humility and truth—to know the things we do really know, especially those things without which we cannot survive as Christians, and to be silent before the great mysteries that remain; to know together the things that truly unite us and to listen respectfully to our genuine differences.

Christians do indeed know something together. We all *pray,* for example. We have even been discovering, on ecumenical occasions and in personal and familial life, the possibilities of common prayer. Furthermore, we

1. For a moving fictional account of the first encounters between the *Tetsot'ine* and Europeans in the nineteenth century see Rudy Wiebe, *A Discovery of Strangers* (Toronto: Knopf, 1994).

have said that Christians know the "holy things" that are set out for the "holy people" in the assemblies of Christ's church, and we know the One who, in the midst of these things and this people, is the Only Holy. They do not thereby understand all the mysteries of the unity or of the disunity of Christ's church. But they do know something a little together, with eyes and hands and lives, in an experienced harmony. And what they know enables their survival and their life.

The Rule for Assembly Prayer

In the search for unity between the churches, we may find fresh assistance by beginning with what we know liturgically. If "church" can be understood as assembly for worship, then a renewed inquiry into the matters that Christians know together even amid the diversity of practice among assemblies will be essential for a discussion of the unity among those assemblies. We have already considered the shared central matters of Christian worship, especially as these matters contribute to the transformation of a group into "assembly" and as they carry the communion of local assemblies with each other, across time and space. But what of the fact that we also "know" an aching disunity? In many places of the world, there are different assemblies of Christians, sharing the same locality but perceiving no linkage to each other. Worldwide "communions" of such local churches frequently do not even recognize each other's existence. How are we to overcome these manifest contradictions to the witness of church as liturgical assembly?

In a liturgical approach to ecumenism, we begin again with the simple fact of assembly around shared central things. We ask again, systematically, whether there is indeed a short list of such things that can be regarded as a "rule for prayer" known by all Christians. We ask why these things are on this short list and consider their meanings, searching there to see if we may find something of the nature of the unity we seek.

The idea of a "rule for prayer" came from such a search. That is what Prosper of Aquitaine (ca. 390–463) was doing when he wrote the classic argument for the necessity and availability of grace for all people, which has come to be summarized in the phrase *lex orandi, lex credendi,* "the rule for praying is the rule for believing." What Prosper actually wrote was this:

> Let us also look at the sacred witness of the public priestly prayers
> which, handed down by the apostles, are celebrated in the same way

in all the world and in every catholic church, so that the rule for interceding should establish the rule for believing. For when the leaders of the holy people perform the mission entrusted to them, they plead the cause of humankind before the divine clemency, and, sustained by the sighs of the whole church, they implore and pray that faith may be given to the unbelieving, that idolaters may be liberated from the errors of their impiety.[2]

So here is *something:* all the churches, all the assemblies of the holy people, regularly—every Sunday, every day—intercede with God for everyone, even their enemies, following the explicit counsel of 2 Tim. 2:1-4[3] and the universal historical practice of Christian gatherings. Or at least they *ought* to so pray, if they are faithful to their vocation as holy assembly. Such interceding for the world is a core characteristic of Christian liturgy. Knowing this profoundly Christian "something," knowing it even a little, supports and establishes this article of catholic faith: that everyone needs God and God's grace, that grace is, *a priori,* available to anyone, and that faith does not come about without grace.

In making such an argument, Prosper was only articulating the faith in a new situation in a way that had been used before him in other situations—in response to the challenges of gnosticism, Arianism, or Pelagianism, for example—by many theologians and teachers of the church. Augustine, Ambrose, Cyril of Jerusalem, John Chrysostom, Irenaeus, Ignatius—each one turned either to baptismal practice or to the fact of real bread and wine used in the Eucharist or to the participatory character of the gathering around the eucharistic table to support, even to *discover,* many basic responses to heresy. In these early centuries, the experienced worship practice of the church counted in the church's theological discussion. Teachers needed to pay attention to worship. As Evagrius of Pontus had said: "If you

---

2. *"Obsecrationum quoque sacerdotalium sacramenta respiciamus, quae ab apostolis tradita in toto mundo atque in omni ecclesia catholica uniformiter celebrantur, ut legem credendi lex statuat supplicandi. Cum enim sanctarum plebium praesules mandata sibimet legatione fungantur, apud divinam clementiam humani generis agunt causam et, tota secum ecclesia congemiscente, postulant et precantur ut infidelibus donetur fides, ut idololatrae ab impietatis suae liberentur erroribus."* Latin text in J.-P. Migne, ed., *Patrilogiae Cursus Completus, Series Prima* (Paris: 1844) 51:209–10 (the volumes of Migne will henceforth be cited as *PL*); *cf.* P. DeClerck, *La "priere universelle" dans les liturgies latines anciennes* (Münster: Aschendorff, 1977), 89; and Geoffrey Wainwright, *Doxology: The Praise of God in Worship, Doctrine and Life* (New York: Oxford University Press, 1980), 225–26.

3. That this reference is what Prosper means by *ab apostolis tradita* is made clear by other writings; see especially Migne, *PL,* 51:664–65.

are a theologian, you will pray in truth; if you pray in truth, you will be a theologian."[4]

But it was not just *any* practice, not whatever one might encounter being done in a supposedly Christian assembly, that was the source for establishing the faith of the church.[5] For Prosper, the *lex supplicandi,* the rule for interceding, which established the *lex credendi,* the rule for believing, was a practice "handed down by the apostles" and "celebrated in the same way in all the world and in every catholic church." We might say that it had biblical grounding, universal acceptance, actual local congregational exercise, and some accompanying sense of God's approval. And it was a *practice,* a thing that was done. The mere fact that it was done—not so much the specific text of its liturgical realization—was the ground for the theological assertion that followed.[6]

In the search for unity between the churches can we make use of Prosper's method? Of course, we will need to recognize that the rule of believing also influences the rule of praying. The teaching of bishops and theologians, especially as that teaching has been a reflection on the meaning of the language of faith alive in the church, has had a critical role both in the reformation of worship and in the expression of the unity of Christians. Furthermore, we will need to understand that diversity in the practice of the churches is not necessarily wrong, nor is it necessarily destructive of unity. Such diversity can be a sign of fidelity and a mysterious gift of mutual enrichment, as the gospel of Jesus Christ is celebrated in different places in different ways. But we can ask what practices among us give an experienced basis for communion between these different Christian assemblies. And we can ask, with Prosper, whether these practices have biblical grounding, universal acceptance, actual local congregational exercise, and some sense of God's approval. We can together know something a little. That "something" will be the rule of prayer in the churches, which has profound ecumenical implications.

4. J.-P. Migne, ed., *Patrologiae Graece* (Paris: 1844), 79:1180b.

5. For example, one recent collection demonstrates a variety of ancient Christian ritual practices—popular and even communal practices—that have not been regarded as source for the "rule of faith." See Marvin Meyer and Richard Smith, *Ancient Christian Magic: Coptic Texts of Ritual Power* (San Francisco: HarperSanFrancisco, 1994).

6. For two fine modern discussions of the *lex orandi* see K. Irwin, *Context and Text: Method in Liturgical Theology* (Collegeville: Liturgical, 1994), 1–43, and Wainwright, *Doxology,* 218–50. It should be noted that the *lex orandi* was an experienced practice—what can be called *theologia prima*—together with reflection on the universality and the meaning of that practice. On *theologia prima* see Aidan Kavanagh, *On Liturgical Theology* (New York: Pueblo Publishing, 1984). On the interrelation of *lex orandi, lex credendi,* and *lex agendi* see Kevin Irwin, *Liturgical Theology: A Primer* (Collegeville: Liturgical, 1990).

In fact, recent experiences in the lives of the churches have been full of this growing common knowledge. The "Constitution on the Sacred Liturgy" of the Second Vatican Council enunciated principles that the movements for liturgical renewal have been bringing alive in the worship assemblies of many churches: active participation of all the faithful, clarity and strength of both word and sacrament, "church" as primarily liturgical assembly, leadership as service to the assembly. Indeed, "word and sacrament" as a brief description of the center of Christian assembly shows up in Methodist, Anglican, Roman Catholic, Presbyterian, and Lutheran circles and in many other places. Evidence of this does not reside only in documents. Many of us have been going to church and finding a new clarity of "word and sacrament" in our churches. That is, we have been finding a new accent on the importance of Scripture reading using a common lectionary in harmony with other Christians, a new sense of the importance of doing baptisms in the midst of the Christian community as it is gathered, and a continued and steady growth in the frequency of the celebration or reception of the Holy Supper.

Furthermore, the Lima Document of the World Council of Churches[7] has helped churches to see not simply the possibility of shared *meanings* in the sacraments but the presence of shared *patterns* in their celebration, in the actual, local facts of their observance. Theologians now not uncommonly end their writings with suggestions for celebration, which they presume can be ecumenically received since the worship patterns among different assemblies have begun so closely to approximate each other. The availability of Roman Catholic worship in the vernacular for almost three decades has meant that many non-Roman Christians have experienced the shock of familiarity when they have visited local Roman Catholic worship, as Catholics have when visiting non-Catholic worship. And the various liturgical resources produced for diverse churches throughout the world in the same three decades—resources that depend on the same liturgical historical scholarship and the same Christian assessments of the need of the present time[8]—look remarkably alike in basic structure and remarkably alike in the commitment to shaping that basic structure into forms that are responsive to the diverse local cultures.

7. *Baptism, Eucharist and Ministry,* Faith and Order Paper 111 (Geneva: World Council of Churches, 1982).

8. Liturgical scholars, who have shared this scholarship and these pastoral assessments, are frequently surprised when they discover theologians still struggling over issues that belong to other pastoral times and seem appropriate only to radically different forms of the liturgy from those celebrated today.

Even some churches that might have originally thought that the sources of liturgical scholarship or of the Lima Document were too "high church" or too narrowly sacramental have found themselves immersed in a renewed accent on the practice and meaning of Baptism and the Lord's Supper. In the United States and Canada, vigorous "evangelical churches" have become interested in what they call "convergence worship," making use of the fruits of the twentieth-century liturgical movement while inviting the classic "liturgical churches" to see their own evangelical callings more clearly.[9] The Society of Friends, the Salvation Army, and others whose rejections of otherwise nearly universal worship practices can be regarded as "critical" or even "catholic exceptions,"[10] have sometimes taken up the calling not of rejecting catholic worship practice but of inviting us all to interpret the practice more deeply and widely: Baptism is the participation in the Spirit-led community; the Word must inform all of our life; every meal is, in some sense, the Lord's Supper. For this insight the non-sacramental Christians need the catholic practice, but the catholics also need the Friends and the Salvationists.

Such a survey is not exhaustive. It only begins to suggest what we together have been coming to know a little. What has been largely missing is serious ecumenical thought that proceeds primarily from this growing common liturgical knowledge. Here, in this liturgical ecclesiology, we can try to establish a little more clearly the central characteristics of the shared rule of prayer. Doing so may enable us to sketch out some of the implications that flow from this rule of prayer for the rule of faith in our own present situation of need.

What is the rule of prayer in the churches? What things in common worship have biblical grounding, universal acceptance, local exercise, and the widespread trust that they are under God's approval? One way to articulate an answer is this: common to the different churches is the deepest structure of the *ordo* of Christian worship, the received and universal pattern or shape and scheduling of Christian liturgy.[11] This *ordo* organizes *a participating com-*

9. See Robert E. Webber, ed., *The Complete Library of Christian Worship*, vol. 3 (Nashville: Star Song, 1993), 122–24, 196–99. For an example of "convergence" interest in Great Britain, applied to music for worship, see Andrew Wilson-Dickson, *The Story of Christian Music* (Oxford: Lion, 1992).

10. Wainwright, *Doxology*, 244. *Cf.* Gordon W. Lathrop, *Holy Things: A Liturgical Theology* (Minneapolis: Fortress, 1993), 157–58.

11. Since the work of Gregory Dix, much of Christian liturgical scholarship has been interested in "shape" and pattern. Alexander Schmemann, in *Introduction to Liturgical Theology*, moved this reflection on pattern toward a reflection on *ordo*. *Introduction to Liturgical Theology*

munity together with its ministers gathered in song and prayer around the Scriptures read and preached, around the baptismal washing, enacted or remembered, and around the Holy Supper. The *ordo* is these things done together, side by side.

From this view, the ecumenical rule of prayer is the teaching and the washing that constitute Baptism in all of our churches. It is gathering, reading Scripture and preaching, interceding, setting out bread and wine together with *eucharistia*, eating and drinking, and collecting for the poor— all of which increasingly constitute the central Sunday assembly in most of our churches. Note that the *ordo* is Scripture reading together with preaching, *eucharistia* together with eating and drinking. It is ministers together with people, choir together with congregation, thanksgiving together with beseeching. It is also the psalms and prayers of the week together with the Sunday assembly, the observances of the year together with the annual *Pascha.* And it is all of this done so that in the power of the Spirit people may be gathered into the grace of Jesus Christ to stand before and bear witness to the love of God as an assembly.

This *ordo,* this way of stating the rule of prayer in the churches, meets Prosper's criteria. Of course, we could discuss the actual current universality of such an *ordo,* the role and meaning of the "critical exceptions" to its universality, and the extent to which this *ordo* may be more a lively goal for renewal in some of the churches than an actual practice. We might also discuss the extent to which this *ordo* currently has the confidence of Christian believers as being under God's blessing.[12] But the practices this *ordo* describes are, indeed, local and congregational, and to the extent we are able to know actual worship history, these simple practices can be seen to be the leading characteristics of most catholic churches throughout the twenty centuries of Christianity. In any case, it needs to be noted that the rule of prayer is determined not simply by biblical texts nor by historical incidence nor by statistical surveys of universality, but by all of these things working together in the living experience of the church and encouraging us toward renewal.

Biblical Foundations for the Rule

To begin with the foundations, this *ordo* is indeed biblical or, to say it with Prosper, "apostolic." It is a way that the Bible is alive in the churches.

(New York: St. Vladimir's Seminary Press, 1975). For further reflection on the *ordo* of the liturgy, see Lathrop, *Holy Things,* and chapter 5 below.

12. Geoffrey Wainwright's criteria for a practice to be part of the "rule of prayer" include biblical origin, universal acceptance in time and place, and holiness or ethical consequence. See *Doxology,* 242–45.

In fact, we begin to come close to the deeper reasons for its centrality—the reasons this "something" we know a little has survived, the force of this rule of prayer for establishing the rule of faith—when we look at the New Testament, refusing to take the biblical roots of worship for granted. For the sake of understanding the reasons for the rule of prayer, one ought to consider more closely the biblical grounding of its leading characteristics: Baptism, Word, and Eucharist.

These core actions of our churches are also found in the biblical record. As far as we can tell, all the communities behind the New Testament writings treasured Baptism, making use of it as the way one entered the church. The reading of Scripture as a liturgical practice is implied by passages in Luke, where the interpretation of Scripture by the risen Lord was probably a model of the church's Sunday meeting; by passages in Paul, where the apostle's own letters were to be read in the gathered assembly; and by the letters to the churches and the opening of the scroll in the Revelation to John.[13] Preaching—like the risen Lord's interpretation of Scripture on the first day of the week—is everywhere assumed. Furthermore, the Christian practice of the Supper of the Lord is assumed by the "do this" of Luke and Paul[14] and by diverse reports elsewhere in the New Testament. For example, that the meal was held every Sunday is reported for the community at Troas and suggested by the first-day model of the Emmaus story: the risen Lord interprets the Scripture and is known in the blessing and sharing of the bread.[15]

There are even passages that hold more than one of these core actions together. At the beginning of Acts, after the Baptism of a great multitude of new believers, the community is "devoted . . . to the apostles' teaching and fellowship, to the breaking of bread and the prayers" (2:42). At Troas, the community gathers on Sunday for preaching and the meal (20:7-12), the same pattern that is found in the disciples' first-day meeting with the Risen One on the way to Emmaus (Luke 24:13-32). In Mark, Jesus uses together the cup and Baptism, central matters that the community knows, as metaphors for the martyr's death (Mark 10:38-39). Paul depends upon the community having Baptism and the meal as central events in order to make the exhortation based on the "baptism" of Israel in the Red Sea and the holy eating and drinking of the exodus journey (1 Cor. 10:1-22) and in

13. Luke 24:27, 32, 45; cf. 4:21; 1 Thess. 5:27; Col. 4:16; Rev. 2-3; 5:1-10.
14. Luke 22:19; 1 Cor. 11:24-25.
15. Acts 20:7; Luke 24:30-31.

order to propose that Baptism and the meal unite Christians in one body and one Spirit (12:13).

None of these passages gives us great ritual detail about what the churches did when they gathered for worship. But this much is clear: in New Testament texts, the risen Christ bids the community to teach and to baptize (Matt. 28:19; *cf.* Mark 16:16), the crucified Risen One is known in the explanation of Scripture and in the meal (Luke 24:30-32; *cf.* John 20:20; Rev. 5:6-7), and preaching is full of the powerful weakness of the cross of Christ (1 Cor. 1:17). These assertions of Christian faith only serve to underline the centrality of these symbolic acts already among New Testament–era communities.

But these assertions also do more. They help us to see why the actions of "the core" *are* the core: because they have to do with Jesus Christ. They are the core because in them we are enabled to encounter the full reality of who Jesus is and what he does, and so we are brought to stand before God in the power of the Spirit as one body in Christ. The core actions are not so much commanded by Scripture or dependent upon a certain view of biblical theology. They are, rather, matters that have lived on in the churches, matters that those churches have seen as "apostolic." They are the means by which the current churches are in communion with those ancient assemblies. When New Testament churches present one of these things as done by dominical command, they present the central matters of their actual practice, matters they saw as having to do with the Crucified Risen One, matters in which we are in communion with them. There are certainly other things that some Christian communities did when they worshipped: ecstatic utterance, for example, or singing. But these things—Baptism, preaching, the Supper—came to be especially central to Christians because they have been seen as intimately bound up with who Christ is.

We see this connection of Jesus with those things that became the church's central actions already in the traditions about his life. According to the Gospels, Jesus himself was *baptized.*[16] He himself came *preaching.*[17] And one of the ways he was most well-known—even notorious—was by his constant *table fellowship* with sinners.[18] From this perspective, the church's gatherings around these very things simply continue the actions of Jesus himself.

But we see the connection of Jesus Christ to the core actions of the church's worship even more strongly in the ongoing tradition of faith that

16. Mark 1:9 and parallels.
17. Mark 1:14 and parallels.
18. *Cf.* Matt. 11:19; Luke 7:34.

participation in these things is participation in him. To be part of the community of preaching, baptism, and the meal is to be gathered, by the power of the Spirit, "into him" and so to stand in him under the grace of the very God who sent him. The core actions of the liturgy establish a community in the dynamic presence of the triune God. Thus in the New Testament, Jesus Christ is the meaning of the Scriptures and the content of preaching;[19] speaking of him is speaking the "yes" to all of God's ancient scriptural promises, of which promises the Spirit in our midst is now "the first installment."[20] Baptism is being formed into the body of Christ by the one Spirit.[21] It is being buried with Christ in order to be raised to newness of life with him, and this resurrection occurs "by the glory of the Father."[22] Jesus Christ hosts the Supper and is himself the very gift given for eating and drinking;[23] to eat and drink with him is to be formed as his body, to drink of the one Spirit,[24] and to stand with Christ as he blesses and gives thanks to God.

The New Testament does not give us a constitution of the church or a service book. It does give us Jesus Christ, seen and known amid ordinary things—water for washing, words for telling important stories and for prayer, a shared meal. It does give us an assembly centered around these things. Just as access to Christ would be difficult and skewed for us without the New Testament books, so also we need the concrete signs of water, communal words, and shared meal. Without them, when we speak of Jesus Christ we could easily be speaking more of ourselves and of our own projections than of the biblical, historic Christ. It is very easy to take a holy figure—"Jesus"—and make that figure a screen on which we show our own ideas or needs. But with these concrete things, we encounter the very *self* of Jesus breaking into our projected ideas:[25] in the teaching, baptizing church "I am with you always" (Matthew 28:20); the Scriptures themselves, read and interpreted in the assembly, "testify of me" (John 5:39); in the meal of the assembly "this is my body" (Mark 14:22). These things are central to us, because Christ is central to us. These things are to us as the very flesh of

19. Luke 24:27; 1 Cor. 1:23; Rev. 5:5.
20. 2 Cor. 1:20-22.
21. 1 Cor. 12:13.
22. Rom. 6:4.
23. Mark 14:23-24 and parallels; Rev. 3:20.
24. 1 Cor. 10:17; 12:13.
25. *Cf.* Edward Schillebeeckx, *Tussentijdsverhaal over twee Jezus boeken* (Bloemendaal: Nelissen, 1978), 31–34.

Christ, the concrete way of our encounter with him who is for us the revelation and the gift of the fullness of God's grace.

Rule for Prayer, Rule for Faith

Several important consequences follow from this deepest, "apostolic" reason for the core actions of Christian worship. When we begin to trace those consequences we begin to see the implications of this rule of prayer for the rule of faith. For one thing, it is clear that we *need* this core, these central symbols. These things we know together have to do with our survival. As the deacon Emeritus and his companions said in the midst of the persecutions of Diocletian (284–305), when they were accused of participating in the Sunday assembly: "We cannot *be* without the supper of the Lord."[26] Now, in late twentieth and early twenty-first centuries, there are a lot of people who are talking about Jesus Christ. That name is used for many religious ideas present in our current cultures—for success programs and for self-realization plans, for politics of the left and of the right, for various requirements for what human beings must be, for ideas about the "soul" and about world-escape. Indeed, some people use the name "Jesus" as if it were a perfect synonym for popular religion or simply for one's own self. Other, more scholarly sorts assume that the only access to Jesus is through current reconstructions of what he might have actually been like, what he might have actually said, reconstructions that are similarly, though more subtly, prey to the pressures of the present politics and religion now influencing the "reconstructor." Yet other peoples in the world still need to hear of Jesus Christ for the first time. The Christian church has classically believed that who Jesus is and what he does are most reliably encountered in "word and sacrament," that is in the Scriptures read next to the bath and meal that are full of Jesus' own, self-giving "I."

According to the Christian faith, in Christ in the communion of the Spirit we meet the God who wipes away tears, gives life to the dead, promises and says yes to the promises, and sets out the food of forgiveness and festival. Thus, we need Christ, the historic biblical Christ, and not simply our own projections and ideas of him. So "church" is none other than the assembly that does these things in which we encounter Christ, in which the Spirit acts. Of course, many other ideas of the meaning of "church" abound in ecumenical discussion. This is the view that arises from the rule of prayer.

26. See above, chapter 1, note 34.

But why *these things,* specifically? Why this *ordo,* this rule of prayer? Why not something else? Why not some other book or some other religious rites? Conch-shell blowing or incense burning or pilgrimages, for example? There is nothing wrong with such rites, per se; in fact some Christians make use of them in their own communities, as accessory to the central things. Furthermore, there are many other beautiful and profound books besides the Bible. But the stories of Israel set next to the ancient books from the earliest church are found by the church as the way to encounter Jesus Christ. The washing that is Baptism and the supper that is Eucharist were already present in his life, as witnessed in the Gospels. Indeed, Scripture reading and interpretation, washing for purity before God, and prayers at meals or the meal-as-prayer were deeply present in the religious culture where Jesus' ministry first occurred. According to the New Testament, he made use of them for the purposes of his own mission. Then these things were received, down through the ages, as gifts from him, done at his command. We might speculate about other possibilities. But we actually have no other means. These are the ones that are historically present in the New Testament and are found nearly universally in the life of the church. These concrete, real things connect us to a concrete, real history of the church.

And they connect us to the concrete, real earth. While we may say that we have these things simply because they are what actually comes to us from the culture in which Jesus was born and from the history of the church, Christian faith has believed that the universal availability of the stuff of these central symbols has been a gift from God. Water is everywhere. Humans need it to live. Baptism is in water, any water, not some special or Near Eastern water. Accessible but strongly symbolic speech, used to convey the deepest human values, is found in every culture. The oral witness to Jesus Christ can be made in that language and the Bible can be translated into it. Festive meals are found universally. The Lord's Supper is held with local bread and local wine—or where these are simply not available or are far too expensive, with locally recognized staple food and festive drink, not with special, imported food. The things in which we encounter Jesus Christ and, in him, God's overflowing grace for all, are accessible everywhere and are easily seen to be signs of the goodness of God's earth, as well as signs for the deep unity God's mercy can establish between the good diversity of the many cultures of the world.

Furthermore, "word," "bath," and "meal" can be seen to be gifts that are inclusive in another sense. Words can be both praise and lament, the recounting of both death and life. Both significations are used in the stories of Israel and of Jesus and both are welcome in the church. A bath can wash and a bath can drown. Both happen in the one use of water in the church. The joyful, life-giving, resurrection meal of the community has the death of Jesus at the center of its memory and the dreadful hunger of our neighbors and of the world as the focus of our resultant mission. The central things of Christian worship are not narrowly "religious" things nor are they concerned only with happiness and success. They welcome us, who gather to do them, to the full truth about ourselves: sorrow and hope, hunger and food, loneliness and community, sin and forgiveness, death and life. God in Christ comes amidst these things, full of mercy.

That these historic, central matters of Christian worship correspond to *mercy* can be seen in the simplest encounter with their forms. Words may be *heard,* coming from outside of ourselves, giving us a new story or reinserting us in an old story, whereby we may understand ourselves and our world anew. Water may be *poured* over us, somebody else thereby immersing us in the bath. Food may be *given* to us—and to lines of other people—pressed into our hands, extended to our lips. These communal gifts, in their very form, show forth and enact the Christian faith that God's grace in Christ is our new story, our bath, our life-giving meal.

But why all of these things? Would not just one be enough? No. The gift is more abundant than that. A set of words alone can easily be twisted into a new law, a list of things we have to do in order to be acceptable to God, unless it is constantly clear that the content of the words is the same content that is washed over us in the bath and given to us to eat and drink in the Supper. Drinking the cup in which Christ says, "My blood, for you," gives us a key to understand the Scriptures. All preachers should strive to see that their sermons say in words the same thing that the bath and the cup say in actions. In the church, words should be edible, like bread, and just as full of grace. And the bread of Christ is to be seen as a "word," indeed one of the strongest words we have to say the truth about God, the world, and ourselves. This is why, in the history of the Christian liturgy, the essential matters are always juxtaposed to each other and are always themselves made up of at least two juxtaposed elements: readings *and* preaching, teaching *and* bathing, thanksgiving *and* receiving the food.[27] The Christian *ordo* is the simple pattern that results when these basic things are done side by side.

27. See Lathrop, *Holy Things,* especially 204–6.

The Central Things and Unity

It now becomes clear that Christian worship has a responsibility to let these things always *be* and *be seen to be* at the center of our gatherings. The word "worship" itself may mislead us into thinking that when we gather we may do anything that seems appropriate to us as "worship"—any sort of singing, any sort of "God-talk," any sort of exercise in a hall with stained-glass windows. But if our gathering is about the grace of God in Jesus Christ and if the communion among our gatherings is to be based on the confession of that grace, we cannot do without word and sacrament. To pretend that "Christian freedom" includes freedom from these things may be only to choose the bondage of our own opinions, our own "religion," our own, unrelieved selves, masquerading as "God."

At the same time, that these things are essential to Christian worship should not be seen as a burden. They are gifts. They should be celebrated as gifts. Indeed, there can be great diversity in the ways an assembly reads Scripture and interprets it, washes those joining the community, and holds a meal. There can be many other secondary characteristics—musical style, architectural or artistic arrangement, patterns of entrance and leaving, leadership—that may make one assembly observing the central things seem very different from another. Yet these assemblies, sharing the rule of prayer, will recognize and encourage each other.

Worship is not and ought not be the same everywhere. Indeed, the unity we seek will always be a communion among local churches. The rule of prayer helps us to see that local churches are none other than the communities that do the word and sacraments. But these communities must enact these central things *locally*: in language and gesture, ritual and song that is locally accessible, unfolding local gifts. These communities are always the catholic church dwelling in *this particular place*. But they are also *the catholic church* dwelling here. The universal gift of word and sacrament give to them something to inculturate, a pattern into which to draw the deepest local gifts.[28]

The *ordo* of Christian worship, the deep pattern we share, is a major means of the communion among these local churches, a principal part of the *koina* ("shared things") which enable *koinonia* ("mutual participation," "communion"). This deep pattern, however, should be used not only as a

---

28. Thus, Gerrit Singgih of Indonesia, in a private conversation, reports that in Java, denominational, contextual, and contemporary ways of worship can be drawn into mutual enrichment by a focus on the *sacraments*. See below, Part Three.

tool for recognition, helping us to see that the other church is indeed truly Christian, but also as a means for mutual encouragement to renewal. As Prosper's argument should encourage all local assemblies to continually recover priestly intercession for the world, so the whole rule of prayer can be the subject of mutual ecumenical recommendation. "Are Scriptures and preaching, *eucharistia* and eating and drinking, teaching and washing clear and central in your assemblies?" we may ask each other. In fact, such inquiries may need to be the first agenda item of an ecumenical movement newly interested in the communion of local churches.

In the manner pioneered by the Lima Document, work should continue to resituate many of the classic disagreements between Christians within the context of the rule of prayer, of the "something we know a little." Much clarity is obtained when baptismal conflicts are placed within the full *ordo* of teaching and washing for the sake of communal discipleship, when ministry is described in reference to actual functions within the assembly, when debates about "sacrifice" are seen to be discussions about the meaning of eating and drinking the gift of Christ in the Holy Supper, and when arguments about action for social justice are rooted in the implications of the Sunday Eucharist. We will be helped in these discussions if bishops and theologians are encouraged to reflect upon and learn from the shared worship patterns of the churches and if the voices of liturgical scholars are also welcomed to the table.

When ecumenical worship occurs—in councils and assemblies of the churches, but also in local instances of mutual reconciliation—it will be of great help if the deep and simple pattern of the shared rule of prayer predominates, with an eclectic use of cultural and denominational material to illuminate and unfold that pattern. We need to move beyond "demonstration liturgies"—showing an ecumenical gathering how one particular group does worship—if these liturgies only serve to obscure the shared pattern and make impossible a common community of prayer. A core realization of the rule of prayer is that the actual gathering of Christians does *its* liturgy. In ecumenical gatherings that shared liturgy can only be the shared *ordo* unfolded with instances of local song or local art that can be received as mutually enriching.

But it is most helpful to remember that the essential purpose of this rule of prayer is to allow the church to speak and sign the mercy of God in Jesus Christ for the sake of the life of the world. Word, table, and bath occur at the heart of a participating community so that all people may freely encounter God's mercy in Christ, that they may come to *faith* again and again, that they may be formed into a community of faith, that they may stand in dignity, life, and freedom before God, and that they may be brought to new love for God's world. When this purpose is not manifest in the exercise of the central things themselves, the deep meaning of the rule of prayer is obscured and betrayed. Even so, God acts in these things. God's life-giving Spirit breaks out of our prisons. But our purpose must be to let the reason for the rule of prayer be apparent in inculturation, be the goal for the urgency of ecumenical *koinonia* and ecumenical theology, and be the theme of ecumenical prayer. The rule of prayer shows a pattern of reading together with preaching that leads to intercessions for the world, of thanksgiving together with eating and drinking that leads to collection for the poor and mission in the world. In fact, all the pairs of the *lex orandi* are understood most clearly when they are understood as yielding such a witness to God's universal mercy. For Prosper and for us, this is the *lex credendi* that the rule of prayer always establishes.

God's grace is alive in word and sacrament for the life of the world: that is the "something" that together we know a little, around which the assemblies of Christians may gather, to which we may continually recall each other. If we each look to ourselves alone, to our own taste in religious ritual, there will not be much hope for assembly showing forth God's mercy for the life of the world. But if, with the remarkable woman of fourteenth-century England, Julian of Norwich, we "look to all together . . . in oneness of charity with all my even-Christians,"[29] if we look at what we know together, there is hope indeed. The rule of prayer—understood as the something we know together liturgically, as the central matters for Christian survival in a continually mysterious world—can be the grounds for a unity among the churches that shows forth God's love for the world.

---

29. The full quotation, in the original Middle English, is found in Marion Glasscoe, ed., *Julian of Norwich: A Revelation of Love* (Exeter: University of Exeter, 1993), 13: "[F]or if I loke singularly to myselfe I am right nowte; but in general I am in hope, in onehede of charitie with al myn evyn cristen."

5

Unity and Liturgical Pattern

In the quest for Christian unity, consideration of the "rule for prayer" is not yet enough if it is understood only as the short list of central matters for Christian assembly. What of the legitimate diversity of our liturgical patterns? How do we find communion with each other within that diversity? Is unity an idea or a feeling for each other, or does it actually find a concrete liturgical form? The very pattern or shape of those central things—the way they are set next to each other in practice—can help us.

In the last decade of the second century, Irenaeus of Lyons wrote a letter, preserved for us in the *Ecclesiastical History* of Eusebius, to Victor, the bishop of Rome.[1] The letter, one of the most important documents of the so-called paschal controversy, was sent in the name of the Christians of Gaul as a passionate appeal for unity within an accepted liturgical diversity, an appeal against Victor's decree that the Christians of Asia, who kept a paschal fast ending on the fourteenth day of the springtime moon rather than on Sunday, were to be considered "all utterly excommunicated."[2] As far as we know, Victor had not demonstrated why the Asian customs violated the gospel, why they constituted "heterodoxy;" they were simply not his practice, nor were they the customs of his predecessors or of many other local churches. Over against Victor, Irenaeus cited examples of ancient diversity in ritual practice that had not broken the communion of the churches. Indeed, for us his text is probably evidence not only of diverse practice in

1. Eusebius, *Ecclesiastical History* 5:24:11–18.
2. The term for "excommunicated" is *akoinonetous.* Ibid., 5:24:9; Greek text in Kirsopp Lake, ed., *Eusebius: The Ecclesiastical History* (Cambridge: Harvard University Press, 1965), 1:508.

the length and times of the paschal fast but also evidence of a time when some churches—notably the Roman church—kept no *Pascha* at all, while other churches had begun to do so.[3] Amidst this argument for liturgical diversity is Irenaeus's famous dictum: "[T]he disagreement about the fast confirms the concord in the faith."[4]

But the "concord" Irenaeus has in mind is not simply agreement about a Christian idea, held in common among people who have utterly different ritual practice. He also clearly envisions a liturgical or ritual unity within a liturgical diversity. The examples of concord he recalls include the time when the earlier Roman presbyters would send the Eucharist to Christians of differing calendrical practice and the time when Anicetus of Rome yielded the thanksgiving at table to the visiting Polycarp of Smyrna:

> [T]he presbyters before you who did not observe [the *Pascha*] sent the eucharist to those from parishes who did. And when the blessed Polycarp was staying at Rome in the time of Anicetus, . . . neither could Anicetus persuade Polycarp not to observe, seeing that he had always observed with John the disciple of our Lord and the rest of the apostles with whom he had passed his time, nor did Polycarp persuade Anicetus to observe, who said he was obligated to hold the customs of the presbyters who were before him. But with things in this state, they were in communion with each other *[ekoinonesan heautois],* and in the church, Anicetus yielded the thanksgiving *[ten eucharistian]* to Polycarp, with manifest respect, and they parted from each other in peace, all the church being in peace, both those who observed and those who did not observe.[5]

These are *liturgical* examples. Here was liturgical unity amid diversity, even disagreement. The recipients of the sent Eucharist clearly knew what to do with it! And Polycarp knew how to give thanks at table. There were shared ritual practices—or at least they were shared enough to be recognized and trusted. Among us, the letter of Irenaeus has also appropriately been found to be early evidence of the *fermentum*[6] and of "concelebration" (understood

3. Thomas Talley, *The Origins of the Liturgical Year* (New York: Pueblo Publishing, 1986), 20–24.

4. Irenaeus, quoted in Eusebius, *Ecclesiastical History* 5:24:13; Greek text in Lake, *Eusebius,* 1:510.

5. Ibid., 5:24:15–17; Greek text in Lake, *Eusebius,* 1:510, 512.

6. Antoine Chavasse, *La liturgie de la ville de Rome du Ve au VIIIe siècle,* Studia Anselmiana, 112 (Rome: 1993), 21–25. On the *fermentum* or the "sending of the Eucharist" as a prac-

as "yielding place" to the visiting presider),[7] both of which practices were means of communion among and within the local churches.

Irenaeus is not alone among ancient Christian writers in this interest in liturgical unity amid liturgical diversity. Tertullian, for example, in a passage in which he clearly acknowledges the great diversity of customary practices among Christians, also writes of unity. One does not have to agree with the final intention of his argument (the veiling of Christian virgins) nor its Montanist leanings to be moved by his questions and his assertion:

> What shall we observe? What shall we choose? We are not able to spit upon a custom which we are not able to condemn. Such customs are not foreign to us because it is not among strangers that we find them, but among those with whom we share [communicamus] the law of peace and the name of *fraternitas*. There is, for us and for them, one faith, one God, the same Christ, the same hope, the same sacraments of the bath [eadem lavacri sacramenta]; to say it with one word: we are one church. So, whatever belongs to those who are of us belongs to us. To say otherwise would divide the body.[8]

This is a passage of great usefulness to us in this time of inculturation and of ecumenical encounter with widely diverse customs in worship. But here as well the unity is not simply an idea that is "the law of peace" or the "one faith." Unity includes, indeed, "the same sacraments of the bath." The very practice of Baptism, too—with its mysteries, rites, and vows—is a means of unity between and in the churches. In fact, for Tertullian, the "law of peace" in which we all "commune" is probably the communion in the very body of Christ itself. And the "one faith" probably includes the signs and actions and rituals of the faith.

tice of unity, see also G. G. Willis, *A History of Early Roman Liturgy*, Henry Bradshaw Society Subsidia 1 (London: 1994), 68–70.

7. Gordon W. Lathrop, "Yielding to Polycarp: Concelebration Reconsidered," *Lutheran Forum* 17, no. 3 (1983): 24–26. See also Robert Taft, *Beyond East and West: Problems in Liturgical Understanding* (Washington, D.C.: Pastoral, 1984), 81–99.

8. Tertullian, *De virginibus velandis* 2:2; text in *Tertulliani Opera*, 2, CCSL 2 (Turnhout: 1954), 1210: "Quid observabimus? quid deligemus? Non possumus respuere consuetudinem, quam damnare non possumus, utpote non extraneam, quia non extraneorum, cum quibus scilicet communicamus ius pacis et nomen fraternitatis. Una nobis et illis fides, unus Deus, idem Christus, eadem spes, eadem lavacri sacramenta, semel dixerim, una ecclesia sumus. Ita nostrum est quodcunque nostrorum est. Ceterum dividis corpus." See also Christoph Stucklin, *Tertullian: De virginibus velandis* (Bern: 1974).

Koinonia and the Liturgy

So how does one hold the balance between liturgical diversity and liturgical unity, between diverse customary practices and the *koinonia* in the faith? And what does this *koinonia*—the communion between Anicetus and Polycarp, the communion in Tertullian's "law of peace," the potential or actual communion between our own very different churches today—have to do with the "shape of the liturgy"?

One should begin to answer these questions by noting that the tension between diversity and unity is very old. The history of liturgical practice has not been a history of steady decline from an original uniformity into a malformed diversity.[9] Rather, Christian assemblies have been marked by diversity from the beginning. The customs attributed to John and Polycarp and the Christians in Asia were different from the customs attributed to the succession of presbyters in the Roman church. Countless other examples, just as old and just as central as the matter of Passover observance, could be educed. We have seen that the Christian ritual community has been, from the beginning, a local community, even an expanded household community, or a surprisingly extended local "club." It is therefore to be expected that local customs and the use of local culture have been as different as households are.

But one should also note that the concern for liturgical *koinonia* is equally old. The inquiry after unity between the churches has been a characteristically Christian inquiry, even when it has been contradicted in generations of inter-Christian polemic. Whatever a history-of-ideas approach to Christianity may understand as the source of this quest for unity—the survival of ancient dreams of empire as a way to hold the newly diverse Hellenistic world together?[10] the influence of Stoic ideals on developing Christian theology and practice?[11]—Christian faith itself has understood the call to unity among the churches and within a local church as an expression of its theology. God, who is triune, is one and is therefore the source and center of the Christian understanding of a world—and a church—that are both diverse and united. And according to the Fourth Gospel, our Lord Jesus Christ prays for those who believe in him, "that

9. See, among others, Paul F. Bradshaw, *The Search for the Origins of Early Christian Worship* (New York: Oxford University Press, 1992), 63–64.

10. See Garth Fowden, *Empire to Commonwealth: Consequences of Monotheism in Late Antiquity* (Princeton: Princeton University Press, 1993).

11. See Walter F. Taylor, Jr., "Unity/Unity of Humanity" in *The Anchor Bible Dictionary*, 6:746–53.

they may all be one" (John 17:21), that the world may believe in him, and so, by the power of the Spirit, in the One who sent him.

Moreover, the actual experience of this unity—or disunity and the search for unity—has been overwhelmingly liturgical. Symbols, shared and enacted or shared and refused, have been the obvious means of our tasting and manifesting both unity and disunity. And the search for unity, while it has often looked like Victor's liturgical imperialism or a regional form of his centrist vision, has also often maintained the balance between honoring the local, particular practice and enabling the wider communion. The passionate search of Irenaeus, his intervention in an act of liturgical disunity and his testimony to evidences of liturgical communion—these partake in a widespread Christian inquiry. Although we are each very different, are we at peace, of one mind and heart in this ritual assembly? The kiss of peace and the communion in the "one body" have sought to assure us. When we visit other assemblies, is the ritual we are invited to share recognizable to us—are we at one with this people? Some accord of the local pattern of worship with the "apostolic pattern" has sought to welcome us. These are classic Christian questions and answers.

But the question does not arise only from "liturgical tourism," although this phenomenon has increased with increased global connections and will increase further as our societies are marked by growing pluralism. The question is really an old Christian one, made newly urgent in this time of bitter human and ecclesial divisions: How does this local church, intended to be the fullness of the catholic church in this place, recognize the practice of that local church "over there" as also the practice of the catholic church in that place? How does one local church recognize another local church in the same place? How do we recognize each other, greet each other, honor each other, send encouragement and assistance to each other, and together invite the world to see our communion in the liturgy? How does the liturgy show forth a "church of churches"?

For Christians, *koinonia* within and among churches must be, at root, a liturgical phenomenon if what we primarily mean by "church" is liturgical assembly. In any case, what we mean by unity is the common participation in Christ of a richly diverse body, not the ideological uniformity of a single idea, the organizational uniformity of a single institution, or even the emotional uniformity of a single feeling of "fellowship." One Baptism welcomes us all into the one body. Indeed, one Baptism welcomes us into the economy of the life of God: in the power of the Spirit, gathered into Jesus Christ with the poor and unclean, we stand before the face of God, as if the rite were an icon of the Baptism of Jesus. Similarly, the Eucharist is the sacrament of unity, gathering us—by communion and participation—into the economy of thanksgiving to the Father and invocation of the Spirit and divine presence with the wretched and the dead, the very economy of the unity of God. Furthermore, while the words we use in prayer and ritual are many, the Word of God is one, empowered by the Spirit to speak the truth of God by speaking the truth of all things in Jesus.[12]

We could answer the question about the mutual recognition of local churches by using the conventional instruments of ecclesial unity. We could inquire about the doctrine of the churches and the possibility of mutual recognition by their theologians or about their shared ministries and the possibility of mutual recognition by their bishops. That would not be wrong. But in so doing, we might too easily forget that doctrine is first of all what we teach and confess and enact in Baptism; creed is first of all baptismal symbol. We might ignore the fact that primary theology is found in the preaching, prayers, and communal actions of the Eucharist.[13] We might overlook that canon is, first of all, the list of books for public, authoritative reading in the assembly. We might fail to recall that bishops are, first of all, local liturgical presiders. Tertullian rightly invited his readers to remember the shared sacraments of the bath. Irenaeus rightly asked Victor to remember not shared theological writings but the Eucharist sent and the thanksgiving yielded. Anicetus welcomed Polycarp to the table.

The earliest use of the term *koinonia* in Christian circles seems to be in a pre-Pauline adaptation of the Hellenistic word, made now to speak of participation in the Christ of the Eucharist, and by Paul's own extension, participation in the Spirit of Baptism and the Supper.[14] The subsequent Lukan use of the word is arguably also liturgical, for it is found in the great catalogue of the public events of the Christian assembly: Those who hear the *public preaching* and are *baptized* devote themselves to the *"apostles' teaching"* and the *koinonia,* to the *"breaking of bread"* and the *prayers.*[15] In most of the term's ongoing uses such a liturgical conception is never far away. Ire-

12. See Catherine Mowry LaCugna, *God for Us: The Trinity and Christian Life* (San Francisco: HarperSanFrancisco, 1991).

13. See Don E. Saliers, *Worship as Theology* (Nashville: Abingdon, 1994), 16.

14. 1 Cor. 10:16; *cf.* 12:13; see John H. P. Reumann, "Koinonia in the Scripture" in Thomas F. Best and Günther Gassmann, eds., *On the Way to Fuller Koinonia,* Faith and Order Paper 166 (Geneva: World Council of Churches, 1994), 42–44.

15. Acts 2:37-42. If *koinonia* here means the sharing of goods between rich and poor, across class lines—as many interpreters today propose—it is an economic sharing rooted in the table fellowship and public preaching of the community.

naeus's assertion about Polycarp and Anicetus—that "they were in communion with each other"—was probably built upon his sense of the authority of 1 Cor. 10:16 in its witness to *koinonia* in that eucharistic body of Christ, which Polycarp and Anicetus indeed shared. Just so, Tertullian's assertion of baptismal unity between peoples of very different "customs" probably built upon an understanding that Eph. 4:4-6, the text he is paraphrasing, is actually enacted by Christians in their strongly similar baptismal rites. So also, the later assertion of the western baptismal creed, "I believe in . . . the holy catholic church, the *communio sanctorum,*" probably originally meant *koinonia* in the "holy things"—participation in the sacraments,[16] the people coming to the "holy things" of Cyril's mystagogy and ancient Jerusalem's liturgy,[17] the church being none other than the assembly of such participation.

It would be possible for us to understand the search for a "shape of the liturgy," which has occupied and enriched much twentieth-century study of liturgical history,[18] to be a search for the concrete means of our *koinonia* with the orthodox Christian churches of the past, means that might also enable restored communion between divided churches in the present. The Lima Document, with its concrete proposals for ecumenical liturgical practice, has shown that this search can bear fruit.

But we have also come to know that Victor's imposed unity should not be foisted on the past any more than it should be used in the present. We need to tell the truth about what we can discover from history. We also need to be able to criticize what we find in history. And we need to find again the genuine means for our communion with the diverse churches of the past as well as the present. Even Prosper's criterion for the rule for prayer—that the prayers are "celebrated in the same way in all the world and in every catholic church"[19]—ought not be taken as a statistical survey of historical incidence but as a witness and encouragement to all Christian assemblies, based in a biblical text (2 Tim. 2:1-4). It ought to be taken as theologically based and symbolically powerful tradition, as an argument for how the Bible has been and should be alive in the churches.

---

16. Werner Elert, *Abendmahl und Kirchengemeinschaft in der alten Kirche, hauptsächlich des Ostens* (Berlin: 1954). *Cf.* Stephen Benko, *The Meaning of Sanctorum Communio*, Studies in Historical Theology 3 (Naperville: 1964).

17. *Mystagogical Catecheses* 5:19-20.

18. The classic study is Gregory Dix, *The Shape of the Liturgy* (Westminster: Dacre, 1945). But there have been many other works; see Gordon W. Lathrop, *Holy Things: A Liturgical Theology* (Minneapolis: Fortress, 1993), 33–34.

19. See above, chapter 4.

So it is good for us now to ask about the shape of the liturgy, the shape which may unite us, by using theological and symbolic tools. Mere history will give us nothing, unless we use Victor's method. Still, our task is also to find a shape that unites us with Christians of the past as well as the present, so it follows that truth-telling history may call us into question and challenge us to go deeper.

The Ditchingham Ordo

But truth-telling history should not cause us to despair of the task. We confess that God gives us unity, that the economy of the life of God surrounds us concretely in the signs and means of God's grace, that our unity is in common participation in Christ. With Prosper, with Tertullian and Irenaeus, we go to the Scriptures and there see again that such participation is found in *common assembly,* especially on Sunday, in *Baptism* and its process, in the *Scriptures* opened to speak of the Crucified Risen One, in *prayers* and intercessions for all people, in the *"breaking of bread,"* and in merciful *signs of witness* to the truth of the world before God. These are the given means of Christian communion.

We have rightly used Irenaeus and Tertullian as witnesses to liturgical diversity in the life of the churches. But we also rightly use them as witnesses to *koinonia* in the context of an accepted diversity. We rightly plumb the depths of the spirit of liturgical *koinonia,* using their texts as openings to those depths. As far as we know, the recipients of the sent Eucharist did know what to do with it. Polycarp certainly knew how to give thanks at table, as the accounts of his arrest and of the prayer he said at his death make abundantly clear.[20] In any case, Irenaeus thought the use of the Eucharist united the churches, in spite of their calendrical diversity. Tertullian thought the same of baptismal practice. These two voices can be taken as witnesses to Sunday, to a common assembly with its ministers, to thanksgiving and eating and drinking, and to a common baptism seen as concrete means of mutual participation in Christ. Indeed Irenaeus fiercely insists that these things unite even when local traditions—even venerable and apostolic local traditions—divide.

Sending the Eucharist to another church may not be possible in our day—though perhaps it should be tried. But these things are possible: mutual recognition of a common pattern—in assembly, Scripture reading,

---

20. *Martyrdom of Polycarp* 7:1-8:1; 14:1-3.

preaching, and prayer, in thanksgiving and eating and drinking, and in Baptism; mutual encouragement to see these things as more central than any local tradition precisely because these things enable our common participation in Christ; mutual standing—in the spirit or in the flesh—at each other's tables and fonts; mutual prayer for each other; mutual welcoming of each other's presbyters and bishops to significant presiding; mutual awareness that what belongs to "those who are of us" belongs to us; and mutual commitment to produce no further books for liturgical use without ecumenical conversation and enrichment.

In August 1994, a small gathering of Christians was convoked from around the world by the Commission on Faith and Order to discuss the relationship of worship to the search for Christian unity. They met at All Hallows Convent, Ditchingham, in East Anglia, England, and they engaged in the first intentional discussion of liturgy to take place under World Council of Churches' auspices in many years. In the end, they issued a report that contains several statements about liturgical unity and liturgical diversity.[21] One might set the Ditchingham Report side by side with Irenaeus and Tertullian, finding the Ditchingham participants also going to the Scriptures to find the central matters for liturgical *koinonia*. In a central passage from the theological section of the report, we find those central matters arranged into an *ordo*, a "shape" set in motion and scheduled, and we find that this *ordo* became the grounds for a mutual conversation among the churches:[22]

> 4. The pattern of this gathering and sending has come to all the churches as a common and shared inheritance. That received pattern resides in the basic outlines of what may be called the *ordo* of Christian worship, i.e., the undergirding structure which is to be perceived in the ordering and scheduling of the most primary elements of Christian worship. This *ordo*, which is always marked by pairing and by mutually re-interpretive juxtapositions, roots in word and sacrament held together. It is scripture readings and preaching together, yielding intercessions; and, with these, it is *eucharistia* and eating and drinking together, yielding a collection for the poor and mission in the world. It is formation in faith and baptizing in water together,

21. For the full text of theological section of the *Ditchingham Report*, see below, appendix 1.

22. "Towards Koinonia in Worship: Report of the Consultation on the Role of Worship within the Search for Unity," 2–8, in *So We Believe, So We Pray*, Faith and Order Paper 171 (Geneva: World Council of Churches), 6–8.

leading to participation in the life of the community. It is ministers and people, enacting these things, together. It is prayers through the days of the week and the Sunday assembly seen together; it is observances through the year and the annual common celebration of the *Pascha* together. Such is the inheritance of all the churches, founded in the New Testament, locally practiced today, and attested to in the ancient sources of both the Christian East and the Christian West.

5. This pattern of Christian worship, however, is to be spoken of as a gift of God, not as a demand nor as a tool for power over others. . . .

7. But the patterns of word and table, of catechetical formation and baptism, of Sunday and the week, of *Pascha* and the year, and of assembly and ministry around these things—the principal pairs of Christian liturgy—do give us a basis for a mutually encouraging conversation between the churches. Churches may rightly ask each other about the local inculturation of this *ordo*. They may call each other toward a maturation in the use of this pattern or a renewed clarification of its central characteristics or, even, toward a conversion to its use.

So by this ecumenical account, by the proposal of the "Ditchingham *ordo*," the *koinonia* of the churches depends upon ecclesial participation in the life of the triune God through the encounter with the crucified and risen Christ. Central, scriptural means for that encounter are given that are thematized and enacted differently but that are present in the life of the churches, are to be received as gifts, are held in a great common pattern, are locally celebrated, are available for the tasks of inculturation. As Tertullian counsels, all of the diversities in the celebration of these things "belong to us." But so does the task of calling each other to the renewed centrality of these things at the heart of our various ecclesial lives. Let the central things indeed be central and *koinonia* follows.

The Shape of the Liturgy

"What shall we observe? What shall we choose?" we now ask again with Tertullian. What notes for the shape of the liturgy in our diverse assemblies follow from these reflections?

With Tertullian we say: we do the "sacraments of the bath." Note that these mysteries are plural. There is more than one thing to be found in baptizing. There is teaching the faith and there is the bath. There is water and the Word. There is *traditio* and *redditio*, the assembly handing on the faith and the candidate confessing the faith. There is giving, blessing, anointing, clothing, illuminating, leading to the table, but interwoven with these, there is also exorcising, stripping, confessing, praying, bearing witness, discipling. Both sides are needed, and the recovery of both profoundly assists the ecumenical dialogue between churches long divided at the bath itself.[23]

This "plurality" is not only true of Baptism. The Ditchingham Report speaks of "the principal pairs of Christian liturgy," of word and table, Scripture and preaching, thanksgiving and meal, even of Old Testament and New, Apostle and Gospel, bread and wine, and also of catechesis and bath, Sunday and week, *Pascha* and the year—indeed, of "assembly and ministry around these things." Regardless of our diversities of practice, we do well to pay attention to the clarity and strength of these pairs at the center of our assemblies. We do well to ask each other about that clarity. Why? Simply said, because "here on earth we can never rightly say the truth of God with just one word, but always only with two words."[24] Our words need to be paired with signs, our baptisms paired with formation in the stories and words, our meals with preaching, our ministers with assemblies, our gatherings with recognized ministers, our feasts with ordinary days, our days with the festal assembly, in order to speak not ideology, not locally protected, denominational truths, but the truth about God as God is known in Jesus. And why will this matter for our *koinonia*? Because there is no *koinonia* except in the truth of God.

There is a stronger way to say this. With Irenaeus, we need to require local traditions, even the traditions of John or of the presbyters of Rome, to take second place to thanksgiving at table and the shared holy meal. We need to require local traditions to circle around and serve the central matters of our communion, the word and sacraments that bear us into the very life of the triune God. The church is always local, but the local reality must be broken open toward the one who holds all localities together and so is the ground of our *koinonia*. Thus, to use the issue that occupied Irenaeus, an annual festival must be understood as a way to set out word, bath, and table in juxtaposition to and in fulfillment of local annual festival meaning. On the other hand, the absence of that same annual festival in another Christian community must not be made into legalistic and divisive pride on one side or the other. After all, we all use Sunday to juxtapose word and

---

23. See below, chapter 6.

24. A. Köberle, *Rechtfertigung und Heiligung* (Leipzig:1929), 295. *Cf.* H. Kressel, *Von der rechten Liturgie: Prolegomena zu einer Morphologie der Liturgie* (Neuendettelsau: 1971), 31; and Lathrop, *Holy Things*, 121.

table to the human cycle of the week. Certainly, by this late twentieth century, almost all Christians have come to keep the annual festival of *Pascha* and to keep it according to the Roman and the Nicene determination that it should coincide with Sunday. But remembering the time before its universal observance may help us to understand what "festival" *is* for Christians, to imagine again how we might deal graciously with the continuing differences among us on the calendar, to rejoice with Christians who find new festivals appropriate for new localities, especially in the southern hemisphere, and to urge them to break open these local meanings toward the Christ who unites us in word and sacrament.[25]

Indeed, should the traditions of John or of the presbyters—or our own versions of sacred local traditions—supplant the central matters in our allegiance, we are rightly accused of idolatry. We do indeed break *koinonia* when untransformed local customs or particular, time-bound customs come to take central place, pushing aside the primacy of those things that, in the power of the Spirit, gather us into Christ and so before the face of God. This is especially so when the local customs destroy the values of the gospel of Christ. If Polycarp did not know how to give thanks to God through Jesus Christ in the unity of the Spirit, if the recipients of the sent Eucharist held no communion, but buried it in their garden or put it on the shields and weapons of their soldiers, there would have been no *koinonia*.

We may ask, especially today, whether time-bound customs regarding the roles of men and women do not profoundly threaten a *koinonia* appropriately grounded in the gifts of God. These customs, ignoring Paul's baptismal, *liturgical* insight that "there is no longer male and female . . . in Christ Jesus,"[26] can be grounded in too great a centrality accorded to the "traditions of the presbyters," or, worse, in a centrist application of a misreading of the "traditions of the presbyters." Let Irenaeus intervene anew, calling us all to read the local tradition appropriately and to balance it with the more-than-local baptismal truth in Christ. Baptized women belong fully to our assemblies, and their presidency in some of our assemblies at the Eucharist is not an appropriate grounds for excommunication or for the breaking of *koinonia*. Indeed, the insistence that the eucharistic presidency of women is grounds for breaking the communion of churches gives inappropriate importance to a local, essentially cultural, and largely unbroken, non-Christian custom.

25. See below, chapter 9.
26. Gal. 3:28.

Such a tension between the local and the more-than-local can be traced in the central matters themselves. At its very beginning, the Christian tradition saw the powerful, intensely local reality of a meal—with its invited male guests, its local food, and its insider customs—broken open by the simplification of the menu present in the Word of Christ and by the juxtaposition of the event to all the scriptural stories so that it became a feast that can feed a multitude with the very presence of Christ who holds all places and peoples together.[27] Without the Word, without the verbal proclamation of "the Lord's death until he comes,"[28] the meal may close in again upon itself. Conversely, without the meal, the Word, even the universally recognized Word of the Scriptures, may be abstract and locally untasted. As we have seen, the history of the place of the Eucharist shows the same tension: the *house* was opened to the poor,[29] the table of the house was opened to the women;[30] but then, in later times, the great public *basilica* was provided with a domestic center, imperial unity not being personal, hospitable, and class-free enough.[31] Analogous tensions can be found in preaching (the "universal" canon, the widely received lectionary, turned into local words), in *eucharistia* itself (widely recognized patterns of prayer proclaimed amidst the local eating and drinking), and in ministry (local, communal, liturgical leaders, recognized more-than-locally).[32]

The same method is to be critically extended to images, to music, and to the remembrance of the saints. In the *iconostasis* or the arrangement of images, the locally powerful image is both welcomed and disciplined to the central purposes of the *ordo.*[33] The memory of the locally powerful hero is juxtaposed and subordinated to the sacramental memory of Christ. The locally powerful music is turned to Christian purpose, often by being jux-

---

27. See below, chapter 8.

28. 1 Cor. 11:26.

29. 1 Cor. 11. See above, chapter 1. One could interpret the fourth-century house church at Lullingstone villa in England in a similar way: the family dwelling was walled off and an entrance provided to the outside; coming here was then coming to the "house of the church," not to someone's dwelling. On the Christian "chapel" at Lullingstone, see L. Michael White, *The Social Origins of Christian Architecture* (Valley Forge, Pa.: Trinity, 1997) 2:254–57.

30. See Marianne Sawicki, *Seeing the Lord: Resurrection and Early Christian Practice* (Minneapolis: Fortress, 1994).

31. Anscar Chupungco, "Eucharist in the Early Church and Its Cultural Settings," in S. Anita Stauffer, ed., *Worship and Culture in Dialogue* (Geneva: Lutheran World Federation, 1994), 85.

32. See Edward Schillebeeckx, *Pleidooi voor Mensen in de Kerk: Christelijke Identiteit en Ambten in de Kerk* (Baarn: Nelissen, 1985).

33. Hans Belting, *Likeness and Presence* (Chicago: University of Chicago, 1994).

taposed to at least one other style of music of wider provenance and always by bringing its power to serve (as must happen with any power in Christian use) an assembly gathered around the central things. When images, saints, and music, or, indeed, when other features of local power—sexual identity, national aspirations, clan or group spirit—are not so disciplined, the health of the local assembly is seriously impaired and *koinonia* with other assemblies, near or far, is made difficult or impossible.

As a result the shape or *ordo* that unites us always carries the relationship of locality and "universality" within itself. It is a washing in local waters to bring our candidates into the catholic church, a reading of the universal canon of Scriptures to speak Christ to local need, a keeping of a local meal that causes us all to participate in each other by our participation in Christ. It is the word and sacrament that unite us, "celebrated in ways appropriate to the dignity and gifts of each local place,"[34] for the care for that local dignity is also a universal Christian concern. Polycarp may respect, though he does not keep, the customs of the Roman presbyters; Anicetus may show the same honor for the tradition of John that he does for the presence of Polycarp. They may do so precisely because they meet in the Holy Supper and its central actions, letting these local traditions circle like planets around that sun. Again, catholic Christians and non-sacramental Christians—the Friends, say, or the Salvation Army—may find their relationship illuminated by this *ordo*: catholics may need Friends and Salvationists and their critique of sacraments to see the connections between Baptism and the Spirit-led assembly, between the Supper and all meals, or the Supper and service and love broken and given away as "body of Christ" to the wretched. On the other hand, these non-sacramental groups will have a deep need for the catholic or sacramental Christians so that the genuine reference to Christ—to the outpoured Spirit of Christ and not just any spirit, to the broken body and outpoured blood of Christ, and to the risen, accessible One who brings us into the life of God—is not lost in the power of their own local spirituality.

So we are given both the central things and the salutary tensions that fill them. What is needed for our *koinonia* in the liturgy is both the word and sacrament, which bear us into the triune God's own grace and life, and the critical method that belongs to the ancient juxtapositions of these central things. Such is the "shape of the liturgy." For us this will be a more profoundly biblical shape, marked by the very dynamic of the biblical witness

34. "A Letter on Koinonia in Worship" from the Ditchingham Consultation, in *So We Believe, So We Pray*, 3.

itself and of its critical method, than the somewhat questionable correlation between the scriptural words "take, bless, break, and give" and moments in the rite.[35]

With Tertullian, we may enact the plural, paired mysteries. With Irenaeus, we may center the powerful, important local on the *koinonia*-giving, more-than-local gifts of God. And with the gathering at Ditchingham, we may discover continually that the pairs always yield a third element—intercessions, a turning to the poor and the marginalized, a mission in the world—as the Scriptures themselves bear witness. Here is a shape of the liturgy for the *koinonia* of the churches.

In the Ditchingham Report, liturgical ecumenism asserts that these churches may rightly "call each other toward a maturation in the use of this pattern or a renewed clarification of its central characteristics or, even, toward a conversion to its use." Then all other diversities in custom and celebration will be our enrichment, flowing in mutual borrowings or, at least, belonging to us in the one church even when they are strange to us. Then our rich differences will only serve to confirm our concord in the faith.

35. Such is Gregory Dix's widely quoted account of the "shape." *The Shape of the Liturgy*, 48.

6

The Practice of Unity

What might a local practice of liturgical unity be like? In the divided situation of the churches, we have not allowed ourselves to imagine such a practice for any number of cultural and theological reasons. But if we were, together, to think through the basic outlines of the classic liturgical *ordo,* we might discover striking possibilities. We might begin with Baptism.

A sense of the meaning of Christian Baptism and of the common shape of its practice throughout the world may be discovered in surprising places. For example, we may find this meaning obliquely in a classic text from the history of the church, a text that is not about Baptism or baptismal liturgy at all, but that only indirectly reflects baptismal practice or uses baptismal imagery. Sometimes the very surprise of such a discovery and the very character of its context may clearly disclose to us the vibrant importance of the basic pattern of baptizing.

Thus in the early second century, while on his way toward trial and martyrdom, Bishop Ignatius of Antioch wrote the following text to the Christians of Rome, the city where he was to die. He wrote not about Baptism but about his impending death:

"Do not speak Jesus Christ yet set your heart upon the world. . . . My desire (*eros*) has been crucified and there is not in me any fire which feeds off material stuff *(pur philoülon),* but rather there is water living and speaking in me, saying to me from within, 'Come to the Father.' I do not delight in the food of death nor the pleasures of this life. I want the bread of God, which is the flesh of Jesus Christ, descended from David, and I want the drink of his blood, which is deathless love *(agape).*"[1]

---

1. Ignatius, *To the Romans* 7:1b, 2b-3. The Greek text is in Kirsopp Lake, ed., *The Apostolic Fathers* (New York: Harvard University Press, 1959), 1:234.

With this remarkable text, Ignatius characterizes the martyrdom he expects and for which he longs, using the imagery of the central matters of the Christian community: the Word of God, the water of new birth into the body of Christ, the love-feast of the Eucharist. Of course, these primal words—water, speaking, bread, flesh, drink, blood, love—have multiple meanings, including multiple religious meanings. But here, in his writing to another church, to an assembly marked by these very things used together, their central Christian liturgical meanings cannot be far away from the sense that Ignatius intends. He seems to wish to convince the Roman church that he does indeed choose to drink the cup his Lord drank, to be baptized with the baptism his Lord was baptized with (*cf.* Mark 10:38-39). He thereby wishes to prevent that church's expected efforts on his behalf. Indeed, he has already said that if he is able to die bearing witness to the Christian faith, he will be "word of God" spoken for others to hear, not just another "cry" evaporating in the needy history of the world.[2] He has already argued, using strong baptismal analogies, that his death will be a birth, an illumination, a patterning after the passion of Christ.[3]

It should be no surprise for us to discover that Baptism and Eucharist could function in the ancient church as metaphors for suffering witness before the world as well as sources for such ethical action. They functioned this way already in the Gospel of Mark. They continued to so function in the church of the martyrs.[4] In a cruel and oppressive time, the distance from eating the bread of God in the community to being "ground as wheat" in the arena was not far.[5]

The Ordo of Baptism

But it may surprise us to note that even in such an impassioned text, in such an existentially charged situation, the bishop from Antioch can be seen to be presenting his metaphor in what we might regard as an *ordo*. From this

2. "For if you should be silent concerning me, I am word of God. But if you should desire my flesh, I shall again be only a cry." Ignatius, *To the Romans* 2:1b. Greek text in Lake, *The Apostolic Fathers,* 1:226–28.

3. "I seek that one who died for us; I want that one who rose for us. The time of birth-labor is upon me. . . . Let me receive the pure light; having arrived there, I shall be a full human being. Permit me to be an imitator of the passion of my God." Ignatius, *To the Romans* 6:1b, 2b-3a. Greek text in Lake, *The Apostolic Fathers,* 1:232–34.

4. See, for example, *Martyrdom of Polycarp* 14:2; 15:2.

5. "I am wheat of God, and I am ground by the teeth of the beasts that I might be found pure bread of Christ." Ignatius, *To the Romans* 4:1b. Greek text in Lake, *The Apostolic Fathers,* 1:230.

view, he is becoming a martyr in a way exactly analogous to the way he has seen many other people become Christians, surrounded by the assembly in the midst of which he has presided.[6] So now he, the bishop, is the one who, having heard the community "speaking Jesus Christ," has left behind the ways of "this life," renouncing "the ruler of this world" and the fire and food of death, in order to turn toward God through that same Jesus Christ.[7] The bishop has been brought again to the water and the Word, though now to the water that speaks from within, in his memory, in words that continue to insert him into the very life of the triune God, in water that is the very out-poured Spirit of God within him (cf. John 4:14; 7:37-39; 19:34). And now, through that water, he turns to the communal meal of God which is the very sharing in Christ's suffering in the flesh, the telling of the truth of all-transforming love. Ignatius is doing all of this—turning from evil, listening to the speaking water, turning to the meal—openly, in the clear sight of the communities of the churches to which he writes, through whose towns he passes. Ignatius is in the midst of the process of becoming a martyr, a process he sees as reflecting the process of becoming a Christian.[8]

Proclamation and conversion, the speaking water, the meal: such was likely the *ordo* of the making of Christians in Antioch. And this *ordo* was then available to be remembered, again and again. Even more profoundly, this *ordo,* this one Baptism, could be understood as having occurred "once for all" in Christ, as continually coextensive with all authentic, witnessing Christian life. One was to live through this pattern repeatedly, not repeating the water-washing but listening to its "voice," acting on its invitation. Furthermore, although Ignatius would speak of this *ordo* as reflecting the practice that he would have known at Antioch, he could also expect it to be understood at Rome; in these central matters the churches were at one.

6. So Ignatius (*To the Smyrnaeans* 8:2a) sees the bishop in the midst of the congregation that is celebrating Baptism and then the Eucharist: "Wherever the bishop appears, there let the full assembly be, just as wherever Jesus Christ is, there is the catholic church. Without the bishop it is not allowed to baptize nor to hold the meal of love." Greek text in Lake, *The Apostolic Fathers,* 1:260. This does not imply that the bishop does everything in such a celebration. He *presides.* For example: "Let that be considered a reliable thanksgiving at table which is celebrated by the bishop or by the one to whom he turns." *To the Smyrnaeans* 8:1b. See above, chapter 2.

7. Ignatius, *To the Romans* 7:1. That Ignatius regarded *Baptism* as "arms" for a life-long struggle with evil can be seen in his letter *To Polycarp* (6:2): "Let your baptism abide as arms, faith as helmet, love as spear, patience as armor." Greek text in Lake, *The Apostolic Fathers,* 1:274.

8. Ignatius himself characterizes his martyrdom as *becoming a Christian* in truth, as being found to be a Christian, not just being called one. *To the Romans* 3:2.

Indeed, the text is a remarkable example of a second-century meaning of "church" that can be helpful to us today. The local church of Antioch is in communion with the local church in Rome. The patterns of the "speaking water" (that is, of the water conjoined with the voice of God) and the meal of God are shared in both places. Between these churches (in fact, between them literally, or geographically), the strikingly self-conscious—even seemingly modern—"I" of the speaker acts in a pattern he has received from his own community's liturgical life,[9] trusting that the community in Rome will recognize the same pattern. Christians are gathered in a local, personal-communal assembly in communion with other personal-communal assemblies, in which mutual understanding is enabled by the common experience of the nearness of the triune God, by the common experience of conformity, in faith and life, to the pattern of Christ's cross and resurrection, and by the shared *ordo*, the mutually recognizable great pattern, of Baptism, Eucharist, and ministry.

We may rightly find ourselves troubled by what seems to be Ignatius's enthusiasm for martyrdom and his world-denying piety. We may prefer Polycarp's greater wisdom of reluctance. But Ignatius is, nonetheless, one of the very early voices to insist on the materiality, the *flesh*, of Christ. Even here, he is not escaping the stuff of the material world: water and food and flesh, for example. He is seeing it reoriented, from death toward God and life. Furthermore, about the actual circumstances of his arrest and death we know very little and cannot judge. We know only his stunning imagery. The doubts, the foreignness, the distance from twenty-first century devotion remain. But in the present ecumenical conversation, we may also find great gifts for our work in this text's hints of the *ordo* of Christian Baptism as it was known at both Antioch and Rome, and in Ignatius's sense of the continual, urgent theological and ethical significance of that *ordo*.

Can we, too, speak together about the baptismal *ordo* of our own local churches in ways that are mutually recognizable? And can we do so with similar passion for that *ordo*'s theological, ecumenical, and ethical meanings? Can we understand together how Baptism—Baptism in its process, Baptism with its continual echoes in the Christian life, Baptism in its unifying work

9. That Ignatius might have intended his "I" to stand for a whole community of Christians, who he believed he carried in himself and represented, can be seen in his description of the bishop Polybius in the letter to the Trallian church. This bishop of the Trallians "came to me in Smyrna, by the will of God and of Jesus Christ, and so rejoiced with me, a prisoner of Christ Jesus, that I beheld the full assembly of you all in him." Ignatius, *To the Trallians* 1:1b; Greek text in Lake, *The Apostolic Fathers*, 1:212. *Cf. To the Ephesians*, 1:3.

among the churches—may be "word of God" amidst the need of the present world, and not simply a "cry"?

In fact, it seems that recently much greater attention has been given to the *ordo* of the Eucharist as an ecumenical inheritance and as an instrument of *koinonia* than to the order or pattern of baptizing. But the Ditchingham consultation also suggested that Baptism has an order and pattern that is meaningful, ancient, and increasingly recognized in the churches. The Report includes these lines in its discussion of *ordo:* "[The shared liturgical *ordo*] is formation in faith and baptizing in water together, leading to participation in the life of the community. It is ministers and people, enacting these things, together."[10]

According to Ditchingham, this *ordo* of Christian worship, including the deep pattern of baptizing, is to be dealt with as a gift, not a demand. Along with the other materials of this *ordo,* the water of Baptism is to be celebrated as a connection between faith and life, gospel and creation, Christ and culture. Furthermore, the juxtaposed matters "of catechetical formation and baptism" are among those "principal pairs of the Christian liturgy" which "give us a basis for a mutually encouraging conversation between the churches," for inculturation, for renewal, for attention to each other's charisms, for local unity. Indeed, the very duality of this *ordo* may help us overcome old disputes. The report continues:

> The *Baptism, Eucharist and Ministry* document is itself a model of such discussion of classic points of division in the light of shared liturgical patterns. Thus, for example, when baptism is seen to be a process of both faith-formation and water-washing, believer baptist groups may be able to see themselves as enrolling their young children in a catechumenate, recognizable to many other Christians, while infant-baptizing groups may find their own life-long call to discipleship and learning refreshed, and both groups will find themselves called to a strong celebration of baptism which shows forth its centrality and meaning. Future Faith and Order discussions could well be formed according to this model, with liturgical studies a welcome partner in the conversation.[11]

So the "Ditchingham *ordo*" includes Baptism in a very simple way. It outlines the baptismal event as two things, side by side, "formation in

10. Ditchingham Report, 3–4, in *So We Believe, So We Pray,* 6–7. See below, appendix 1.
11. Ditchingham Report, 11, in *So We Believe, So We Pray,* 8.

faith" and "water-washing," leading to a third thing, "participation in the life of the community." Does that correspond with what we have seen in Ignatius? Yes, if we note, by putting this simple pattern next to Ignatius's, that the process of baptizing must be "known" the way the Yellowknife people "know something a little." So, interpreted through Ignatius, "formation in faith" includes both "speaking Jesus Christ" and the renunciation of the ways of evil and death. The "words" that belong to formation in faith, to teaching and learning, are also alive and continue in the water-event itself. Here, in the power of the Spirit, these words say to the one who is baptized into Christ's death: "Come to the Father." And this baptismal *ordo* has lifelong significance. The "voice" which the baptized hears through the interior, remembered water says nothing else than what is to be heard in the Word of God throughout the Christian life. The "meal of God," in both of its senses—as celebration in the assembly and as sharing in the cup of Christ through suffering witness in the world—is the primary form of "participation in the life of the community." The water leads to that meal, and the meal tells the truth about the world as it is before God.

Put roughly, in schematic form, the Ditchingham *ordo* for Baptism is:

—formation in faith;
—water-washing;
—participation in the life of the community;

though the lifelong call to learning and discipleship places the continued formation in faith *after* the water as well as before it. The pattern we may discern in Ignatius shows the same outline:

—proclamation, conversion, turning from evil;
—the "speaking water";
—the meal of God/witness in the world.

Of course, the very fact that we may discern the pattern in his account of his own potential death is a testimony to Ignatius's view of the lifelong significance of the baptismal process.

But can we discover this shape of Baptism elsewhere? Is it discoverable in actual liturgical evidence, not just in allusion or in the discussions of twentieth-century ecumenism? Is it present in the earliest centuries of the church? Indeed, is it present in the New Testament itself? Finally, is it present in our communities? If it is, does such a simple outline help us in our tasks of mutual recognition and mutual encouragement?

The Baptismal Ordo in the Primitive Church

In fact, there is a striking correspondence between this pattern and what we may discover in the work of Justin, a layman or catechist who was teaching in Rome about four decades after Ignatius was killed there. We have in Justin's work the first full, direct description we possess of what happens in Christian Baptism. The description occurs in Justin's first *Apology*, a defense of Christian faith and practice addressed to Antoninus Pius, then the Roman emperor.

What we find there can be summarized as follows: Those who hear what the Christians are teaching and believing, who come to believe these things themselves, and who promise to live accordingly are taught how to pray. The community prays and fasts with them. These candidates are then led to a place where there is water and are bathed in the triune name of God, in a washing that is called "illumination." They are then led to the place where the whole assembly is gathered, making intercession. These prayers are concluded—and the newly baptized are welcomed—by the kiss of peace. Then the Eucharist is celebrated, the newly baptized also participating in the meal. Justin then continues: "And for the rest, after these things we continually remind each other of these things. Those who have the means help all those who are in want, and we continually meet together. And over all that we take to eat we bless the creator of all things through God's Son Jesus Christ and through the Holy Spirit. And on the day named after the sun, all, whether they live in the city or the countryside, are gathered together in unity."[12] There then follows the account of the Sunday Eucharist, of the sending of communion to the absent and food and support to the poor, and of the meaning of Sunday. So the book, Justin's defense of the faith, ends.

We could summarize this baptismal process with the very pattern we find in Ignatius, echoed at Ditchingham: *formation* in the faith or conversion; *washing* with water associated with the Word and name of the triune God; and *participation* in the life of the community, including now the continual mutual remembrance of Baptism, the remembrance of the poor, the com-

---

12. 1 *Apology* 61–67. Greek text in J.-P. Migne, ed., *Patrologiae Graece* (Paris: 1844), 6:420–32. For a translation and discussion of the full text, see Gordon W. Lathrop, *Holy Things: A Liturgical Theology* (Minneapolis: Fortress, 1993), 61–64.

munal meetings, the meal-thanksgiving, and as the event incorporating all of this, the Sunday Eucharist. We can also say that several things implicit in Ignatius are made quite explicit here: Proclamation and teaching precede the water, but they also follow; indeed, a "continual reminding" is a strong part of the *ordo*. The baptismal events occur in the community and lead to participation in the community's life; the meal is at the center of such participation.

Such lifelong meaning of Baptism and such communal resonance are obviously present in Ignatius. But here, in Justin, the whole matter is set in motion, even in procession, and accompanied by prayer. The resultant pattern could be listed in this way:

—teaching the faith and inquiry about conduct;
—praying and fasting of candidates and community;
—procession to the water;
—washing;
—procession to the place of community prayer;
—Eucharist;
—continual reminding, in Sunday Eucharist and in care of the poor.[13]

In fact, this primitive order for making a Christian ultimately becomes the order of the "catechumenate," known to us from many sources from the third century on:

—inquiry about willingness to change conduct;
—hearing the Gospel/teaching the words for faith;
—prayer (and fasting);
—washing;
—the meal;
—"mystagogy," the learning of the mysteries in which one was now participant;
—and the resultant weekly assembly, witness and care for the poor.

13. It is of considerable interest that, armed with this pattern, we can discover something like the same *ordo* in the probably earlier Syrian book, the *Didache* or "The Teaching of the Twelve Apostles." If we assume that this ancient "church order" begins with catechesis for those who are coming to be baptized, the resultant order of the book is strongly familiar. See Aidan Kavanagh, *The Shape of Baptism* (New York: Pueblo Publishing, 1978), 36–37.

Such a process came to be associated with the Christian keeping of *Pascha* and thereby came to influence profoundly the evolving shape of Lent and Easter. This process itself was ultimately represented by the developed form of the western Christian "catechism," in which specific central texts came to stand as symbols for parts of the process and as tools for continual reinsertion in baptismal faith:

—the Ten Commandments;
—the creed;
—the Lord's Prayer;
—Baptism (for example, the Great Commission);
—Holy Communion (for example, the *verba institutionis*);
—confession and forgiveness/daily prayer/duties.

Furthermore, our third-century witnesses (the *Apostolic Tradition,* Tertullian, the *Acts of Thomas*) begin to show that at this time some ritual signs of the outpouring of the Spirit in Baptism—or some signs that the baptized were being made a people of priests and kings—were being added to the process, in different places and with slightly differing meanings. The most frequent such sign was the anointing with oil. We do not really know the age or the provenance of this practice: Was it drawn from the mysteries or from gnosticism? Was it an intentional addition of an impure agent (oil) to the bath of purity, in order to sign that bath's radical new meaning in Jesus Christ? Was it a sign of hospitality and welcome, drawn to baptismal practice from meal practice or from the use of the baths? Was it simply an enacting of the biblical words about the Spirit? Or was it all of these and more? In any case, it is important to note, regardless of any favorite theory, that this anointing comes to interpret the process itself, to mark its movement as a new Christian is brought from "darkness" into the "priestly people of God," not to be another thing altogether, not to create a new structure.

The third century also begins to give us evidence of the baptism of "those who cannot answer for themselves." Here too, however, the basic structure of Baptism remains the same. Prior to the bath, teaching and formation in the faith are given to those who bring the children, those who answer for them. The children are welcomed into the life of the community. Indeed, the third-century evidence about such baptized children shows that they were also brought to participation in the Eucharist. And the pattern of "continual reminding" was, of course, exactly what was called for in the ongoing catechesis of baptized infants.

It is also important to note that the root structure—faith formation, the water, participation in the community—could be unfolded in very different ways, even in the ancient world. In Syrian and subsequently in Armenian Christianity, for example, we have evidence of slightly different accents—a different role for the community and great importance for post-baptismal instruction.[14] The primitive pattern here could be summarized as follows:

—a conversion takes place, miraculously, sometimes in encounter with a lone apostle;
—the apostle prays for the convert(s);
—a seven-day fast occurs;
—on the eighth day there occurs anointing of the head, immersion, Eucharist;
—followed by introduction to the community and instruction in ethics.

Of course, such a baptism looks rather more like the baptism of the Ethiopian eunuch (Acts 8) or like the order of Matthew 28—"baptizing them" followed by "teaching them to obey"—than it does the baptisms of the day of Pentecost (Acts 2). But even here, the core structure, although weighted differently, is the same: encounter/proclamation/conversion/formation in faith leads to water bath, leads to meal/communal life/further instruction.

But does this core structure itself have a biblical origin? Can we find it in the Scripture? Of course, the New Testament is not a book of rituals. Nor does it give clear evidence of ancient Christian practice. But scriptural evidence gathered indirectly suggests that the deep structure here is also the same. This root pattern may, in fact, be seen in widely divergent parts of the New Testament. Thus, the baptisms of the day of Pentecost follow from Peter's preaching and lead those baptized to "devote themselves to the apostles' teaching and fellowship, to the breaking of bread and the prayers" (Acts 2:42), as well as to distribution of goods "to all, as any had need" (Acts 2:45). Paul, too, depends upon Christian Baptism leading to the meal in order to make his analogy to the crossing of the sea leading to eating the manna and drinking from the Rock (1 Corinthians 10).

14. *Cf.* Kavanagh, *The Shape of Baptism,* 40–42. See also Gabrielle Winkler, *Das Armenische Intiationsrituale* (Rome: Oriental Institute, 1979). The anonymous writing, *Asenath,* in its picture of the conversion and reception into Israel of the Egyptian wife of Joseph, may also give us insight into the patterns of second- and third-century Syrian baptisms.

Furthermore, if 1 Peter may be considered to be a baptismal catechesis and a church order, then here the order of making Christians is also the same. Proclamation of the resurrection and teaching about ethical transformation (1:3-21) leads to "purification" (1:22) and "new birth" (1:23). This purification through the Word of God, which may be a reference to the water bath, leads in turn to communal love (1:23; 2:1); to eating and drinking (2:2-3); to participation in the community, the royal priesthood, the people of God (2:4-10); and to moral instruction (2:11ff). The order of 1 Peter can also be seen to be formed by the process of the baptismal *ordo*.

That such an order is significant, that it is not simply the self-evident way that baptisms might be done, can be gathered from the washings that may have surrounded the origin of Christian baptizing. Several first-century groups seem to have practiced a full-body washing in running or deep water for the sake of ritual purity and in order to be ready for—even to compel—the coming day of God. Amid such washings, John's baptism seems to have functioned as an astonishing proclamation of the nearness of the reign of God through the prophetic sign he enacted when he did the washing himself rather than encouraging others to bathe themselves. John the baptizer signed the nearness of the God who would come to wash a people of God's own.[15]

Similarly, Christians also washed with water toward the coming day of God. Like John's baptism, the Christian bath was not self-administered. But unlike all of these washings, Christian Baptism was not repeated. It was not finally about purity. Its eschatology was new and surprising. It led to participation in Jesus Christ, to death and resurrection, and hence to what was regarded as "unclean"—to the meal of his body and blood, to engagement with the poor and the outsiders—not to the pure life, cut off from others. It was not about personal purity but communal participation in Christ. It led to the day of God by incorporating the baptized into the community that tasted the down payment of that day in the presence of the Crucified Risen One and in the Spirit that was poured out from his cross and resurrection. It was itself an eschatological reality by being drawn into the very life and name of the triune God. All the many images and meanings for Baptism in the New Testament—washing for the wedding, illumination, forgiveness, entering the temple, surviving the flood, being clothed in Christ, and so on—can be taken as celebrations of this eschatological reality.

15. See further below, chapter 7.

Every Baptism into Christ thus participates in the meaning of the stories of the Baptism of Jesus himself (Mark 1:9-11 and parallels): the candidate goes into the water with Christ, the Spirit descends, and the voice of the Father calls this one a beloved child, a participant in the body of Christ.[16] Such is Baptism "in the name of the Father and of the Son and of the Holy Spirit" (Matt. 28:19). But the Christian arises from these waters not to fasting and temptation, the foreshadowing of Jesus' cross that follows the Jordan story, but to participation in the community of the meal and mission of Christ. And every baptism into Christ participates in the meaning of the stories of his death and resurrection, his final "baptism" (Mark 10:38; Luke 12:50). The candidate is buried in these waters together with Christ, in order to be raised with him. The Christian arises from these waters to participation in the world-changing, witnessing, communal assembly around the Risen One, together with those who are in him.

Christian Baptism is therefore not a purity rite that can be repeated and repeated. Christian Baptism is an event in the name of God, filled with the presence of God (Matthew 28:20). Unlike the other washings, then, Christian Baptism called for teaching and formation in that name. And it led to remembering the meaning of this new washing and teaching its ethical consequences. It led to the assembly. The new character of *this* washing could be expressed by *this ordo*: teaching, washing, and community participation, or said differently, conversion, the "speaking water," the meal. This washing was henceforth water that speaks with the voice of God, not simply our own cry for help. This washing was henceforth in water that had been itself washed by Jesus Christ and so by the triune God.

It needs to be noted, therefore, that "baptism in the name" did not always mean that a formula, like those in Matthew 28:19 or Acts 2:38, was actually recited over the use of the water. Such a conception gives far too small a meaning to the phrase. It seems unlikely that in the New Testament the phrase means "recitation of a formula" (*cf.* 1 Cor. 1:13-15). Furthermore, we have clear evidence of early baptisms where no such formula existed.[17] While the recited name has come to function at Christian Baptism in a foundational way, the use of such a text is actually a symbol that condenses the whole *ordo*. Baptism in the triune name involves learning to

16. On the baptism of Jesus as the primitive model for Christian baptismal theology and practice, see Kilian McDonnell, *The Baptism of Jesus in the Jordan* (Collegeville: Liturgical, 1996). Ignatius, too, taught that the baptism of Christ and his passion together made of "the water" a new thing: Jesus Christ "was born and was baptized, that by his passion he might purify the water." *To the Ephesians* 18:2b. Greek text in Lake, *The Apostolic Fathers*, 1:192.

trust in God by being washed into the crucified Christ and being raised to live in the community of the Spirit. The *ordo* is itself trinitarian. The *ordo* stands for the divine name.

Baptism in the triune name is none other than that one washing that is no longer a purity rite, a prayer for God, a cry for help, but is rather a participation in the very life of the present God of the Gospel, the God seen at Jordan, known in the resurrection, poured out as the Spirit. The "name" is both the content of the teaching which must be juxtaposed to the washing and the powerful presence of the gracious God who makes of our water the very threshold of the eschatological day.

Baptism in the name of Jesus Christ, Baptism in the triune name, and Baptism in the Spirit, therefore, are exactly the same thing. They are an ancient human water rite transformed to be the making of Christians-in-community. They make Christians in such a way that the act itself becomes a lifelong pattern of living.

In the New Testament, therefore, Baptism imposes no distinction from the rest of needy humanity. It is rather open identification with all in Jesus Christ and in the mission which is through him. It is the washing that makes Christians to be "unclean" with Christ, who welcomes the impure (Mark 2:15) and the unwashed (Mark 7:2) and the unclean (John 4, 5, 9) and the dead (John 11). It is the bath that constitutes his witnesses in the world.

Baptismal Practice and Ecumenism

The biblical pattern, found in Paul (1 Cor. 10) and in Peter (1 Peter 1-2), ought still be used by Christians in their baptismal practice and catechesis. The ancient assembly of the people of God, the community of royal priests for the world, was formed by being led across the sea to hear the Word of God at Sinai and, in the elders, to eat and drink with God (Exodus 19–24). This ancient people was re-formed by being led across the blossoming desert to hear the Word of God, eat together, and send food to the poor (Nehemiah 8). So now, in Christ, the new assembly, the royal priestly people, is formed by being led through the water to word and table and so to a life of witness in the world, to an identification in love with all peoples.

In recent decades, many different Christian communities have been rediscovering something of the vigor of this ancient pattern for baptizing. Churches have been acknowledging that Baptism is a process, a continuum,

17. See, for example, *Apostolic Tradition* 21.

as well as a once-for-all event; that catechesis and proclamation belong to Baptism; that Baptism involves the strong, identity-changing use of water; that Baptism takes place in the assembly and leads to participation in community and lifelong witness. Such recognition has also led Christians of one church to acknowledge the presence of the same recovered pattern in other churches as well. We are invited to find in each other the living, trinitarian pattern of the baptized, just as the Roman church was invited to recognize that same pattern in Antioch through the person of Ignatius.

But the *ordo* can also propose to us concrete possibilities for further renewal and unity in our baptismal practice. The *ordo* can lead us to ask these questions in our own local assemblies: Can we, in each of our communities, actually hold Baptism and formation in the faith together? Can we welcome again the ministry of catechists and baptismal sponsors in our midst? Can we see the creeds as baptismal symbols; can we see central doctrines as having baptismal locus? Can we teach a living trinitarian faith, based on the churches' experience of the triune God in the "speaking water"? Can we restore a strong role to the water, recovering immersion fonts where possible? Can we see the events of the actual baptismal celebration as recapitulating the whole process of Baptism, indeed the whole Christian life? Can we let any strong secondary symbols used in the rite—prayer over the water, oil, light, new clothing, or other symbols adapted from diverse cultural surroundings—assist in unfolding the meaning of the *ordo* itself? Can we let the whole assembly—or as many of its members as possible—gather around our fonts (or at rivers, lakes, or oceans!), welcoming the newly baptized into the community and to participation in the Eucharist? Can we bring all the baptized, including the children, directly to the meal of God? Can we enable a "lifelong catechumenate," a continual re-learning of the faith, a continual re-hearing of the voice in the water? Can we actually connect Baptism and ethics, Baptism and mission? Can we re-member the *ordo*, holding together those things that much baptismal practice has torn apart: teaching and bath, water and meal, individual salvation and communal meaning, eschatology and this present world, adults and children, faith and discipleship, one-time event and all of life? Can we unfold this whole *ordo* in each local place in ways appropriate to the dignity and gifts of that place? And can we do these things by teaching, love, and invitation, by opening up what is already present in the churches, not by constraint and compulsion?

To press the questions even more deeply, the shared *ordo* may give us the basis for a concrete practice of unity. We may ask: If Baptism constitutes the assembly that is the church, ought not the Christians in a given locality enact that truth? Can we not do much of the process of Baptism together? Could a renewed catechumenate be undertaken by many or even all of the Christian assemblies in a given local place? Could we be present at each other's baptisms? Could we do baptisms on the great feasts and do them side by side? Could we even consider constructing a single font for the local churches in our towns and cities?[18]

The actual liturgy for the Baptism itself, in all of our churches, may then most wisely include these things: the presence of the local church, including the ministerial leadership of that community and witnesses from the larger *koinonia*; a recapitulation of the process that has led to the water, including the confession of trinitarian faith by the community, by the candidates, and by the sponsors of those who cannot answer for themselves; prayer; as full a washing with water as possible; a testimony to the new identity of the baptized in communion with both the local church and the whole catholic church; and a direct flow into the Eucharist and mission.

The *ordo* may also assist us to re-address, with a new wholeness, old points of Christian division. For example, when Baptism is a process, the disagreements between "baptists" and "catholics" may be turned into mutual admonition and mutual enrichment, as the Ditchingham Report has indicated. Furthermore, when the central event of the *ordo* is a *bath,* we all may yield the practical point of immersion to the baptists. We may encourage and rejoice in the fullest use of water that is possible, while in the spirit of the ancient *Didache,* not enforcing the matter legalistically.[19] After all, this Christian Baptism must be a strong sign of the new identity of a participant in the assembly, not a legalistically applied purity rite.

Further, when adult Christians are always, like the bishop of Antioch himself, still becoming real Christians, when the Word alive in the water is always still speaking interiorly in Christian lives, when Baptism leads to community and to ethics, then the mutual witness of sacramental and non-sacramental Christians may also be mutually heard. Quakers, Salvationists, and some non-baptizing Christian groups of Asia and Africa need the churches who actually, physically perform the *ordo.* They need *ordo*-like catechesis and community formation, so that their own spirituality does not

18. So suggests the Ditchingham Report, 12.

19. "But if you do not have living water [i.e., running water, river water], baptize in other water, and if you are not able to use cold water then use warm [the reference is probably to public baths]. But if you do not have either, pour out water on the head three times." *Didache* 7:2-3; Greek text in Lake, *The Apostolic Fathers,* 1:320.

become gnostic. But the sacramental churches also need the witness of those for whom the only water is that of the interior speech of the Spirit and for whom the resultant life of self-giving service is "participation in the Body of Christ." Astonishingly, Ignatius and his witness might be a meeting place for both.

Further, when the entire process of the *ordo* is trinitarian, when the tri-une name is the "shape" of Baptism, when faith in God by identification with Jesus Christ leads to the community of the Spirit, then disputes about what has been legalistically termed the "formula" of Baptism may not be so church dividing. Indeed, if the process of baptizing itself is trinitarian, we may be able to recognize both of the biblical "formulae" as well as baptisms without a formula. We may be able to enter more profoundly into the discussion of appropriate and orthodox language to express the mystery of the Trinity in our day, including criticism of the ways in which "Father" and "Son" have been used to express both the subjugation of women and a faith which is neither orthodox nor even Christian.

Further, when participation in the entire *ordo* is participation in the eschatological gift of the Spirit, when passing through the water brings us into the community of the Spirit, we may be able to rejoice in signs of the Spirit added to the rite: laying on of hands, anointing with oil, sealing. But we may also be able to resist either separating these signs from the *ordo,* as if they were themselves a new and distinct thing, or castigating those Christians who do not use these signs, who rest instead in the Spirit's action through water and the word.

Many other such questions may also be illuminated as we take the re-membering of the *ordo* into consideration. Indeed, if *church* is primarily litur-gical assembly, then an inquiry about shared baptismal practice and its mean-ing is not a luxury. Rather, such inquiry is a basic undertaking needed for the renewal and the maintenance of the unity of the churches. Furthermore, common work on these questions and common restoration of the *ordo* may help us to let the astonishing, gracious gift of Baptism into Jesus Christ stand forth as a word to our time, amid our need, answering our cries.

The Ordo of Eucharist

But the *ordo* of Baptism leads to the meal. The Sunday assembly for the celebration of the Eucharist continually reminds the baptized of "these things." Baptism joins people to that assembly. Further questions for local ecumenism between assemblies of Christians follow. How can the Eucharist indeed be the sacrament of unity? How can its celebration unite us rather than be the occasion for an intense and painful exhibition of our disunity? How can its celebration always be truly local, the catholic church dwelling in this particular place, among these particular people where the celebration is held? And yet, how can the profound structures of its unity also enable a real and welcomed diversity between us?

The urgency of these current ecumenical questions is sometimes heightened when, with this perspective in mind, we read ancient texts about the unity of Christian eucharistic practice amid an accepted diversity. If Ignatius and Justin enabled us to think about the baptismal *ordo,* the text from Irenaeus, quoted above,[20] may remind us of a time when the meal could still be shared, even amid diversity between the churches. According to Irenaeus, Polycarp and Anicetus were in communion across disagreement and difference in tradition, even *apostolic* tradition. They shared a *pattern:* thanksgiving at table and the rite of communion. Or at least they shared a pattern sufficiently deep and basic to enable Anicetus to yield the thanksgiving at table to Polycarp and to enable the communion to be sent. Can we recover the possibility of doing something of the same thing?[21]

On recent ecumenical occasions throughout the world, the so-called Lima Liturgy[22] has provided a possible answer to these questions of communion amid diversity. What this liturgy has given us is not so much a pattern as an actual text. While it has had no official standing in any church, it has a growing history of ecumenical use. The text has become a place in which diverse churches can meet each other.

In fact, the text had a quite specific origin which enabled the history of its use. Fine liturgy is always local, and the Lima Liturgy was no exception. It was drafted by Frère Max Thurian for the 1982 meeting of the Faith and Order Commission in Lima, Peru, the meeting at which the document *Baptism, Eucharist and Ministry* was adopted. Thurian drafted the liturgy, as the texts of its prayers so frequently disclose, with the consensus of that document and the spirit of its drafting body quite clearly in mind. It was further edited by a small ecumenical committee at the meeting for which it was intended. So the Lima meeting itself was the "local" origin of

20. Eusebius, *Ecclesiastical History* 5:24:15-17. See above, p. 118.
21. On the development of the *ordo* of the Eucharist in the primitive church, see Lathrop, *Holy Things,* 43–52.
22. See Max Thurian, ed., *Ecumenical Perspectives on Baptism, Eucharist and Ministry,* Faith and Order Paper No. 116 (Geneva: World Council of Churches, 1983), Appendix II, 225–46.

this liturgy.[23] From that origin—and then from the use of the same liturgical text at the Vancouver Assembly of the World Council of Churches in 1983—other communities drew courage and fostered interest in their own use and adaptation of the Lima Liturgy. The excellence of the liturgical text, the history of its origin, and its resonance with widespread ecumenical experience all contributed to its wider use.

But the Lima Liturgy had a local origin in another sense as well. Frère Max brought to the drafting task not only his participation in the Faith and Order work and his careful attention to the content of its dialogues. He also brought his years of experience in the formation of the liturgy of Taizé. In many ways, the Lima Liturgy is the fruit of the local, ecumenical life of the Community of Taizé. Its nearest textual neighbor is to be found in the eucharistic Liturgy of Taizé,[24] and its widespread success is not unrelated to the respect and trust so generally accorded to the work of that community.

The text of the Lima Liturgy thus represents a local liturgy—from Taizé and from several specific ecumenical gatherings and their common life—that spread more widely in its use, a text that allowed many churches to meet in mutual recognition and *koinonia*. Because of its origin in the work of these scholars and these monks, this text has become a kind of depository not only of ecumenical insights, but also of many of the fruits of nineteenth- and twentieth-century liturgical studies and the liturgical movement. Healthy liturgical texts often begin as the texts of one local church which are then borrowed by other assemblies.

One can, of course, criticize the actual text of the Lima Liturgy.[25] But the liturgy cannot be criticized for not solving the deeper questions of

23. It would be fruitful to consider the sense in which this meeting, like many ecumenical meetings, had the character of assembly, of "church." To the extent that such gatherings have a center in word and sacrament, are gathered in the triune presence of God, and bear witness in the world, they are, in some sense, a temporary local church.

24. See *Eucharistie à Taizé* (Taizé, France: 1972).

25. The very liturgical studies that are represented so clearly in its conception might, for example, raise these questions: Can the diverse lay and ordained leadership roles, so important to Christian assembly, be more clearly indicated than they have been in the Lima text? Might the penitential rite be better placed before the entrance hymn or psalm rather than in the main body of the liturgy itself? Can the *kyrie* be used as a clear—and perhaps more extensive—litany of entrance? Can the *collect* function more strongly as the prayer of entrance? Can the text itself give some ecumenical attention to lectionary suggestions? Might hymnody play a more important role? Might there be alternate forms for intercessions allowing for free and local prayers? Is the placement of the *peace* in the communion rite, rather than as a seal to the intercessions, really a good choice for ecumenical assemblies? Could the offertory prayers be eliminated, given the presence of a strong *anaphora* and, there-

mutual eucharistic sharing. It gives the churches a possible place to meet. It does not resolve the ecclesial issues of mutual recognition or mutual sharing of ministries. Its use does raise the fascinating question about what a local *church* actually is. Is not a gathering of people who celebrate the Eucharist together—perhaps even people from differing confessions and disciplines—to be regarded as in some sense a "church"? What is the local church that holds the Supper in an ecumenical assembly making use of the Lima Liturgy? And who are the ministers, liturgical leaders, and servers who belong to the liturgical action, who rightly serve this local church? While the use of the Lima Liturgy does heighten these questions, the text itself cannot be expected to give answers.

But there is a deeper criticism to be made of the Lima Liturgy. Or rather, there is a trajectory of development which might rightly carry forward the work that Lima began. The *ordo* of the liturgy—the shape of the Eucharist and of its prayer at table as well as the ways that shape may be enacted in diverse cultural situations—was implicit in the text of Lima. Now explicit attention to *ordo*, rather than text, may challenge ecumenical eucharistic celebrations to go beyond Lima.

Liturgy is an event with a shape. It is more than a text. It is the flow of a communal action that expresses its meanings in gestures and concrete signs as well as in words. Indeed, the meanings of the liturgy come to expression in the continual juxtapositions of words with sign-actions.[26] So the liturgy of the Eucharist is made up of word-service set next to table-service in order to express the truth of Jesus Christ, in order to gather all people into the grace and life of the triune God. Further, the Eucharist's word-service sets Scripture readings next to preaching, and so leads the community to intercessory prayers. Its table-service sets *eucharistia*, thanksgiving at the table, next to eating and drinking the gift of Christ, and so leads the community to mission. Around these central matters occur movements of gathering, collecting for the poor, and sending—significant in

---

fore, the absence of the necessity for any further prayer over the gifts? Can the strongly thematic character of the prayer texts be avoided or reduced, yielding more attention to the always central yet perpetually changing theme of the Scriptures of the day in relationship to our salvation in Christ? In general, could there be fewer words? See further the friendly and helpful critique of Robert Gribben, "The 'Lima Liturgy'—an Ecumenical Liturgical Text," *One in Christ* 20, no. 3 (1984): 249–56. See also "The Ditchingham Consultation Report," Appendix 1, in Best and Heller, eds., *So We Believe, So We Pray: Towards Koinonia in Worship*, 22–24.

26. See Lawrence A. Hoffman, *Beyond the Text: A Holistic Approach to Liturgy* (Bloomington: Indiana University Press, 1987).

their juxtaposition to word and table. The whole action is done by a participating community together with its ministers, thus bringing to expression
the Body of Christ. This event is usually held on a Sunday or festival, juxtaposed to our "ordinary" days, so that Christian eschatology—the presence
now of God's promised future for the cosmos—may be proclaimed. Such is
the shape of the liturgy.

This liturgy is always celebrated locally. It goes together with a local
church. It takes place in local speech, in the midst of the gifts and the problems of local cultures and traditions, reflecting its light on local needs. Inculturation of the liturgy is one of the oldest traditions of the church, found
already in the making of the Christian sacraments out of the meals and
washing rites of late-antique Judaism and continued in the adoption of new
languages and in the extensive influence on Christian worship exerted by
Hellenistic mysteries, imperial buildings, and court rituals.[27] And this inculturation must continue, in each new place, treasuring and transforming cultures new and old, dominant and threatened.

Yet the universal character of the gospel of Christ and the very unity
of the triune God also call every celebration to reflect the shared deep-pat-
tern of the liturgy and the shared transcultural gifts of water, word, and
meal. It is astounding that these latter material things—always local gifts in
their actual origin, yet always universal in human resonance and recognition—have been made into the bearers of the central Christian meanings
and, by the promise of God and the power of the Spirit, bearers of the very
presence of Jesus Christ. Liturgy also is catholic, "universal."

In the midst of this liturgy, thanksgiving at the table has an *ordo* as well.
It is made up of praise and beseeching, like all classic Christian prayer.[28] In
eucharistia, the praise especially remembers the mighty deeds of God in the
past, making memorial of the events of our salvation in the death and resurrection of Christ. The beseeching especially asks for the presence and
power of the Spirit, for the one who brings the promise of God's future
into our own time and meeting, transfiguring this very assembly and meal.
This great pattern of prayer at the table has been worked out in a variety of
sub-patterns, some of them especially marked by different choices in the
placement of the "institution narrative," the *verba institutionis,* of the Supper
of Christ. Outlined in large strokes, we can say that the Eastern, Antiochian

---

27. See Anscar Chupungco, "Liturgical Inculturation and the Search for Unity," in *So
We Believe, So We Pray,* 55–64. See also S. Anita Stauffer, ed., *Worship and Culture in Dialogue*
(Geneva: Lutheran World Federation, 1994).

28. See Lathrop, *Holy Things,* 55–59.

sub-pattern places these *verba* in the "praise" part of the prayer, as a public proclamation and confession of the amazing gift of Christ, while letting the "beseeching" part of the prayer focus on the *epiclesis,* the invocation of the presence of the Spirit. The Alexandrian and Roman sub-pattern, on the other hand, places the words of Christ at the Supper in the beseeching part of the prayer, using these very words to beg God to fulfill the promise and gift of Christ now and surrounding these words with the language style of ancient Roman petitions to the emperor. In the Roman use, only a vestige of the *epiclesis* remains. Both patterns are legitimate developments.

But the large number of modern eucharistic prayers throughout the world and in many churches have primarily been modeled on the Antiochian pattern. This may be so because of the perceived sense that the church needs to acknowledge its dependence on God by the use of a full *epiclesis.* Or it may be that the imperial language and the use of the *verba* in beseeching are simply not understandable today. Rather, the medieval misunderstanding perdures: placing the words of Christ in the Roman position, following a vestigial *epiclesis,* seems to indicate that the presider's recitation "confects" the sacrament and creates the presence of Christ.[29]

We do not know the pattern of Polycarp's thanksgiving at table,[30] but we can see that these reflections on *ordo* do connect us with the ancient report of Irenaeus. It is not a text that unites Polycarp and Anicetus and their churches amid their disagreement and diversity; it is a shared pattern.

The Eucharistic Ordo and Ecumenism

One can see that these reflections on *ordo* are, to some extent, already represented in the Lima text itself. The Lima Liturgy is marked by the very shape of the liturgy discussed here, although its character as *text* may obscure

---

29. "Unfortunately, this pattern has several disadvantages. It neglects the stronger of the ancient traditions. It also interrupts the flow of the narration of the wonderful things God has accomplished in creation and in history. It fails to emphasize the basic helplessness or praying attitude of the assembly and thus fails to help avoid a 'magical' notion of the institution narrative. Finally, this pattern could rob the *epiclesis* of one of its greatest strengths—the ability to underline the unity between 'consecration' and communion. The fact that this pattern continues to be imposed on Roman Catholic eucharistic prayers calls for serious reconsideration." John H. McKenna, C.M., "The Epiclesis Revisited," in Frank C. Senn, ed., *New Eucharistic Prayers: An Ecumenical Study of their Development and Structure* (New York: Paulist, 1987), 183.

30. However, Polycarp's reported prayer at death (*Martyrdom of Polycarp,* 14) does show a pattern of thanksgiving and beseeching over a cup and may well disclose the ancient shape of *eucharistia.*

that fact. Furthermore, the Lima Liturgy had a local origin, and, encouraged by the drafter of the text himself, continual adaptations of the text—adaptations based in a sense of the liveliness of its root shape—have been made in new local situations.[31]

Still, the *ordo* may press our experience of the Lima Liturgy as the only "ecumenical liturgy" toward a further development. In truth, the text of Lima is experienced as just that, as *text,* not as pattern or shape. That fact limits its usefulness in new local situations, its accessibility to inculturation. And the *anaphora,* the eucharistic prayer of Lima does not represent the mainstream of rich, current, ecumenical development in eucharistic praying, including the development in Roman Catholic circles, and it does run the risk of the medieval misunderstandings of "consecration."

A way forward may be found in these two proposals: Take the *shape of the liturgy* as a profound ecumenical meeting place, as a basis for renewal, recognition, inculturation, and gestures of communion. And let there be an ecumenical exchange of the current *eucharistic prayers* of widespread usage and excellence, an exchange that allows the euchology of many churches to be echoed throughout the world, in many local situations.

We might note that the *Baptism, Eucharist and Ministry* document itself proposes a list of elements of eucharistic liturgy, arranged generally in the manner of the shape of the liturgy.[32] And we might especially look at the many churches and groups of churches that have based the materials they have given to local congregations on a liturgical outline.[33] The *ordo* in the American Episcopal *Book of Common Prayer* may stand as an example, not exactly the same as others, but sharing the great common *ordo:*

The People and Priest
Gather in the Lord's Name
Proclaim and Respond to the Word of God
Pray for the World and the Church
Exchange the Peace

31. See Thurian, *Ecumenical Perspectives on Baptism, Eucharist and Ministry,* 233. Even the *eucharistia* of the text, while modeled most strongly on the Roman pattern, has been influenced by the Antiochian use: the epiclesis is indeed before the *verba,* but it is by no means fragmentary or vestigial; it is a full, strong prayer for the power of the Spirit.

32. *Baptism, Eucharist and Ministry,* Faith and Order Paper 111 (Geneva: World Council of Churches, 1982), Eucharist 27.

33. See, among many other examples: *Erneuerte Agende* (Hannover: 1990), 32 and 42; *With One Voice: A Lutheran Resource for Worship* (Minneapolis: Augsburg Fortress, 1995), 8–9; and *Book of Common Worship* (Louisville: Westminster/John Knox, 1993), 33 and 46.

Prepare the Table
Make Eucharist
Break the Bread
Share the Gifts of God[34]

A mutually accepted *ordo* for the Eucharist can provide for both local inculturation and widespread ecumenical recognition. An *ordo* can provide us with a place to meet.

Recent proposals have also suggested that eucharistic praying, in whatever local form, follows a pattern.[35] Many eucharistic prayers—from ancient sources, such as Hippolytus or Basil,[36] or from modern composition[37]—have been used by more than one church, across persistent formal divisions. Those who reflect on the future of ecumenical eucharistic celebration, those who actually plan such events, and those interested in local eucharistic unity should pay attention to these patterns and these prayers.

It is time for local churches—as well as communions of churches—to note the similarity of their liturgical patterns for Sunday gathering and to engage with each other in discussions of the meaning of assembly around that *ordo*. Such recognition will inevitably bring along a double mutual encouragement: We need to urge each other to continual renewal so that the central characteristics of the *ordo* may stand forth in clarity in each assembly. And we need to continue to ask each other whether those characteristics are being unfolded according to "the dignity and gifts of each local place."

There will probably continue to be several different eucharistic assemblies in each local place. Eucharistic assembly can be large or small—as the history of both house churches and basilicas demonstrates—but it will never quite be the massive, universal assembly of eschatological imagery. It will always be partial, a symbol of the God who is gathering all people into unity. It will always remain firmly in this world, using our dynamics of

---

34. *Book of Common Prayer* (New York: Seabury, 1979), 400–401.

35. *Book of Common Prayer*, 404–5; *Book of Common Worship*, 156.

36. *Eucharistic Prayer of Hippolytus* (Washington: ICEL, 1983); cf. *Lutheran Book of Worship, Ministers Edition* (Minneapolis: Augsburg, 1978), 226; *Book of Common Worship*, 150–51. *Eucharistic Prayer of Saint Basil* (Washington: ICEL, 1985); cf. *Book of Common Prayer*, 373–75; *Book of Common Worship*, 146–49.

37. *Eucharistic Prayer A* (Washington: ICEL, 1986); cf. *Book of Common Worship*, 142–45. See also "Eucharistic Prayer V," *With One Voice, Leaders Edition* (Minneapolis: Augsburg Fortress, 1995), 63–64. This prayer is also forthcoming in the liturgical book of the United Church of Canada. Many other examples, internationally, could be educed.

assembly. Neighborhoods, like-mindedness, denominational connections, economic class, ethnic identity—all of these will help to determine who gathers in a particular assembly. These characteristics are not wrong, unless they become the primary, unbreakable reason for an assembly in which there is no openness to the other. As part of the dynamics of human belonging, such characteristics can be ways that the gifts of culture, tradition, and locality come into the assembly.

Still, the shared *ordo* will be a major means by which these dynamics of human belonging are broken open to become a symbol of the gathering God. Word and table give an assembly a center which points beyond our dynamics of belonging. The scriptural Word, read and preached, does not belong to any denomination or group. It comes from outside of our group, calling us all into the life of God's grace. The prayers articulate the assembly's turn toward a wider world. And the welcome to the table must never be determined by any of our dynamics of belonging. This is not the communion of our denomination or ethnic group or class. We are all needy guests; none of us is host here.

Furthermore, the eucharistic *ordo* can provide occasions for signs of communion to be shared among local assemblies. The Scriptures can be read according to a shared lectionary. The preachers and other liturgical ministers can prepare for their responsibilities in local ecumenical text study groups. The prayers of the assembly can include petitions for the other assemblies. The thanksgiving at table may draw from the growing ecumenical corpus of eucharistic prayers or patterns of praying. The collection of money or food may be partly intended for local ecumenical work among the sick and the hungry. We may all be occasional guests in the other assemblies, breaking open the usual patterns of belonging. And two or more local assemblies may sometimes celebrate a common liturgy, the host presider yielding place at the table to a guest presider, in the ancient manner of Anicetus yielding to Polycarp. These could be contemporary ways that we, too, send the *fermentum* between diverse assemblies in one locality, signaling to each other that we know that, by God's mercy, we are all eating from one bread and drinking from one cup. These could be ways that we help each other to understand that the church is a witnessing assembly in this place, in which diversity enriches our common *ordo*—not a collection of religious shops where different people may buy diverse religious goods, each according to their personal taste.[38]

38. Such possible local efforts at mutual recognition and mutual encouragement among assemblies have been assisted by parallel efforts in publishing houses that have themselves

Such local practices, arising from the baptismal and eucharistic *ordines*, will not all be possible for every assembly of Christians. And even when they are possible, these practices will not solve all the problems of our continuing disunity. But surely some of these practices would be possible for any Christian group—presence at each other's baptisms, say, and the prayer for the other local assemblies at each Eucharist. Even this would assist in making our disunity more poignant. Even this might help us to see something of those great patterns which Polycarp and Anicetus shared but which we share as well. It might invite us again to overcome our continuing divisions, being transformed by God's mercy into a richly diverse communion of churches, all of whom find *koinonia* in our Lord Jesus Christ through his gift of holy bath, holy word, and holy table.

The goal of such *koinonia,* of course, is not simply the unity of the churches. The churches are each the holy assembly, in communion with all the assemblies in every place, in order to bear witness to God's mercy for all the world. The assemblies are intended to provide symbols whereby we may all understand and walk together in God's good world, before God's face, in thanksgiving and love. The unity of the churches in their liturgical life, in the shared pattern of their central symbols, is intended as sign and instrument of human unity in the earth.

Ignatius, ever the source of rich images for our Christian life, wanted to regard his journey in chains toward martyrdom, which he also compared to the baptismal process, as a kind of "song."[39] He was singing the assemblies, as if he was a bard or Homeric poet, praising the astonishing reality of the churches gathered in every place. The song was also a prayer for unity. Ignatius prayed that there might be, in each place, in each of these assemblies, the unity between their actual human experience—the "flesh"—and the Spirit that came from the Risen One, the unity between faith and love, and the presence of the unity between Jesus and the Father. On the grounds of this triune life, into which the assembly's liturgy draws our experience,

been influenced by the ecumenical ferment and have published ecumenically accessible texts for use in the great shared *ordo,* together with patterns for those major liturgical texts which might be developed locally. In this regard, the American Presbyterian *Book of Common Worship* is exemplary. Even without this commitment from publishers, however, Christians will continue to borrow materials and adapt materials from each other's books. As Tertullian says, "Whatever belongs to those who are of us belongs to us."

39. "I sing the assemblies, in which I pray there may be the unity of the flesh and spirit of Jesus Christ, who is always our life, the unity of faith and love, to which nothing is to be preferred, and, above all, the unity of Jesus and the Father, in whom, enduring and escaping all the threats of the ruler of this age, we shall reach God." Ignatius, *To the Magnesians* 1:2. Greek text in Lake, *The Apostolic Fathers,* 1:196.

the churches are given unity with each other and made witnesses of God's gift of life for the world. We can begin to taste the unity of faith and love in the communal patterns of Baptism and the Eucharist. We can continue to live the unity of faith and love in witness and mission.

But if the unity of the assemblies exists so that the world itself, in spite of all threats, may come before God and so live, then we must turn to ask how the liturgy of these assemblies is situated within the cultures of that world.

PART THREE

Holy People
Liturgical Assemblies amid Earth's Peoples

THIS IS THE PRINICIPAL ITEM, AND THE HOLIEST OF
HOLY POSSESSIONS, BY REASON OF WHICH THE
CHRISTIAN PEOPLE ARE CALLED HOLY; FOR GOD'S
WORD IS HOLY AND SANCTIFIES EVERYTHING IT
TOUCHES; IT IS INDEED THE VERY HOLINESS OF GOD.
— *Martin Luther*
"On the Councils and the Church"

7

Assembly, Baptism, and Culture

In his "Treatise on the New Testament, that is the Holy Mass" of 1520, Martin Luther proposed that the ability to distinguish what is central and constitutive in the Eucharist from what is additional and secondary in its celebration is "the greatest and most useful art."[1] Since in the same treatise he asserted that Christ appointed "but one law or order for his entire people, and that was the holy mass,"[2] this sorting of the central and the secondary was, for Luther, immensely important to the life of the church. The center of the Supper—and thus, of the very existence of church—is the gift of Christ in the proclaimed word and in the thanks-

---

1. *Luther's Works* (Philadelphia: Fortress, 1966), 35:81. This American translation is henceforth cited as *LW.* The German is:"*die groeste nutzlichste kunst.*" D. *Martin Luthers Werke* (Weimar: 1914), 6:355. This German edition is henceforth cited as *WA.*

2. *WA,* 6:354; *LW,* 35:80–81. The full quotation is:"Christ, in order to prepare for himself an acceptable and beloved people, which should be bound together in unity through love, abolished the whole law of Moses. And that he might not give further occasion for divisions and sects, he appointed in return but one law or order for his entire people, and that was the holy mass [*"nit mehr den eyne weyss odder gesetz eyngesetzt seynem gantzen volck das ist die heylige Mess"*]. (For although baptism is also an external ordinance, yet it takes place but once, and is not the practice of an entire life, like the mass.) Henceforth, therefore, there is to be no other external order for the service of God except the mass. And where the mass is used, there is true worship [*"recht gottis dienst"*]; even though there be no other form, with singing, organ playing, bell ringing, vestments, ornaments, and gestures. For everything of this sort is an addition invented by men. When Christ himself first instituted this sacrament and held the first mass, there was no tonsure, no chasuble, no singing, no pageantry, but only thanksgiving to God and the use of the sacrament. According to the same simplicity the apostles and all Christians for a long time held mass, until there arose the various forms and additions, by which the Romans held mass one way, the Greeks another. And now it has finally come to this: the chief thing in the mass has been forgotten, and nothing is remembered except the additions of men!"

giving-bread and blessing-cup of the church's gathering. Lovely and important as they may be, none of the additional, peripheral materials—forms of music, vesture, or ceremony, for example—can be made into laws, into the only right ways to get to God. When such ceremonial materials are presented as if required by God, as if necessary for grace, the church itself is threatened, even destroyed.

It is not that one does without music or ceremony! Luther clearly says, "I neither wish nor am able to displace or discard such additions." Indeed, Luther himself praised music, created and reworked hymns and the music of the liturgy, and seems to have rather loved some aspects of late medieval liturgical ceremony, even when he could joke about those same aspects.[3] No, what he longed for was to distinguish these formal and ceremonial matters from the center, which is thanksgiving and Christ's gift, to require them to serve that center, and to forbid them—or their absence![4]—from becoming a new law or a ground for boasting.

This major critical principle of liturgical hermeneutics, a corollary of the doctrine of justification and the application of that doctrine to worship, still stands as a resource for current thought about worship and culture. It proposes to the churches that in worship the center must be clear: the assembly must gather around the gift of Christ in word and sacrament. At the same time, this principle urges us not to make a law out of western or northern cultural forms which have long been associated with Christianity and which, more recently, have come to be deeply associated with economic power. Rather, it welcomes the gifts of the many cultures of the world: their languages, their music, their patterns of festivity and solemnity, their manners of gathering, their structures of meaning. None of these is to be despised. All are to be honored.

But liturgical hermeneutics also urges that these cultural patterns must not become their own new law or usurp the place of the center; they must rather come into the "city" to gather around the "Lamb" (Rev. 21:22-27); they must be broken to the purpose of the gospel of Christ. Cultural patterns of all sorts—southern and northern, western and eastern, rural and urban, specifically local and increasingly worldwide—are welcome in the assembly. But they are not welcome to take the place of the Lamb. They are

3. *Cf. WA,* 18:113; *LW,* 40:131: "[I]n the parish church we still have the chasuble, alb, altar and elevate as long as it pleases us."

4. See *LW,* 40:131: "We do as the papists, but we do not tolerate their teaching, commandment, and constraint. We refrain from doing like the Karlstadtians, but we do not tolerate the prohibition."

not welcome to obscure the gift of Christ in the Scripture read and preached, in the water used in his name, and in the thanksgiving meal.

This much is implied by the "greatest and most useful art" of Luther's liturgical hermeneutics. This agenda for the relationship of liturgy and culture in our present time can be seen as a faithful reading of the ecumenically important seventh article of the Augsburg Confession:

> It is also taught among us that one holy Christian church will be and remain forever. This is the assembly of all believers among whom the gospel is preached in its purity and the holy sacraments are administered according to the gospel. For it is sufficient for the true unity of the Christian church that the gospel be preached in conformity with a pure understanding of it and that the sacraments be administered in accordance with the divine Word. It is not necessary for the true unity of the Christian church that ceremonies of human institution should be observed uniformly in all places.[5]

But how shall we actually apply this principle of liturgical hermeneutics? What gifts of the cultures should come into the assembly of Christians? And how are these gifts to be used or "broken" to the purpose of the gospel?

Unlike Luther or Melanchthon, the writer of the Augsburg Confession, we cannot uncritically adopt the renaissance conception of historical development as a pure and simple early core subsequently clouded by "additions." We will need to see that, from their very beginnings, the Christian practices of Baptism and the Eucharist were marked by the use of complex local cultural phenomena. But at their best, in the proposals of the Gospels and Paul, these were cultural phenomena criticized and turned to a new purpose. It is not so much Luther's or Melanchthon's historical assertions we adopt, as their method of critique and distinction, their theology of Christ's gift in the midst of our diverse ceremonies, our diverse cultures.

Liturgy and Culture

"Culture" is "the symbolic-expressive dimension of social life." So at least one group of scholars has recently proposed.[6] This definition is useful

5. Emended from Tappert, trans. and ed., *The Book of Concord: The Confessions of the Evangelical Lutheran Church* (Philadelphia: Fortress, 1959), 32.
6. Robert Wuthnow, James Davison Hunter, Albert Bergesen, Edith Kurzweil, *Cultural Analysis: The Work of Peter L. Berger, Mary Douglas, Michel Foucault, and Jürgen Habermas* (Boston:

as we reflect on liturgy, an obvious case of socially significant symbolic expression. But this definition is also useful because it helps to make clear how almost all of us in the contemporary world live in a variety of cultures. That is, we participate in many different systems of symbolic expression which are socially significant.

From one point of view, then, Christian liturgy itself might be regarded as an instance of "culture." Its ritual forms have been a "language" for the communication among Christians of meanings about themselves and about the surrounding world as seen before God. Its words, gestures, and ceremonies—its hymns, preaching, sacraments, prayers, communally recited creeds—have been a means to pass on to newcomers and children and to reinforce among lifelong believers the Christian community's wisdom about and understanding of God and the world. Its symbolic acts have been the basic units of a social communication. Still, Christianity is not an economy, it has not prescribed the way one distributes land or tills the earth or hunts or cooks food, it is not a pattern of child-bearing, not the organization of roles necessary for community survival, not the way one shapes a language to speak of these things and symbols to endow them with meaning. It is better to say that the Christian symbolic language functions in analogy to culture, *like* a culture, in perpetual dialogue with the cultures among which its assemblies stand.

For we all do live amidst many other complexes of symbolic communication which have their own ways of indicating world-meaning and shaping our identity. We speak diverse languages, tell different stories, know different seasons, eat different foods with diverse conceptions of hospitality, arrange community leadership differently. Some of us live with several different languages, calendars, sets of stories. Insofar as we are Christians, we believe all these diversities are largely good, signs of the manifold riches of God's good earth.

Cultures exist as complexes of symbolic reinterpretation. The analysis of cultures must always involve "relating *specific* symbolic acts to the broader symbolic *environments* in which they occur."[7] In the case of the culture-like character of Christian liturgy, that means relating local liturgical particularities to such patterns as may be perceived to link the history of Christian

Routledge and Kegan Paul, 1984), 259; *cf.* 3: Culture is "the symbolic-expressive aspect of human behavior," including verbal utterances, gestures, ceremonial behavior, ideologies, religions.

7. Wuthnow, et al., *Cultural Analysis,* 209, interpreting the work of Habermas.

worship or the geographical spread of Christian assemblies. But just as importantly, this linking of specific symbol and symbolic environment means that we must see the relationship between enacted Christian rituals and the many places—the regions of the world and the traditional and changing ways people live in them, the diverse languages, new social norms, diverse persons, new symbol-systems, new *cultures*—where the Christian assembly gathers to do the enacting. Christianity is a missionary religion on all of the continents, a *translation* religion, and there is nothing more traditional to its symbolizing life than the interior urge to relate its central symbols and its formative history—its own symbols and its faith—to ever changing cultural situations.[8] The Christian assembly takes place locally, and while it is deeply interested in its catholic linkages to all in every place, its local rootedness is also essential to its identity.[9]

It is important for us to say that Christian worship has cultural characteristics, for the word "culture" is too frequently used in our day only as a kind of sacred symbol for one's own ethnic or national identity, sensed as threatened and therefore set over against all the others. From this construction, an inquiry about "liturgy and culture" will be read as a kind of challenge: "How is your Christianity going to take my identity seriously?" On the other hand, there *are* threatened cultures in the world, and humanity would be generally impoverished by the loss of their specific wisdom. At its best, Christian worship can be seen as a place of dialogue and interpenetration where diverse symbols may carry and communicate both the meaning of the world and the identity of individuals.

But it is also important to say clearly that the Christian assembly is not in itself a culture. To speak of the "politics of Baptism" and the "economy of the Eucharist" is to speak analogically. For Christians, the way in which the Eucharist distributes food symbolically is in a critical dialogue with all ways of distributing and sharing food and the cultural symbols of meal keeping that may reinforce and interpret that distribution. The way that Baptism establishes identity is in a critical dialogue with all cultural symbolizations of identity, especially those that interpret ethnicity, class, rank, and gender. The Christian assembly is not a "culture" itself, except as it may exist in certain monastic or sect-like situations. Even there, the Christian community will be only partly independent, only partly withdrawn from engagement with local culture. It is better to see how the assembly sets out

8. See Anscar Chupungco, *The Cultural Adaptation of the Liturgy* (New York: Paulist, 1982).
9. See above, chapter 2.

the central symbols of the faith in a rich dialogue with the many ways local people are using to pass on a manner of living to their children.

Christian worship, then, itself has cultural characteristics. It has its own identity-giving and world-interpreting structures, and yet the meanings and identity it conveys belong to Christians who live within many actual cultures. Thus Christianity is most frequently a symbol-system in contrast to or in cooperation with surrounding symbol-systems, perhaps exercising influence upon those systems, perhaps utterly unrelated to them. This interaction of symbols or its absence is, in fact, acutely and poignantly experienced: the individual Christian, the baptized member of the local liturgical assembly, lives a life that is in touch with several cultures and struggles to sort out their meanings and their use in interpreting reality.

In this struggle, of course, Christians are not alone. Almost everyone in the world today lives within an actual situation of the confluence and conflict of culture-symbols. Aboriginal people find themselves speaking and writing in English to each other in order to teach their classic cultural sense of the land. Native American people build casinos in order to preserve their tribal economic integrity. Europeans and European Americans experiment with Tibetan Buddhism to answer a sense of spiritual anguish and vacuity. The list could go on. In this situation, however, the great, universal double danger is that in the name of security, people will try to build rigid boundaries around local meanings, refusing anything strange or any exterior criticism and giving up on wider human meaning, or that, in the name of modernization and efficiency, local wisdom and local gifts will be lost or turned into the commodities of the pretended universal "culture" of consumerism. Unfortunately, a kind of Christian ideology can be used to serve both tendencies. To engage now, at this moment in world history, in reflection on vigorous assembly liturgy and its relationship to cultures is to engage in an immensely important human undertaking against both of those dangers.

But the Christian interest in the discovery of permeable boundaries between cultures is not based only on the general hope for mutual respect and fruitful human exchange. The Christian interest in cultural interpenetration arises especially from the deep desire to speak and ritualize the truth about the mercy of God so that this truth may be heard everywhere. And this interest is founded in the trust that there are certain specific central signs which, if they are allowed to speak largely and clearly, in "the fullness and integrity of the sign,"[10] are capable of universal human address, full of the

---

10. Martin Luther, "Ein Sermon von dem hochwürdigen Sakrament des heiligen wahren Leichnams Christi und von den Bruderschaften," *WA*, 2:742: *"und der gentze und*

truth of that mercy, capable of calling all people to faith in that life-giving God. Christians believe that they bear a responsibility to conserve faithfully this Christian heritage of words and signs for God's mercy while at the same time plumbing the depths of that mercy as it comes to expression in ever new terms. When speaking of the astonishing grace of God, every cultural system is inadequate, every set of social symbols comes in for critique and radical reordering. Yet, Christians believe, God can transform our varying means of communication into bearers of saving grace, can inhabit and dwell amidst our symbol-systems. This is always happening locally. The universal liturgical patterns of Christians are always and only done *here*, in a particular local place, amid these particular people and their many cultures.

As we have seen, Christians have a wide—if not universal— agreement about the most central of their identity-creating signs. These are the washing or bathing that gathers a person into the Christian assembly, the reading and preaching of the Scriptures, and the thanksgiving meal that the assembly holds weekly as the memorial of Jesus. Christians call these signs "word and sacrament" and believe that they are set out in a participating community so that the "gospel of Jesus Christ" may be heard by needy human beings. Christians have taken the very accessibility and ordinariness of these central signs—water used for bathing and a new beginning, public speech in an understandable yet symbol-laden vernacular, a communal meal—as a gift of God enabling the universal mission of the church and opening the door of dialogue with all cultures. Given the centrality of these ordinary things, that dialogue must at least begin with an inquiry into the local meanings of water, with the use of the symbolic powers of the local vernacular, and with an awareness of local meal-keeping practices.

Again, the New Testament does not give us anything other than hints about the actual ritual practice of these central things. It assumes the presence of Baptism, preaching, and Supper. It does not describe them. What the New Testament can do is to suggest how the basic Christian symbolic acts are set within their broader symbolic environment. Helped by such commentators as Paul and Luke—and perhaps John—we can see the meanings and importance of the things that have become the central symbolic acts of the Christian liturgy. But at the same time, following on suggestions in many texts, we can reflect upon how these things are themselves *critical reworkings of cultural/symbolic materials from the early Christian environment*. The New Testa-

volkömenheyt willen des zeychens." Cf. WA, 2:727, on immersion baptism as "eyn rechts volkommens zeychen geben."

ment can thereby offer us a model for the ongoing relationship between the Christian assembly and the many cultures, a model for the permeable but focussed character of the Christian analogue to culture: the assembly.

The Origins of Christian Baptism

In order to explore the ways in which primitive Christian symbolization related to its cultural/symbolic environment, we need to have some awareness of that environment. We now know that "Hellenistic" culture, the heritage of Greek expansionism under Alexander the Great, pervaded the lands of the eastern Mediterranean, including Palestine, the very lands of Christian origins. The Hellenistic period in this area was marked by a widespread search for world-coherence, evidenced in such phenomena as the unifying dominance of the Greek language, the priority given to Greek customs, the syncretistic flow and mixing of religious ideas, and the longing for the ideal empire.[11] This longing for coherence probably ought to be seen as a negative witness to the general experience of disorder and chaos. At the same time, significant resistance was offered to this vision of "universal" coherence by the survival of local cultures. In Palestine, this resistance took both linguistic and religious forms. Such forms, however, were never "pure," but always evinced the culture conflict of the times. The popular use of Aramaic, for example, brought with it a sense of local Semitic identity, but it also brought the memory of *empire*, the older, pre-Greek empires for which Aramaic was the *lingua franca*. And such movements as those of the Sadducees, the Pharisees, the Zealots, and the Essenes were themselves marked in different ways by the very Hellenism they were seeking to counter. The early Christian movement arose within this tension and interpenetration of cultures.

It has been long and widely recognized that Christian Baptism was not created *ex nihilo*. All of the Gospels and Acts presume that the baptism of John preceded the Christian practice.[12] Indeed, the very fact that baptism among Christians was to take place in the name of Jesus (Acts 2:38; 8:16; 10:48) or in the name of the Father and of the Son and of the Holy Spirit (Matt. 28:19) indicates that *this* particular baptism was now taking place with a new content. But the bathing action itself and its potential for sym-

11. See Garth Fowden, *Empire to Commonwealth: Consequences of Monotheism in Late Antiquity* (Princeton: Princeton University Press, 1993), 3–36.

12. Matt. 3:11; Mark 1:7-8; Luke 3:16; 7:18-30; John 1:25-26, 31, 33; 3:22, 26; 4:1-2; Acts 1:22; 13:24; 19:4.

bolic meaning were already known, at least among those who had encountered or heard of John. One might compare the sense that a pre-existent washing practice could now be "in" or "into" Christ with the way Paul could say that walking under the protection of the cloud and crossing the sea was being "baptized into Moses" (1 Cor. 10:2).

But where did the "baptism of John" (Mark 11:30; cf. Acts 19:3) come from? According to the synoptic tradition, Jesus himself asks this question. The answer to his question is not simple. It was surely both "from heaven," in that according to Christian faith it came truly with God's own authority as the beginning of the gospel, and at the same time, from human cultural origin, in that there seems to have been an important symbolic use of water-washing before John. This is an answer very like the implied answer to the questions about Jesus' own origin in Mark 6:1-6. Indeed, Mark's (11:27-33, parr.) "baptism *of John*" could be read as referring to the specific symbolic water-washing that John uses in the name of God, implying that there were others. The same implication is in fact present in Paul's question to the disciples in Ephesus: "Into what then were you baptized?" (Acts 19:3). There seem to be other answers available to that question than the baptismal way of John or the Baptism in the name of Jesus. In fact, the Letter to the Hebrews (9:9-10) asserts that "the present time" has its "various baptisms" which function only "until the time comes to set things right." These may be various ritual washings required in the Torah[13] and still practiced in the "present time" of the author of Hebrews. Called "baptisms," they are in any case full-body washings and may be some development of the Torah-washings in the religious culture of the time.

Twentieth-century scholarship has sometimes been willing to identify a variety of baptizing/washing movements in the Hellenistic cultural environment of the origins of Christianity.[14] In any case, one cannot ignore Josephus's report of his own teacher, Bannus (does the name mean "bather" from the Greek *balaneus* or the Latin root *baln-*?), who in the middle of the first century, "lived in the desert, wore clothing supplied from trees . . . and washed many times in cold water both day and night for purification," [15]

13. Cf. Ex. 40:12; Lev. 8:6; 14–15; Num. 19:13.
14. See especially Joseph Thomas, *Le mouvement baptiste en Palestine et Syrie* (Gembloux: Duculot, 1935); Georg Kretschmar, "Die Geschichte des Taufgottesdienstes in der alten Kirche," *Leiturgia* (Kassel: Stauda, 1970), 5:9, 52, and Kurt Rudolph, *Antike Baptisten* (Berlin: Akademie-Verlag, 1981).
15. Josephus, *Life* 1:2:11. Greek text and translation available in Todd S. Beall, *Josephus' Description of the Essenes Illustrated by the Dead Sea Scrolls* (Cambridge: Cambridge University Press, 1988), 12–13.

nor his several reports of the repeated full-body washings of the Essenes.[16] Most modern scholars identify these Essenes with the community of Qumran and its ancient library.[17] We know from these Dead Sea Scrolls that very similar washings are reflected in several of its texts,[18] only now the texts supply the eschatological significance of this repeated accent on purity, a significance Josephus would be almost certain to have suppressed.

Thus the Qumran Manual of Discipline speaks of the *eschaton*, first using the bath as a metaphor:

> In the mysteries of God's understanding and in his glorious wisdom, God has ordained an end for falsehood, and at the time of the visitation he will destroy it forever. Then truth, which has wallowed in the ways of wickedness[19] during the dominion of falsehood until the appointed time of judgment, shall arise in the world forever. God will then purify every deed of man with his truth; he will refine for himself the human frame by rooting out all the spirit of falsehood from the bounds of his flesh. He will cleanse him of all wicked deeds with the spirit of holiness; like purifying waters he will shed upon him the spirit of truth[20] to cleanse him of all abomination and falsehood. And he shall be plunged into the spirit of purification that he may instruct the upright in the knowledge of the Most High and teach the wisdom of the sons of heaven to the perfect of way. For God has chosen them for an everlasting covenant (1QS 4:18-22).[21]

But only shortly thereafter in the text the metaphor has yielded to the reality of the community's bathing practice: the disobedient ones in the community "shall not enter the water to partake of the pure meal of the saints, for they shall not be cleansed unless they turn from their wickedness" (1QS 5:13-14).[22]

---

16. On washings occurring before the common meal, see Josephus, *Jewish War* (henceforth, *JW*)2:8:129; on washing as part of the process of joining the community, see 2:8:137-38; on washing after defecation, see 2:8:149; on washing after contact with strangers or junior members, see 2:8:150; and on washing before or instead of offering sacrifices, see *Antiquities* 18:1:19.

17. See the parallels listed in Beall, *Josephus' Description of the Essenes*, 123–27.

18. 1QS 3:5-9; 4:18-23; 5:13-14; CD 10:10-13; 11:21-22; *cf.* CD 3:16-17; 1QH 8:4-22.

19. *Cf.* the remarkably similar image in 2 Pet. 2:22.

20. Beall, *Josephus' Description of the Essenes*, 56: "He will cause the spirit of truth to gush forth upon him like lustral water."

21. Translation from G. Vermes, *The Dead Sea Scrolls in English* (Harmondsworth: Penguin, 1962), 77–78.

22. Vermes, *The Dead Sea Scrolls in English*, 79.

Indeed, given the washing practice reflected in the scrolls, it is not surprising that the observant community, awaiting the day of God, should regard itself as planted by the "secret well," the waters of life (1QH 8), near a cistern "rich in water" (CD 3:16). "The cistern," says the Damascus document, "is the Law" (CD 6:4).

In addition to these witnesses, ancient Jewish and Christian sources as early as the second century list a variety of groups who seem to be identified by their accent on repeated and central washings: the daily baptizers, the Masbotheans, the Sabaeans, the Banaim, the morning bathers.[23] Two ancient texts, recently identified as, most likely, Jewish first-century writings, give central importance to full-body washing in a river.[24] And some scholars believe the root baptizing traditions of the much later Mandeans of Mesopotamia must be traced to the Transjordan during the time of the origins of Christianity.[25] While what is called "proselyte baptism" is probably a much later phenomenon,[26] New Testament texts do point to washing traditions among the Pharisees (Mark 7:3-4) and Jewish purification rites requiring a good deal of water in stone jars (John 2:6 mentions 120–180 gallons). What is more, archeological evidence also points toward a considerable interest in bathing at about this time. Cisterns with stairways that

23. See Thomas, *Le mouvement baptiste,* 34–45, and Rudolph, *Antike Baptisten,* 8–10.

24. *Sybilline Oracles* 4:65 and the *Life of Adam and Eve* 6–11; in the latter the rivers are the Tigris for Eve and the Jordan for Adam.

25. See Kurt Rudolph, "Mandean Sources," in Werner Foerster, *Gnosis* 2 (Oxford: Clarendon, 1974), 132, 140–43, and "Die Religion der Mandäer," in Hartmut Gese et al., *Die Religionen Altsyriens, Altarabiens und der Mandäer: Die Religionen der Menschheit* 10, 2 (Stuttgart: Kohlhammer, 1970), 445–52.

26. The oldest clear reference is in the Babylonian Talmud. No convincing evidence can be found for the first century. See Adela Yarbro Collins, "The Origin of Christian Baptism," *Studia Liturgica* 19, no. 1 (1989): 32–35. If *Asenath* is indeed a Jewish text and is to be dated between 100 B.C.E. and 115 C.E., as C. Burchard proposes ("Joseph and Asenath," *The Old Testament Pseudepigrapha* [New York: Doubleday, 1985], 2:187-88), then a flood of light would be cast on the origin of Christian Baptism, so many of the practices of later, especially Syrian-Christian initiation being present there: the use of Sunday or the eighth day, the importance of virginity, the bridal imagery, the initiator as a syzygy of the Lord, preparatory fasting and almsgiving, washing in living water, revelation of mysteries, the kiss, the meal, and, especially, this whole process as initiation. Since we lack exterior means of dating the text, however, and precisely because of these parallels as well as the presence of other imagery and language until now found only in Christian sources, it seems much wiser to regard *Asenath* as a romance of Christian provenance, close in community of origin to the community of the *Didache* and close in spirit to the later *Acts of Judas Thomas,* also a romance. If this proposal is correct, however, *Asenath* remains a text that should be studied for its importance to the second- and third-century development of Christian baptism. Note that in *Asenath* 14 the protagonist washes only her face. This should be compared to *Didache* 7:2-3 and *Acts of Thomas* 132 and contrasted with *bYoma* 87a.

seem to be designed for full-body bathing and that utilize, at least in part, an unbroken access to fresh rainwater are found in considerable numbers at Jerusalem, Jericho, Herodium, Masada, and at Qumran itself as well as elsewhere.[27]

These various "baptisms" cannot be used easily to construct a genealogy of Christian Baptism. There have probably been rather too many naive attempts to say that John's baptism (and with it the subsequent Christian practice) derive directly from one or the other of these sources. On the other hand, neither should the presence of these practices in the cultural environment of early Christianity be ignored. There may have also been rather too many "protestant" assertions[28] that such ritual practices have nothing to do with the origins of Christianity. The sense alive in the second-century church, that Christian Baptism was situated amid many other washings, seems instead to be the case. Thus Clement of Alexandria asserts that the Lord has, "by means of the one baptism, taken over (*perilabon,* gathered up, supplanted) the many baptisms of Moses" (*Stromateis* 3:82:6). And both Justin (*1 Apology* 62) and Tertullian (*De baptismo* 5) see in a variety of Hellenistic-era washings an empty shadow of Baptism into Christ. We are today simply able to be a little more precise about the character of these Hellenistic and Mosaic washings in the cultural surroundings of the origins of Christianity.[29]

But we can be only a little more precise. We cannot clearly identify "baptizing sects." Even the history and the shape of the "Qumran community" are debated issues: the Dead Sea library may have been exactly that, a *library,* not the careful description of contemporary communal practice. But we are able to say that washing for purification and, at least sometimes, washing for purification in view of the expected day of God were ideas and practices that were in the air, were *available cultural symbols.* The availability of this symbolism may have been due to many things: the influx of Iranian water devotion; the development and use of Roman bath technology in

27. John Peter Oleson, "Water Works," *Anchor Bible Dictionary,* 6:887. See also Eric M. Meyers and A. Thomas Kraabel, "Archaeology, Iconography and Nonliterary Written Remains," in Robert A. Kraft and George W. E. Nickelsburg, *Early Judaism and Its Modern Interpreters* (Philadelphia: Fortress, 1986), 181; and Beall, *Josephus' Description of the Essenes,* 56–57.

28. For a critical appraisal of "catholic" and "protestant" presuppositions in research on Christian origins see Jonathan Z. Smith, *Drudgery Divine: On the Comparison of Early Christianities and the Religions of Late Antiquity* (Chicago: University of Chicago Press, 1990).

29. Kretschmar, "Die Geschichte des Taufgottesdienstes," 5:9.

Palestine; the importance of water narratives (the creation, the flood, the exodus, the entry into the land, the lustrations given in the Torah) and of eschatological water imagery[30] in the Hebrew Scriptures; the longing (seen in the movement of the Pharisees but also at Qumran) to generalize—laicize—the priestly purity and thus the priestly access to God; and probably most importantly, the experienced disorder of the Palestinian world. The imposed order of the Roman occupation and the interior sense that the "times were evil" could have led many people to wash and wash again, seeking order in purity and in the coming judgment of God. In any case, we ought to bring some cultural sympathy to imagining the reasons for the multiplication of baths.

What we know of some of these baths includes these characteristics: They were full-body washings[31] in cold, flowing or rain-originating, stone-held water. They were repeated, even exaggeratedly multiplied.[32] They probably *did not* involve oil, which was taken as a symbol of impurity.[33] They could involve white or "pure" clothing,[34] sometimes kept on during the bath. They preceded communal eating.[35] They could be part of the process of entering a community,[36] but then only as yet another purification or as an entering into the way of purification. They set off the bathed from strangers or juniors, from the "impure"[37]—the bath being a symbol of the law[38] and only appropriately used by the ethically pure and observant. Indeed, ethical behavior was to follow from the bath or no amount of water, not even oceans, would be able to cleanse.[39] In such evidence as we have, these intensified baths seem to involve only men (with the exception of the *Life of Adam and Eve*—and even then, Eve does not complete the washing and is tempted away from it!). If the practice did apply to men only, then the ritual bathing of women does not seem to have qualified for eschatological intensification.[40] And the baths are performed by the bather him-

30. Isa. 4:2-6; 35:6-7; 44:3; Ezek. 16:1-14; 36:24-28; 47:1-12.
31. *JW* 2:8:129; CD 10:10-13; *Sybilline Oracles* 4:165; *Life of Adam and Eve* 6–11.
32. Thus Bannus and the daily baptizers.
33. *JW* 2:8:123; cf. CD 12:15-17; *Life of Adam and Eve* 41–42.
34. *JW* 2:8:123, 129, 131, 137; cf. Bannus.
35. *JW* 2:8:129 and 1QS 5:13.
36. *JW* 2:8:137-38; cf. 1QS 6:13-23.
37. *JW* 2:8:150; 1QS 5:13; Mark 7; cf. 1QH 8.
38. CD 6:4.
39. 1QS 3:4-5.
40. For a history of such washing, see Shaye J. D. Cohen, "Menstruants and the Sacred in Judaism and Christianity," in Sarah Pomeroy, ed., *Women's History, Ancient History* (Chapel Hill: University of North Carolina, 1991), 273–99.

self;[41] there is no evidence of a "baptizer." Finally, these repeated baths seem best understood as an enacting ahead of time of the bathing that God is coming to do, when truth and the spirit are poured out[42] amidst all the falseness and disorder of the times, as a preparation for becoming part of the pure remnant on that day, perhaps even, by a kind of sympathetic magic, as a prayer for and urging of that day.

If even a few of these characteristics were generally understood, then the way that John the Baptist makes use of this cultural/symbolic "language" is stunning. The baptism of John has much in common with these intensified Hellenistic Jewish baths: full-body washing in flowing water, ethical implications, the evocation of "the day," even his own simplified manner of life. We do not know if his bathing included women, though Luke speaks of "crowds" coming to him and of the "people" being baptized (3:7, 10, 15, 18, 21). Nor do we know if he intended to form a group of disciples, a community, though the latter seems to exist in New Testament witness and in some subsequent tradition.

The invitation to this bath, however, is public, not withdrawn and communal. And this bathing is not in just any stone cistern; it is at the *Jordan*,[43] as if for the people to come through that water again was for them to be formed into Israel coming into God's land, newly, at this end of days.[44] The very location—as well as the *washing*—hearkens to the sense of disorder that has been proposed here as a possible social setting for the multiplication of baths. But John's baptism does not seem to be multiple. In any case, *he* does it; he is the baptizer. In the Hebrew Scriptures, occasions when someone is passively bathed include the priest-making of Aaron and his successors (Ex. 40:12-15; Lev. 8:6-13), the preparation of Jerusalem as the bride of God (Ezek. 16:1-14), and the promised eschatological washing of the people (Isa. 4:2-6; Ezek. 36:24-28), *not* the ordinary bathings of ritual purity. While the first two may have figured in John's meaning, it is probably the last which is signified by his acting to bathe.

---

41. Bannus; CD 10:10-13.

42. 1QS 4:18-23.

43. Although once John is reported as baptizing at Aenon (Aramaic: "springs"), which may or may not have been near the Jordan (John 3:23).

44. That "Jordan" could function in such a symbolic way in the times of John is clear from a painful story recounted in Josephus. The *Antiquities* (20:5:1; *cf.* Acts 5:36-37) tells of a certain Theudas who, probably in the mid-first century, gathered people at the Jordan with the promise of crossing it in what was to be manifestly a new "conquest," a new parting of the waters to claim the land for God. The Roman cavalry killed and imprisoned the people who gathered with him and carried Theudas's head to Jerusalem.

By a kind of prophetic sign then,[45] John indicates and anticipates *God's* coming to wash the people. Both the location and the practice of having people be the recipients of Baptism point to the imminence and centrality of God's action rather than private human action for the sake of ritual purity. John calls for repentance, for "turning around" in the water to see the coming God. John's practice receives the current interest in baths and radically reinterprets it by the juxtaposition of profound biblical imagery.

But for Christians the chain of reinterpretation goes on. According to the entire gospel tradition, Jesus comes to Baptism. Simply that coming, whereby he becomes the pattern and the content of all Christian Baptism, is what the Christian tradition has meant by the "institution of the sacrament." Christians do not believe that Jesus invents Baptism, but rather that Baptism is even more radically reinterpreted in him than the many baths were reinterpreted in John's singular prophetic practice.

Jesus is baptized, thus all three of the Synoptics witness (Matt. 3:13-16; Mark 1:9-10; Luke 3:21). By that action, Jesus also stands with all the people amid the current oppression and disorder, in need of the eschatological coming of God. He stands there as surely as he was later crucified, crying out to God, according to Mark (15:34-35), in a cry that was also a cry for the *eschaton.* He is baptized and, according to these same Synoptics, this washed one is made unclean, both by his associations and by his utterly unclean death.[46] He is baptized with the sign of the coming day of God, yet his obvious inheritance is not that glorious day but the same fate as the Baptist (Mark 6:17-29; 9:11-13). By these means, the Synoptics indicate that the Jesus tradition as they know it has received both the baptism of John and the situation of disorder and pain that made it urgent.

The same assertion is made in a different way in the Fourth Gospel: Jesus baptizes (John 3:22, 26; 4:1-2). The Baptism Jesus enacts, or rather—in what comes down to the same thing—the Baptism that the disciples of Jesus enact in his name, is simply John's baptism continued.

But this Baptism of the Christian community is also John's baptism utterly changed. The assertions of both the Synoptics and of the Fourth Gospel are, of course, already interpretations, *theologoumena,* but they do make clear the universal tradition that Christian Baptism is made out of John's baptism. They also make clear the deep-going reinterpretation that the washing tradition now undergoes. We cannot say with certainty whether

---

45. See Collins, "The Origin of Christian Baptism," 35.
46. Mark 2:15-17; 7:1-5; 15:27; *cf.* Matt. 11:19; Luke 7:34; Gal. 3:13.

or not the historical John actually preached, "I have baptized you with water; but he will baptize you with the Holy Spirit" (Mark 1:8), or some variant thereof. He could have done so, of course, meaning *God* as the coming Mighty One.[47] Other contemporary users of the bath also expected the coming God to pour out the Spirit like water (1QS 4; see above) or like fire. Such language was simply another image for the expected day. But in Christian use, the meaning is clear. *Jesus* is the coming Mighty One; his baptism transforms Baptism itself, making it the very presence of God (the voice and the dove); and henceforth Baptism into him is the outpouring of the Spirit, the dawning of the day of God, one's beginning to hear the voice of God, the joining of the holy assembly before the coming God. Such is the inevitable meaning of the account of Jesus coming to John's baptism when it is told in the midst of Christian communities still doing baptisms as central, identity-giving events.

Christian Meaning for Baptism

But the meaning is more radical yet. In Mark, for example, the day that dawns at the baptism of Jesus and is again glimpsed at the transfiguration (9:2-10) comes at the cross. At the cross the one who is known in secret as the Son (1:10-11; 9:7) is proclaimed openly (15:39). Elijah—and thus the day of God that Elijah goes before—has come in an unexpected way (9:11-13; 15:36), in the Baptist and in the cross. Jesus does drink the new cup of the dominion of God (14:25), and it is sour wine (15:36). No wonder the unwashed (7:2) and the impure (2:15) are welcome into him. No wonder one who appears like a candidate for a washing appears before and after Jesus' *death* (14:51-52; 16:5).[48] Jesus and his cross *are* Baptism for the young man as also for all the impure. At Qumran, a community of ritual bathers could say, "The cistern is the Law" (CD 6:4). In the Markan tradition, the washing is Jesus' death (10:38-39). The grace that the Baptist proclaimed has been continued and radically deepened. The impure and un-holy are gathered into the assembly that reads this Gospel.

Something very like this radical interpretation is also present in the Fourth Gospel. Here the Baptist himself sees the descent of the Spirit on Jesus and hears the voice (John 1:32-34). Here a woman from among the unclean Samaritans and a sick man unable to get to the washing pool and a

47. *Cf.* Collins, "The Origin of Christian Baptism," 30.

48. See the discussion of the "secret gospel of Mark" in Thomas Talley, *The Origins of the Liturgical Year* (New York: Pueblo Publishing, 1986), 207–9.

cast-out blind man are welcome to the water that is from Jesus (4:1-42; 5:2-18; 9:1-41), indeed, the water that *is* Jesus (9:7; *cf.* 17:3). But what finally replaces the tradition of washing, giving more than the purity and order for which it reached, is the new wine of Cana (2:1-11), a "sign" pointing forward to Jesus' death and resurrection. For the water that flows from Jesus' heart (7:37; *cf.* Ezek. 47:1-12), the very presence of the outpoured Spirit, flows from the Crucified One (19:30-35) who is risen (20:20-22). Indeed, the slave-service of the crucified is all the washing one needs (13:1-11), the full meaning of both Baptism (13:10) and the Supper (13:2-4).

These texts of Mark and John may best be seen as interpretations of Baptism, interpretations vigorously present in churches that were practicing this washing rite as the way to constitute their assemblies. These interpretations come alive when they are seen against the background of the cultural interest in washing in the environment of earliest Christianity. One could read these texts, however, not simply as reinterpretations but as refusals of the washing rite. Cana and the footwashing story in John and the cross as baptism in Mark might suggest one needs no actual washing rite at all. But that would be to misread what is a much more interesting proposal. In Mark, Jesus *is baptized,* the paradigm for all subsequent baptisms. The added conclusion of Mark therefore rightly includes Baptism in the instructions of the Risen One (16:16), while rightly placing it only on the side of promise, never on the side of requirement and threat and purity regulation. And in John, Jesus himself *baptizes* and invites to the water.[49] The rite is not set aside. Rather, the meaning of the footwashing—of the cross—is exactly what must always be added to the bath (13:10), thus utterly transfiguring the bath. Culturally significant material, including the "language" of washing rites, has been received in these accounts of the tradition of Jesus, has been criticized and even destroyed, and yet has been reused for the purposes of a Christian proclamation of eschatology, grace, and the presence of God's all-washing mercy in Jesus. The cultural symbol of washing for the day of God has been "broken."[50] Its power to evoke hope for God in the midst of dis-

49. John 3:5 might also be considered. Although "water" here could mean ordinary birth from the womb, it might also mean that water which is full of the Spirit, that water which, with the Spirit, flows from the Crucified Risen One. The ambiguity could be intentional.

50. See Paul Tillich, *Dynamics of Faith* (New York: Harper, 1957), 52–54. For Tillich, in a "broken myth" the terms of the myth and its power to evoke our experience of the world remain, but the coherent language of the myth is seen as insufficient and its power to hold and create as equivocal. The myth is both true and at the same time untrue, capable of truth only by reference to a new thing, beyond its own terms.

order and death has been used, but its conceptions of purity and "insider-hood," indeed its deep-rooted anxiety, have been rejected.

There are many other interpretations of Christian Baptism in the New Testament. Most of them can be traced to varying ways of asserting that the *eschaton* is occurring in Jesus Christ and is encountered in the washing which is into him and the assembly which that washing establishes. Thus Baptism is preparing the community for marrying God (Eph. 5:26; *cf.* Ezek. 16:1-14). Baptism is the making of a new people of priests (1 Pet. 1:22—2:10). Baptism was prefigured by the flood and in it a community stands with the resurrection of Christ in appeal to God (1 Pet. 3:21). Baptism is the coming of the eschatological promise and the forgiveness of sins to those who are being added to the assembly (Acts 2:38-41). Baptism is rescue from the darkness and transfer to the dominion of Christ, in whom is forgiveness of sins (Col. 1:13-14). Baptism is rebirth and renewal for the unrighteous through the outpoured Holy Spirit (Titus 3:5-6). It is enlightenment, tasting the heavenly gift and sharing in the Spirit (Heb. 6:2-4). It is entering through Jesus into the new sanctuary, bodies washed with pure water (Heb. 10:22). Baptism is all people, men and women, Jew and Gentile, being clothed in Christ (Gal. 3:27-28). Baptism is being plunged into Jesus' death; it is being buried with Christ in order to be raised with him in newness of life (Rom. 6:1-11; Col. 2:12). It can easily be seen how especially this last Pauline conception powerfully corresponds to the eschatology and the theology of the cross that are present in both Mark and John.[51]

None of these accounts gives us clear information about the actual ritual practice of Baptism in the New Testament communities. It should not surprise us, however, if so rich a field of meaning depends upon the strong signs of an evocative ritual practice. In any case, if Christian Baptism is a critical re-use of available cultural "language," then the ritual practice we have seen among the self-baptizers and with the Baptist will also hover behind the Christian use. Thus, Christian Baptism will also ordinarily have been a full-body washing in flowing, cold water. Paul's burial metaphor requires some such usual practice as does the death metaphor of the synop-

---

51. Being washed in the blood of Christ (Heb. 9:14) or having one's robe washed in the blood of the Lamb (Rev. 7:14) may be other ways to speak the same meaning: the ritual washing has its fulfillment in the death of Christ. Some similar meaning, related to John 19:30-35, may be behind the mysterious assertion of the three witnesses—the Spirit, the water, and the blood—in 1 John 5:8. In any case, the Pauline sources are not the only New Testament texts that link Baptism and the death of Christ. Oscar Cullman (*Le baptême des enfants* [Neuchatel: Delachaux et Niestlé, 1948], 15–16) was right: the death of Jesus can be called the "general baptism."

tic Jesus (Mark 10:38-39; Luke 12:50). Christian Baptism may have sometimes involved new, clean clothing.[52] It also led to the community meal.[53] It bore within itself ethical consequences.[54]

But at their best, these were now the ethics of love and mercy, not the ethics of separation. And the Baptism that led to them was also utterly different from the available cultural language, with a difference corresponding to Christian faith in Jesus Christ and Christian eschatology. It was now not the Jordan that was the appropriate place of Baptism, but wherever there was water (Acts 8:36), for the eschatological reality is Christ, not the recovered land. Ultimately, the amount or temperature of the water used was also not to be rigidly measured, though "living water" remained the ideal (*Didache* 7:2-3).[55] For exactly the same eschatological reason, there was now *one* Baptism, not multiple washings (Eph. 4:5; *cf.* Heb. 9:9-12). This one Baptism, together with the continuation of the Baptist's practice of having people passively washed (Acts 8:38; 1 Cor. 1:14), was intended to speak clearly of the final grace of God coming now upon people in Christ, constituting them as community. In fact, entrance into the community of the last day in Christ (Acts 2:41-42) now became the specifically Christian use of the washing rite. This bath was for all people—women and men, Gentile and Jew, slave and free—at least as its implications were finally understood in the Gentile mission.[56] From a Markan or a Johannine point of view, now the *rejection* of women, of the outsiders, or of the ritually unclean would, paradoxically, be "unclean." And since the point of this Baptism was now faith in the crucified and risen Christ and the making of a community of witnesses, not ritual purity, the bath itself was accompanied by teaching and preaching (Acts 1:14-22; Matt. 28:19-20).

There may have been, already in some of the communities of the New Testament, specifically new and Christian use of signs to accompany this washing. The use of fire or light (Heb. 6:4), of the laying on of hands (Heb. 6:2; Acts 19:6), perhaps even of oil (1 John 2:20, 27; 2 Cor. 1:21) or of signing (Rev. 7:3-4; *cf.* 2 Cor. 1:22; Eph. 1:13; 4:30) could be inferred as standing behind some of the references of the New Testament. But we do not know. Anointing with oil at Baptism might easily have followed from the

---

52. *Cf.* Gal. 3:27; Col. 3:9-10; Eph. 4:22-24; Rev. 7:13-17; 22:14; Mark 14:51-52; 16:5.
53. 1 Cor. 10:2-3; Acts 2:41-42; *cf.* 1 Cor. 12:13; Rev. 22:14; Heb. 6:4-5; 1 Pet. 1:22—2:3.
54. Rom. 6:4; Heb. 6:4-8.
55. See above, chapter 6, note 19.
56. *Cf.* Gal. 3:27-28; John 4:1-42; 1 Cor. 12:13; Col. 3:11.

name "Christ," from the explicit rejection of the old purity rules and from the sense that Baptism into Christ was the new form of that old passive washing whereby priests were made (Ex. 40:12-15; Lev. 8:6-13) or the new form of that old prophetic metaphor in which Jerusalem was prepared to be married to God (Eph. 5:26; cf. Ezek. 16:1-14). The actual ritual beginnings of anointing among Christians, however, remain unclear.

When noting what may be said about baptismal liturgy from the texts of the New Testament, it is important to indicate once again that "baptism in the name" (Matt. 28:19 and Acts 2:38, etc.) probably does not mean that an explicit formula of words was recited by the baptizer during the bath. Paul uses the same terminology in 1 Cor. 1:12-17, and it is unlikely that anyone would have imagined the formula: "I baptize you in the name of Paul." Paul means, rather, that were *he* to have baptized, those baptisms could have been regarded as in the presence and power of Paul and through his agency, that is, "in the name of Paul." He wishes to make clear that all true baptism is in the presence, power, and agency of Jesus Christ. This eschatological meaning of the washing is what "Baptism in the name of Jesus Christ" is intended to express. In the same way, Baptism "in the name of the Father and of the Son and of the Holy Spirit" is not baptism with a certain formula but that same Baptism, described in the beginning of Matthew's gospel (3:16-17), in which the Spirit descends and the voice speaks and the Son is revealed. In other words, this washing is Baptism as the Christian community does it, with the old washing rituals now broken open to speak God's grace in Christ.

The old washing rituals did not always stay broken. Suppressed or transformed materials from the cultural environment could reassert themselves much as the later basilica could reassert its original meanings to the detriment of its transformation by the Christian assembly. So the idea of purity and obedience could pop up again (2 Pet. 2:20-22), as could conceptions of purity and insiderhood (2 Cor. 6:14-7:1) or, much later, the practice of self-washing[57] or the perceived need for multiple washings.[58] And the Christian conviction that this washing in Christ is full of the eschatological outpouring of the Holy Spirit could be turned into a new ritual requirement if we read the laying on of hands in Acts (8:17; 19:6) as a liturgical descrip-

57. This practice was present in Syria, if *Asenath* is a Christian document. See above, note 26.

58. This practice occurred among those Christians influenced by the Parthian Jewish prophet Elchasai; cf. 2 Cor. 7:1. See Rudolph, *Antike Baptisten,* 13–17. See also G. P. Luttikhuizen, *The Revelation of Elchasai* (Groningen dissertation, University of Groningen, 1984).

tion rather than a literary feature associating earlier washings with the apostolic church.

Baptism and Culture

But then the very beginnings of baptism may give us a key to the relationship between the Christian assembly and the many cultures of the earth. Baptism provides that assembly with both a center and a method.

Christian practice welcomed the cultural symbolism of an eschatological resistance movement: full-body washing to be ready for the day of God. But it rejected repeated washings, self-washings, and washing only for men because it reinterpreted the "day of God" to be the presence and gift of the crucified Christ, thereby reinterpreting "purity" to be nearness to Christ, reception of the grace of the triune God. The symbol was now a "broken symbol." The resultant washing became the way to enter into Christ's community, his "body," the ragged community which was the reinterpreted "holy people."

The use of this washing in new situations led a continuing history of inculturation. Christians unfolded the power of this entrance into the assembly by adding a long period of teaching the faith before the bath and by adding the use of anointing, the laying on of hands, exorcism, clothing, fire, and the leading to the meal at the time of the bath. Such use of the "word," of the "name" of God, as God is known in Christ, of the instruction next to the bath, and of the welcome to Christ's table were necessary in order to make clear, especially in non-Jewish situations, that *this* washing makes us a communal witness to faith in God. The other "additions" all expressed a kind of ceremonial astonishment—in new cultural situations, borrowing and reinterpreting symbols known especially in the mysteries— that washing could be washing into life and grace before God in Christ.

Thus, we may say that insofar as the liturgical practice of the earliest Christian communities can be reconstructed, we see that those communities made use of the strong but broken symbol of washing. They used that old eschatological symbol now as the entrance to their community and as one of their central and identifying practices. The cultural symbolism of washing was thus received and turned to the purpose of proclaiming God's grace in Christ.

Christians today, who similarly practice Baptism as central, do well to ask whether their practice is similarly *strong* and *broken*. Is our baptismal practice marked by a full use of water and its attendant signs, by a full panoply of interpretive images, and by a full reception of the human long-ing for order, salvation, and enlightenment which such images signify? At exactly the same time, is our baptismal practice always turned to the speaking of grace, resisting the use of the water rite to create separation, works-righteousness, and ideas of cultic purity? Baptism constitutes the "holy people," who are naked and needy, being forgiven, being drawn from death. Baptism gathers an assembly into Christ and so into identification with the situation of all humanity, not into distinction and differentiation. Paradoxically, Baptism is the washing that makes us unclean, with all the unclean and profane ones of the world. In Christ, Baptism makes us part of humanity, witnesses to the grace of the triune God for us all.

This very use of cultural/symbolic material from the environment of the origin of Christianity proposes to us a model for the ongoing cultural dialogue of Christian worship. Anything brought in to the assembly can be received with the same sympathy for its meanings, but also with the same powerful critique as seems present in the Christian use of the ancient washing practice. Can we find the same help from a consideration of the Eucharist?

8

Assembly, Eucharist, and Culture

The New Testament itself evidences an awareness that the cultural treasures of the nations are to be both welcomed and criticized in the life of the church. Thus, the Fourth Gospel makes use of themes and symbols drawn from contemporary Jewish Tabernacles observance[1] or current Greek Dionysian myth.[2] But it also critically requires both sets of cultural material to yield to Christ, the true water-source, the true revolution in religion. Not the repeated libations in the temple at the feast of Tabernacles, but the "water" from Christ's heart, from his death will water the whole earth (John 7:38-39; 19:34-35). Not Dionysian drunkenness or continued Jewish purification rites, but the "wine" of Christ's "glorification," of his cross will both gladden and cleanse us, assuaging all thirst (John 2:4-11; 13:1; 19:28-30). Baptism and Eucharist can be seen as assembly celebrations of these assertions of Christian faith, assertions made for the life of the world. In Christian worship as well as in John's Gospel, both Jewish and pagan cultural symbols are freely used and strongly criticized.

If the church can be understood as in some sense like the city of God that the Revelation of John sees as "coming down out of heaven" (21:2), then the reception of the nations into that church can be explicitly described as both welcome and critique (21:24-27). Into God's city—and by extension into the church—the nations come, the kings with their "glory"

---

1. John 7:37-39. On the custom of pouring out water in the Temple during the feast of the Tabernacles, perhaps as a rain-making prayer or as an eschatological symbol, see C. K. Barrett, *The Gospel according to St. John* (London: S.P.C.K., 1962), 270–71. *Cf.* Ezek. 47:1-12; Zech. 14:8.

2. John 2:1-11. On the incognito wine-maker as Dionysus, whose ecstasies were intended to overthrow established religion, see Barrett, *The Gospel according to St. John,* 157–58.

and the people with their "honor." This weighted burden brought by rulers and people, this carried treasure, can be interpreted as the cultures of the nations. The apocalyptic image is, of course, an elaboration of the old prophetic hope that the nations would at last come to Jerusalem as to the center of the earth, coming to the holy assembly before God (Isa. 2:2-4; 25:6-9), bringing their wealth for the building and sustenance of the city (Isaiah 60). But the bringing of "the cypress, the plane, and the pine, to beautify the place of my sanctuary" (Isa. 60:13) also implies the coming of the craftspeople—and therefore the coming of the culture—of the nations (*cf.* 1 Kings 7:13-14). Their "skill, intelligence, and knowledge" is to enter into the city in praise of God and God's light-giving mercy. In the Christian vision of the Revelation, that light is to be seen in the "Lamb" in the midst of the city; the nations bring their "glory" not to the temple but to Jesus Christ who is at the center of the praise of God's new city.

But in the Revelation text, the vision of the open gates and of the welcomed treasures of the peoples is immediately paired with an evocation of powerful critique. Not only must the royalty and the wealth of the nations, their cultures, be reoriented to the utterly new, non-royal central presence of God and the Lamb, but also "nothing unclean will enter" the city (Rev. 21:27). The "treasures" are both reoriented and sifted; not every cultural phenomenon is welcome, certainly not those that serve "abomination or falsehood," not those incapable of serving God and Christ at the center.

Except for the centrality of the Lamb, the Revelation text does not give us clear criteria for the critique of cultural gifts, for what is "abomination." But it does give us an image for what much of the rest of the New Testament actually does in reorienting and sifting cultural materials. The interesting thing, for our purposes, is that the Revelation image is one of welcome and critique in the context of *worship:* the nations come streaming toward that which, in the Christian vision, replaces the temple, toward God and the Lamb at the center of the open-gated city. Similarly, in John, the Tabernacles libations, the "six stone water jars for the Jewish rites of purification," and the Dionysian practices all are ritual matters. Each of these ritual symbols is re-used verbally in the Gospel to proclaim the meaning of Jesus. And for us, they can at least suggest some meanings surrounding the actual use of water-washing and wine-drinking in the church.

But as we have seen in considering the critique and reorientation of those water-washings that became Christian Baptism, much of the New Testament does have an idea of what constitutes the "unclean" that may not enter. It is exactly the opposite of what usually constitutes religious and ritual uncleanness. For Mark or Paul or John, for example, that is "unclean" which excludes the unclean, the outsiders, the women, or the crucified. That is "unclean" which limits the free gospel and which thus cannot be ordered to the centrality of the Lamb. Not every cultural phenomenon is welcome in the city of God. Insofar as the church and its worship mirror that city, this critical sorting must occur in Christian liturgy as well.

Meal Practice and Culture

Among the treasures of the nations are their meal practices. Meals create and express a human group. Meals are complex symbols, not just functional edibles. They are a primary form of culture, passing on the primary values of the group. To know what a people eats, who eats it, in what order and when, is to know a great deal about a society.[3] To know what stories are told at a community's meals and what symbols function there, passing on what values, is to know the heart of a culture.[4] Meals *are,* concretely, communities and their survival. Meals are far more than simply enough food to get through the next hours. They symbolize and participate in social relationships, hierarchies, inclusion and exclusion, the boundaries around a group and the transactions across those boundaries.

It comes as no surprise, then, that the story of Israel, the narrative of that community's identity, can be told in the terms of a series of symbolically important meals: Abraham and the angels at Mamre,[5] the Passover and the manna,[6] the meal of Moses and the elders before God on Sinai, prototypical of all the meals of sacrifice in Israel,[7] the feast and the "sending of portions" from the "great synagogue" at the time of return from exile,[8] and the promised great meal on the mountain,[9] to name only the most important. Such stories, of course, do not establish a clear pattern for the actual celebration of a meal. But they do determine a tradition of meaning: this community's national identity is reconfirmed and celebrated in common meals.[10]

3. See Gillian Feeley-Harnik, *The Lord's Table* (Philadelphia: University of Pennsylvania Press, 1981), 11: "In establishing precisely who eats what with whom, commensality is one of the most powerful ways of defining and differentiating social groups."
4. See Feeley-Harnik, *The Lord's Table,* 6–18.
5. Gen. 18:1-15.
6. Exodus 12; 16.
7. Ex. 24:9-11.
8. Neh. 8:10-12.
9. *Cf.* Isa. 25:6.
10. For an interesting history of Judaism conceived as a history of its meals, see Jacob Neusner, *A Short History of Judaism: Three Meals, Three Epochs* (Minneapolis: Fortress, 1992).

Hellenistic Judaism seems to have recalled such stories while using an essentially Greek pattern for the actual manner of communal eating. The characteristics of the *deipnon* and the *symposion,* the general Mediterranean way of eating, were mixed with a memory of the sense that eating was always before God, as a people.

Ancient classical sources allow us to make some generalizations about this Mediterranean pattern for a meal.[11] Houses included a dining room, often the most important of rooms, sometimes decorated with significant imagery[12] and usually arranged for reclining at the meal. A banquet, which may be taken as the paradigmatic example for all meal practice, involved a host and invitations: the meal was for a select group, often only free men.[13] Women, though often excluded from the meal, were sometimes among those who provided entertainment or even sexual companionship during the post-meal drinking party.[14] Seating arrangement at the table indicated rank. The meal was preceded by washing of the feet, by a servant, and washing of the hands: "water over the hand, tables brought in" says one ancient synecdoche for what modern English would express with the phrase "we dined."[15] The actual eating, the "tables," seems to have followed this order: sometimes an appetizer course, with conversation; then the *deipnon,* the meal itself; then the removal of the tables, the bringing of the mixed wine–cup, the ritual libation to the gods, and the *symposion* or common drinking and entertainment (or among the philosophically inclined, drinking and conversation). Of this order of the meal, Plato reports: "Socrates took his place on the couch; and when the meal was ended, and the libations offered, and after a hymn had been sung to the god, and there had been the usual ceremonies, . . . they were about to commence drinking."[16]

Many of these very characteristics recur in the shape of Jewish meal practice at the time of Christian origins, as it can be reconstructed from the New Testament and other ancient sources. Among the Jews dining rooms,[17]

11. For the following, see Dennis E. Smith, "Greco-Roman Meal Customs," in *The Anchor Bible Dictionary,* 4:650–53; and Dennis E. Smith and Hal E. Taussig, *Many Tables* (Philadelphia: Trinity International, 1990), 23–28.

12. As, for example, in the floor mosaic of the rape of Europa, which was situated just before the *triclinium,* the three-sided dining room arranged for reclining, at the Roman villa in Lullingstone, England.

13. *Cf.* Plato, *Symposium* 176e.

14. *Cf.* Mark 6:22.

15. Athenaeus, *Deipnosophists* 14.641d, quoted in Smith and Taussig, *Many Tables,* 25.

16. Plato, *Symposium* 176a, translated in B. Jowett, *The Republic and Other Works by Plato* (Garden City, N.Y.: Anchor, 1973), 323.

17. Josephus, *The Jewish War* (henceforth, *JW*) 2:8:129; Mark 14:14.

invitations[18] and the closed male group,[19] washing,[20] reclining,[21] rank at table,[22] and the two-staged banquet, with the mixed cup "after supper"[23] were also common features of meals. At meals, Hellenistic Judaism was culturally *Greek*. Indeed, even the daily sacrifice in the temple could be described in the Greek pattern: a meal for God (Sirach 50:12-13), a libation for God (50:14-15), and an "entertainment" (50:16-19)!

But this cultural material had undergone a transformation to serve the purposes of primary Jewish values. There was to be no idolatry here, so the libation after *deipnon* and before *symposion* became the blessing of *God* over the mixed cup. The Greek ceremonial moment at the end of the *deipnon* became over time the great place for the Jewish *Birkat ha-Mazon,*[24] the lengthy prayer of thanksgiving and supplication which many scholars see as the prototype of Christian *eucharistia* at table.[25] Indeed, all food was to be taken with thanksgiving, and this fact yielded the sense that the meal is taken before God. Furthermore, the principal ceremonial food was now not only wine but also bread, recalling the bread of Abraham's and Gideon's meals with God, the bread of the Passover, of the exodus, and of the temple. So not only the *symposion* but now also the *deipnon* was begun with ceremony; the meal was always inaugurated with a blessing over bread, as a kind of perpetual first-fruit ritual.[26] The meal was thus a reconstitution of the people as God's people and a reinsertion of those at table into the faith of Israel, the faith that God has made the world and redeemed the people. Because of this transformation, the washing had also become a religious ritual, an enactment

18. Luke 14:12-14.
19. 1QS 5:13; 6:20-22; *JW* 2:8:129; Mark 14:17-18; 16:14.
20. *JW* 2:8:129; 1 QS 5:13; Mark 7:1-21; Luke 7:44; John 13:5.
21. Matt. 9:10; Mark 14:3, 18 par.; *Mishnah Berakoth* 6:6.
22. 1QS 6:4; Matt. 23:6; Luke 14:7-11.
23. Luke 22:20; 1 Cor. 11:25.
24. See already Jubilees 22:6-9, where Abraham eats and drinks and then blesses God in a three-fold prayer, praising God for creation, thanking God for salvation and protection, and beseeching God for the future. This is the very pattern found in the much later *Birkat ha-Mazon,* in the prayer of Polycarp over his own death as over a libation-cup at the end of a meal in the *Martyrdom* 14, and with an inversion of the first two parts, in the prayer after the meal in *Didache* 10. Note also that the pattern of Sirach 50 is meal, libation, hymns, and prayers.
25. Thomas J. Talley, "From Berakah to Eucharistia: a Reopening Question," *Worship* 50 (1976): 115–37.
26. *JW* 2:8:130-31: "the baker serves the loaves in order . . . the priest prays before the meal . . . both when they begin and when they end, they honor God as the supplier of life." Translation in Todd S. Beall, *Josephus' Description of the Essenes,* 17. *Cf.* 1QS 6:4-5; 10:14-15; 1QSa 2:17-21. Note also the priority of the blessing over bread in *Mishnah Berakoth* 6:5.

of the purity necessary to be part of the people.[27] At Qumran "the purity of the holy men" came to be a standard term for the communal meal,[28] and such a term would have been widely understandable. Furthermore, the Greek philosophical symposium, the conversation over wine after the *deipnon,* in certain circles was to become a discussion of *torah,* a teaching of the "philosophy" of Israel.[29]

In the context of Christian origins, then, meals were already complex cultural symbols. Determined in pattern by the dominant Greek culture, these meals were also events in which Jewish identity was reconstituted by bread, by prayer, by ritual purity, and by teaching and narrative memory. The very fact that the meal prayers came to be addressed—perhaps already in the first century—to God as *melech ha-olam,* "king of the universe," and to beseech for the reign of God gives evidence of the depth of this complexity. These meals took place in a distressed social situation, full of military oppression and apocalyptic longing. The prayers at meals could be seen as an interior, religious response—even as a protest—to the horrors of that other *melech,* the one who ruled the Roman empire.

The Origins of Christian Eucharist

From a Christian point of view, this Hellenistic Jewish meal practice, this concrete cultural pattern, was a treasure that was "brought into the city." Indeed, it came to the center of the life of the churches. And the sorting occurred. Exactly as we have seen with Baptism and its relationship to the cultural symbolism of washing, in the Eucharist the New Testament communities both continued and critically re-formed Hellenistic Jewish meal practice. Both a *yes* and a *no* were spoken to the complex cultural symbolism of the meal we have here briefly explored.

The Eucharist of the church is rooted in the fact that the churches were meal-keeping assemblies[30] that remembered the meal keeping of Jesus and believed that they encountered the risen Christ "in the breaking of the bread."[31] These meals, of course, would have been in the general cultural mold of Mediterranean/Greek practice. They were held in dining rooms or,

27. *JW* 2:8:129: "[T]hemselves now pure, they go into the dining-room, even as into some holy shrine." Translation found in Beall, *Josephus' Description of the Essenes,* 17.

28. See Beall, *Josephus' Description of the Essenes,* 56.

29. Sirach 9:15-16; 32:3-6; John 13-17; Acts 20:7, 11; *cf.* 1QS 6:2-3.

30. Acts 2:42, 46; 20:7, 11; 1 Cor. 10:16-21; 11:17-34; *Didache* 9:1; 14:1; *Martyrdom of Polycarp* 7:1; Pliny the Younger, *Letters* 10:96.

31. Luke 24:13-35.

at least, in houses, perhaps using the largest available room or the enclosed and partially covered courtyard of the house. In any case, "the church in the house of so-and-so"[32] should probably be understood as another indication of the meal-fellowship that met at a certain house. The clubs, associations, *hetaeriae* which Christians called "the assembly" were largely gatherings for a meal. There would have been hosts at these meals—perhaps originally the householder or the *paterfamilias* of the extended family—responsible for the arrangements and the rituals of the meal. The meals themselves involved a use of wine after the *deipnon*[33] and, perhaps, a continuing conversation.[34]

But these meals of the church were also marked by particular Jewish transformations of the *deipnon* practice. Also in the Christian community there was prayer over bread at the outset of the meal.[35] Also among Christians the ritual of the libation and its hymnody had become the thanksgiving and petition after supper.[36] Here too, the sense may well have prevailed that a meal was taken before God, that a meal involved a reinsertion into faith that God made the world. It is these meals—meals which came to be held especially on Sunday,[37] meals which were probably marked by a good deal of diversity in actual practice—that were the primitive form of Eucharist. In the earliest period of the church, we cannot make any easy distinction between *agape* meals and Eucharist;[38] there is only the *deipnon/symposion* of the churches.

But why was the church a meal fellowship? One might answer, exteriorly, that the Christian movement was a society, a club, and the most obvious means available to such a society in Greek culture was the shared meal. Surely a deeper answer, however, one closer to the meaning of these meals for Christians, is that Christians remembered the meal practice of Jesus. At the center of that memory, as at the center of concentric circles of meaning, they came to remember the association of Jesus' death and resurrection with meals and, most especially, his own words of promise and gift at a meal.

---

32. *Cf.* Rom. 16:5; 1 Cor. 16:19; Phlmn. 2; Col. 4:15.

33. See above, note 23.

34. See Acts 20:7, 11.

35. Mark 6:41 par.; 8:6 par.; Luke 22:19; 24:30; 1 Cor. 11:23-24; *Didache* 9:3.

36. See above, notes 24 and 25. *Cf.* the prayer of Polycarp after supper in *Martyrdom* 7:3-8:1.

37. Acts 20:7; *Didache* 14:1; Pliny the Younger, *Letters* 10:96. *Cf.* Luke 24:13-35, 36-43; Rev. 1:10; 3:20.

38. See the work of Bernd Kollmann, *Ursprung und Gestalten der frühchristlichen Mahlfeier* (Göttingen: Vandenhoeck und Ruprecht, 1990).

It was these words—and their association with the principal ceremonial foods and ceremonial acts of the Hellenistic Jewish *deipnon/symposion,* the blessing over bread at the beginning and the lengthy thanksgiving over the cup at the end of the meal—that enabled the Christian Eucharist to survive the banning of supper clubs imposed upon the Christians in the persecutions. The bread blessing of the beginning and the wine prayer of the end of the meal, accentuated by Jesus' words, could be simply moved to the morning, away from supper, away from the symposium, away from the tendency toward the insider club, away from the looming, Greek-cultural tradition of drunkenness.[39] The food of the meal, the actual food the church was accustomed to take together, could then be given away.[40] The Eucharist was finally more than a Hellenistic supper and symposium, even more than such a supper with Jewish overtones. It was the meal-gift of Jesus Christ alive in the church. We can follow this transformation by paying some attention to accounts of the historical Jesus and to the writings of Paul, Mark, John, and Luke.

We cannot say much with certainty about the historical *Jesus.* But the widespread attestation, in many different sources, of the striking character of his meal practice makes that practice one of the more likely things than can be attributed to him. As in all Hellenistic Jewish practice, he prayed over bread at the beginning of the meal.[41] For Jesus, then, the meal was an event of the people before God. Indeed, the meals of Jesus seem to bear a special witness to the tortured situation of this Jewish cultural symbol of faith in the God of creation and covenant. Echoing the Jewish meal prayers which speak of the "kingdom of God," the meals of Jesus enacted a prophetic sign of the profoundly needed nearness of the reign of the *melech ha-olam.* So in Mark 2:18-20, Jesus and his company do not fast but rather feast, in celebration of the presence of the "bridegroom," an old prophetic image for the presence of God in Israel. And the petition of Jesus' prayer for "daily bread" may well be a way in which he sees the hoped for "day of God" already imaged in the shared meals of his company.[42] It is as if the company around Jesus is already the *assembly* of the end times.

---

39. 1 Cor. 11:21-22, 34; 2 Peter 2:13; Jude 12.

40. Thus, when we first find clear evidence for the Christian Eucharist no longer being a full meal but a bread and wine rite after a word-service, we also find, in the same description of the Eucharist, reference to a collection for the poor: Justin Martyr, *1 Apology* 67. See Lathrop, *Holy Things: A Liturgical Theology* (Minneapolis: Fortress, 1993), 44.

41. *Cf.* Mark 8:6; Luke 24:30.

42. See above, chapter 1, pp. 33-34.

Unlike the Hellenistic Jewish feasts, the feasts of Jesus welcomed 'the many' to participation in these signs. He ate and drank with sinners. "Forgive us as we forgive," he also taught his disciples to pray. If meals were indeed signs of God's coming day, then Jesus welcomed sinners to life-giving participation in that day. He rejected the rules of purity, intended to accentuate the identity of the very people the meal was meant to constitute. There are women at his meals. While the Gospels show him visiting the dining rooms of the righteous on invitation, he is also shown visiting the dining rooms of sinners or welcoming the outsiders into other dining rooms or using no dining room at all. The great "feeding" stories have him outside, with no walls to limit the approach of the thousands. And a dining room, a Hellenistic *triclinium,* will hardly be sufficient to hold the people of the highways and byways, the lame, maimed, and blind who figure in his meal parable. The assembly of this meal practice is a surprising assembly.

The churches seem to have continued these meals of Jesus. Sometimes the invited, closed group of the Greek *deipnon* or the group-constituting concern for purity found at Qumran could emerge as a central ecclesial meal practice as well: witness the factions of Corinth (1 Cor. 11:21-22) and the fierce critique of meal participants in Jude and 2 Peter (2 Pet. 2:4-13; Jude 8-12). But for the most part, the old sense that eating with Jesus enables outsiders and sinners to participate in God's day and that Jesus' invitation is wide did maintain its crucial centrality for the great writers of the New Testament tradition. Only now it is the Crucified and Risen One with whom the church eats. It is the blood of Christ that is for "the many;" his cross is their participation in the meal of God's kingdom (Mark 14:24-25).

Paul's criticism of the Corinthian meal practice is a criticism of factionalism, of the socioeconomic exclusiveness of those who actually get to eat and drink (1 Cor. 11:17-34). This critique is so strong that it leads Paul to propose that full-scale food consumption take place away from the Christian gathering, while the bread and cup that bind "the many" into one body (10:16-17) remain. If the Corinthian community was also following the practice of keeping this communal meal on Sunday, which we can detect elsewhere, it is fascinating that we find the same Paul who urges the elimination of banquet and drinking also urging the Corinthians to set aside gifts for the poor on the first day of the week (16:2; *cf.* 2 Cor. 8–9). But the center of this critique is Paul's assurance that the shared bread and cup are participation in the body and blood of Christ, are the proclamation of the death of the Lord until he comes. The bread of the beginning of the Jewish *deipnon* and the blessing-cup of the Jewish *symposion,* now associated with Christ's presence and gift, are enough to stand for the whole meal, enough to unite "the many" into one body.

In Mark, one finds repeated reference to Jesus' meals,[43] doubtless as a challenge to the church, not unlike Paul's challenge to Corinth, to find the center of the meaning of its meal practice in the crucified Christ. The whole of Mark's Gospel seems to ask, "Are you able to drink the cup that I drink" (Mark 10:38), while giving away the bread to sinners and outsiders (7:28)? In Mark, of course, the new cup of the kingdom of God is none other than the cup of Christ's death (14:25, 36; 15:36); it is finally in and because of this death that the outsiders and sinners are welcome to God's meal.

Indeed, if the practice of the church was a regular *deipnon* and *symposion,* it is important to note that it is at a reclining meal that a woman proclaims Jesus' forthcoming death (14:8). This unnamed woman at Bethany signs in love what is done in hatred and lust, shame and abuse, by and to her anti-type, the daughter of Herodias. Recall that this girl, providing the entertainment at Herod's *symposion,* obtains the death of John the Baptist in the midst of the meal (6:17-29). This grisly foreshadowing of the Last Supper helps us to see the more clearly that the final meal of Jesus has no *symposion;* the bread and cup and their meaning are given in the midst of the supper, and the meal ends with a hymn instead of the mixed cup and conversation or entertainment. Here, the *symposion* cup is the cup of the garden (14:36) and the surprising, spoiled-wine drink of the cross (15:36), which *is* the arrival of the kingdom of God.

These three banquets—at Herod's birthday, at Bethany, and at Passover—are reported in Mark not to establish a rubrical pattern of Christian celebration, but to propose the deepest meaning of the church's meal practice. At Passover, the bread and cup are set out in the middle of the meal, rather than framing it, and the *symposion* is moved to the garden in order for us to understand, in a manner appropriate to Mark, that the cross welcomes all—"the many," the sinners, the women—to God's table. In a way much like Paul, Mark strongly criticizes an exclusive symposium of invited, powerful, or "pure" men. It is very likely that Mark's church continued to keep their meal-cum-symposium; these Christians also would have had the cup "after

43. Mark 2:15-28; 3:20; 5:43; 6:31, 34-44; 7:1-23, 27-28; 8:1-9, 14-21; 10:38-39; 11:12-13; 12:39; 14:3-9, 12-26, 36; 15:36. It is also of interest that the two great parables that frame the ministry of Jesus in Mark, that of the sower (4:1-20) and that of the vineyard (12:1-12), use the imagery of the production of *bread* and the production of *wine.* see Bas van Iersel, *Reading Mark* (Edinburgh: T. and T. Clark, 1989), 155–56.

supper." Such was the available meal practice. But they could only have understood that practice more profoundly after reading Mark.

The critical transformation of the meal is also to be found in John. Here, what is in the midst of the meal, giving the meaning to the meal, is Jesus' washing of feet (John 13:1–5). This washing is the more noticeable since, just like the bread and cup in Mark's report of the Last Supper, it is not where it belongs in Hellenistic meal practice—at the beginning, at the welcome of the guests. And it is the more noticeable since it is done by the host. This slave-service is, in John, a sign of the cross. Just as in Mark, this literary device should not be understood as ecclesial rubric but as an indication of critical meaning: the church's *deipnon* is nothing if it is not focused on the cross. The very first action of the arrival of Jesus' "hour," that time toward which the whole Gospel has been leaning in pre-figuration, is the meal made into foot-washing. So Jesus' cross-service *is* the presence of the water made into new wine (2:4); it *is* the pouring out of the Spirit like water (7:39). In John, the *deipnon* becomes the footwashing, an image the more powerful since the Johannine Jesus has already said that he gives his flesh and blood to eat and drink (6:53–58). And in John, the *symposion* becomes the "farewell discourse" and "high-priestly prayer" (13:31—17:26), a discourse marked by talk of going away and coming again, of Jesus' death and resurrection, and centered in the image of the vine (15:1–11), as is fitting to this wine-accompanied meal tradition. Again, the Fourth Gospel is not proposing a pattern for liturgy or rejecting the practice of the church's meal. It is breaking the cultural symbolism of the meal, requiring it to speak the meaning of Jesus Christ's cross and resurrection. Henceforth, in the Johannine community, the *deipnon* and the *symposion* are to be seen in new depth.

This growing awareness of the gift of Jesus, this finding of the center of the concentric circles of eucharistic meaning, yielded the Eucharist in the churches. The Eucharist did not have two sources, an *agape* and a cross-cult meal.[44] It had many sources—the many meal-keeping Christian communities, in many associations and houses, with their own versions of Greek/Mediterranean meal practice—and yet, a single source—the gift and presence of Jesus Christ juxtaposed to that meal practice. Its origin was in a breaking of Hellenistic meal meanings to the purposes of the gospel, a breaking found already in the meal practices of Jesus and received and understood and believed in the texts of Paul, Mark, and John.

44. Pace the influential classic study of Hans Lietzmann, *Messe und Herrenmahl* (Bonn: A. Marcus and E. Weber, 1926). For a more recent two-meal theory, see Xavier Léon-Dufour, *Sharing the Eucharistic Bread* (New York: Paulist, 1987).

The Lukan texts[45] give us a relatively clear idea of what may have been the actual meal practice of one church. Here the Hellenistic Jewish bread before the meal (sometimes with the *kiddush* cup of the festival, as well; see Luke 22:17)[46] and wine "after supper," together with their associated prayers, come to recognizable expression. It is also true that Luke helps us see the growing association of the meal with the Word: perhaps as a symposium conversation in Luke 22:21-38 and Acts 20:11, but also as something that looks a great deal like a word-service, the reading of texts and preaching, in Luke 24:13-27 and Acts 20:7. It is this latter pattern that prevails in the church's ongoing life. But it does so at least in part because Mark and John and Paul have seen the gift of the bread and cup as something larger and more important than the closed-room, invited-guest, stomach-filling event of a supper club. Indeed, the word-service conjoined with the bread and cup rite, found in the second-century church, is a faithful development of the meals of Jesus with which the church began.

Eucharist among the Broken Symbols

For central texts of the New Testament, then, the Eucharist is one of the broken symbols of the Christian faith. It is made out of received cultural material, still full of the power to hold the human experience of the world into such meaning as that culture conceives. But that material is also criticized, reoriented, sifted, seen as insufficient and equivocal.

Faithful Christian meal practice received current cultural symbolism. The Hellenistic meal enacted a community, ordered that community in rank and meaning, ritualized some contact with the gods, used wine to establish relaxation and, in some circles, conversation about values. The Hellenistic Jewish meal transformed that symbolic/cultural tradition to serve biblical faith. The community was seen to be Israel before God, and this sense came to expression in meal prayers. The washing before the meal was thus a rite of ritual purification before entering a holy place. Bread came to ritual importance. Idolatry was resisted. Thus, the libation to the god became the thanksgiving and beseeching addressed to Israel's God over the cup after the meal. The whole meal practice proposed eschatological meaning in a troubled time. Christians, too, used the *deipnon* and the *symposion*, found this gathering to be a regular center of order and mean-

45. Luke 22:14-20; 24:30-31; Acts 20:7-11; but also all the Lukan meals and meal metaphors. See Arthur A. Just, Jr., *The Ongoing Feast* (Collegeville: Liturgical, 1993).
46. *Cf. Didache* 9:2.

ing that created and expressed a community, used bread and wine and ran the risk of rather too much wine, prayed at table, resisted idolatry, and with the Jews, believed that their meals had something to do with the last day of God.

But faithful Christian meal practice also resisted the cultural power of the banquet, in both its Greek and its Hellenistic Jewish forms. At their best, at least according to the counsel of Paul and Mark, Christian meals sought to enact openness and grace and to resist cultic concepts of purity.[47] Christians did this, if in nothing else, by becoming a community of men and women at table, by taking a collection for the hungry, and by understanding that the cup was "for the forgiveness of sins" (Matt. 26:28). They did this even though the evangelical ideal of the open-air meal and the streaming thousands was not possible and the unity of rich and poor at table may not have been frequently realized. They nonetheless built a critique of the closed meal-society into their tradition: the bread and cup was for "the many"; this meal was the assembly of grace. They accentuated the bread and wine while giving the rest of the food away. If at first they used a dining room for their meals, this dining room needed an open door, like the modern Jewish Passover has. Faithful use of the meal finally exploded away from the reclining society and out of the dining room into a remodeled and enlarged room[48] or into the courtyard and then into the basilica. They did all this by proposing that the *eschaton* is Jesus Christ crucified and the assembly that is with him. And so they filled their meal prayers with reference to him, through whom alone, in the power of the Spirit, they could stand before Israel's God. Because of this Christocentric meaning, the Eucharist came to be juxtaposed to the Scriptures read as of the crucified and risen Christ and to be linked especially to Sunday.

Christian practice welcomed, at its heart, the food symbolism found in some instances of the Hellenistic Jewish cultural synthesis—that meal which, by its prayers over bread at the beginning and over wine at the end of the meal, proclaimed the creation faith of Israel. But it rejected the closed circle of pure men as the appropriate community of such praise because it found the deepest gift of the meal to be the very presence of the crucified Christ. In Christ, all people—women, outsiders, Gentiles, children, sinners, a multitude coming from East and West—are being brought before the God

---

47. In addition to texts considered above, see Acts 10:9-16 and Gal. 2:11-21.

48. So the house of the church at Dura Europas had to be remodeled. See L. Michael White, *The Social Origins of Christian Architecture* (Valley Forge, Pa.: Trinity, 1997), 2:124–29.

who made and saves all things. The assembly is already a witness to that bringing.

Besides meal practice, many more cultural symbols were similarly drawn from the Hellenistic Jewish matrix of primitive Christianity in the formation of Christian patterns of worship: observance of the week and of *Pascha,* the shape and postures of prayer, the very idea of assembly, Scripture reading and preaching, roles in leadership, and music, to name some. But our concern here has been to look at the origin of the central liturgical practices of Baptism and Eucharist in order to find in these broken symbols a way to continue to think about the presence of the churches among the cultures of the world.

The juxtaposition of the event of Jesus Christ to old washing rites and old meal practice, at a specific historical and cultural moment, has given to the churches both a center and a method. The center is this: Christian assemblies gather around a washing rite now done in Jesus' name, around the Scriptures read so that the cross and resurrection which brings all people to God may be proclaimed, and around the thanksgiving over the shared bread and cup. These things are not optional if the assembly wishes to be Christian. They are indeed fragments of an old, first-century culture, handed down generation to generation over the ages. But transformed by the gift and promise of Christ, they are also means of grace, the central ways we may hear and encounter the gospel, concrete witnesses in material reality of our historic salvation.

By God's great mercy, these central things are also richly accessible in new cultural situations: they are stories, a water bath, a meal. As long as the central patterns of their use and the critical character of their transformation in Christ are maintained—as long as they are marked by the open assembly, by the accent on grace, by the rejection of purity and insiderhood, by the connection to concern for the poor—they may indeed be done in new ways, appropriate to new cultural situations. The Scriptures will be read in whatever local vernacular is appropriate for foundational stories. Baptism will be exercised in such a way that the local community can recognize that this great washing matters profoundly, is overwhelmingly gracious, and is inextricably bound to Christian preaching and teaching about God. The eucharistic meal will be shared in ways that connect to local meal practice, perhaps with local staple food and festive drink, especially when that practice is richly hospitable. In any case, the central things will be done strongly and clearly.

The recovery of the centrality of these things will enable and encourage the healthy use of cultural gifts in our assemblies. The first agenda item for a renewed interest in worship accessible to local culture will be renewed scriptural knowledge and strong biblical preaching, new clarity about the baptismal *ordo,* and the establishment of the Lord's Supper as the principal service in all of the churches every Sunday. Then there will be a reliable place, a center filled with Christ's transforming gift—rather than, say, western nineteenth-century cultural fragments or the untransformed apotheosis of our own present society—around which all of our cultural gifts may be gathered.

But, at the same time, the juxtaposition of Jesus Christ to the ancient cultural material of washing and meal also yields the church a method for that gathering. New cultural material, entering into the assembly around Christ, coming into the meeting around the central things, will need to be received with the same love and sympathy and the same criticism accorded to that washing which hoped for God's day and to that meal which expressed the faith of Israel. The church's method will need to be marked by welcome and critique, by the open gate and the warning, "Nothing unclean may enter there!" (Rev. 21:27), by yes and no.

Yes and No to Culture

If strong local religious meanings were operative in the original Christian uses of the bath and the meal, they can continue to be welcome in the church in new situations. A quality in music or a kind of instrument that traditionally suggested to local ears a significant connection to the spirits may now be used to sing to God in Christ by the power of the Spirit. Ways to gather, to arrive together in a meeting, or ways to orient the meeting toward the directions of the earth that are locally experienced as enabling an important meeting—these may now be used to communicate that this meeting is before the God who created the earth and gathers us together into unity. Many other locally significant practices—festal garments or the taking off of the shoes, an empty and chairless room or a richly decorated one, dancing, the use of locally significant colors and materials, the observance of local times, local ways of setting a table and local festive vessels—all may be welcome here. Christians will be especially drawn to authentic and strong *symbols,* meaningful objects and practices that intensify and often subvert ordinary experience, calling ordinary experience toward transformation.

Just as we always need local words to be able to speak, we will always need something of local metaphors simply to gather. The transformation of patterns of meeting also belongs to the yes and no of Christian faith. As we have seen, in the early centuries the churches took the form of associations and supper clubs, though they became much more than that. Indeed, their "supper" was finally moved to the morning. In modern North America, the churches are easily seen as "volunteer religious societies," groups that care for essentially private spiritualities, a conception especially available in Enlightenment-engendered democracies with no state church. Here too, the churches must be much more than the culturally available category, although accessibility to the people in the culture may require beginning with this category. This category, of course, must be appropriate to the gospel and not in fundamental opposition to it. The form of a church in a given culture will need to start somewhere between "house" and "open gathering." It cannot be "men's club" or "warrior society" or "sacrificial cult" or "temple."

Christians may have a special interest in seeing that insights that have belonged to minority cultures and have been enshrined in their languages and symbolic systems should not be lost. Dominant cultures, especially those with widespread economic power and most especially that growing international culture called "consumerism," can be blind to or forgetful of the need for harmony between the human community and the surrounding natural world or the urgency of strong local community for the maintenance human well-being. Sometimes the local Christian *yes* to indigenous cultural practices will look like a certain "romanticism" insofar as it maintains practices that are threatened and on the verge of disappearing: *yoiking* among the arctic and sub-arctic Sami, for example, or the use of certain tree leaves to sign cleansing and reconciliation in West Africa, or the use of pollen and sage in prayer on the North American plains, or the use of ancient instrumentation associated with small tribal groups in Asia, or the use of face painting as blessing in Australia. Yet the very rareness and indigenous quality of these practices may enhance their power to suggest the holy to our present time. The otherness of the practices may assist us all in subverting the power of uncriticized dominant cultures. And their age may stir everyone's memory of nearly forgotten values, nearly forgotten symbols. After all, the old Jewish washing from which Christian Baptism was made and the meal-thanksgivings spoken in praise to the *melech ha-olam* amidst the lands of Caesar's rule were also minority symbolizations, resistance symbolizations.

The culture-patterns created around and in churches that were missionary founded and that have gradually mixed local language, local symbolic behavior, some local musical style with received westernisms are also to be respected and honored. These patterns may be experienced as belonging to the beloved history of Christianization, a history which sometimes includes overtones of liberation. In some places—for example, among the *Dalit* in India—people who became Christian had not been included within the purview of classical cultural systems and only found dignity in the received western Christian patterns. On the other hand, fierce adherence to old western patterns may carry something of the sense that the local culture is defeated, lost, failed, especially because of the dominance of western technology and economy in so much of the current world. But the Christian community cannot allow economic and technological victories to determine its values. Christians have long been taught to value that which "the world" despises, beginning with the cross of Jesus Christ. Hidden in "failed" symbols may be values urgently needed in the modern world.

International "youth culture" may present its own special problems. To the extent that rock music and MTV represent a widespread criticism of dominant cultural values, the kind of criticism to which young people of every age are frequently called, the Christian community needs to take it seriously. Such music frequently sings out longings for global peace and for the care of the earth. That does not mean that "rock," with its accent on star performers and community as group-conformity, is immediately useable in Christian assemblies, but something of its symbolizing may come in. Christian musicians who know the gospel and the spirit of the liturgy need to experiment with such welcoming. But the rock music culture is also a colossal and international business, a vast example of consumerism, and its seeming subversion of dominant values may be only a shallow pretense. Young people of our day need to be invited to deeper critique. Sometimes they need to be invited to remember cultural treasures of their own, which both they and the worldwide community need.

In any case, since God created all things, since all things hold together in Christ, since all things have been reconciled to God by the blood of Christ's cross (Col. 1:17, 20), all things are welcome in the Christian meeting. Human cultures are none other than the rich variety of human beings passing on their traditions about how the community lives with each other and with the earth. By the doctrines of creation and redemption, Christians say yes to these cultures.

But they also say no. Christians also confess that we are all together caught in sin, in alienation from God, in the fall. When "all things" are placed at the center, instead of the One in whom they hold together and are reconciled, they fall apart. Festivals, new moons, sabbaths, or the four directions, local leaves, certain ways of gathering or singing, the ways the missionaries did it, the drum or the organ, European hymnody, youth culture, television culture—none of these can be insisted upon (Col. 2:16-22). Nor can local purity laws: "[D]o not handle; do not taste; do not touch." What matters is Christ, who liberates us from all laws pretending to present us to God. What is central is the body of Jesus Christ, in comparison to which all other ritual practices are like shadows. "Nothing unclean may enter there."

So all things are welcome in this assembly, but they are welcome to enter into the economy of "the grace of our Lord Jesus Christ, the love of God, and the communion of the Holy Spirit" (2 Cor. 13:13). They are not welcome to make themselves the center. Cultural practices, which reflect a people's identity, cannot be used so that identity is made the primary matter, excluding all people who do not share that identity. For this reason, national flags or cultural heroes or local rulers may sometimes come to church, but they may neither be made the center of church nor be given a place that reflects a power uncriticized by the all-redeeming cross of Christ. The welcoming of the cultural treasures of the peoples into the praise of the mercy of the Holy Trinity will need to reflect a profound sense of the doctrines of *creation*—that all things are made by God and owe praise to God alone—of *sin*—that all things are fallen and in need of God—and of *justification*—that by the cross, all things have been once and for all reconciled to God. Cultural treasures cannot be used to reintroduce the assembly to legalism or to the necessity of making sacrifice in order to please God. Here the dogmatic tradition of the churches has maintained the critical *no* of the faith, and the liturgical assembly needs to be in dialogue with that tradition.

While cultural symbols that suggest spirit or godliness to local participants will be welcome, they will also need to be criticized. The Christian community is not just interested in *God,* any god, it is interested in the gracious God known by the power of the Spirit in the crucified and risen Christ. Suggestions of "god" or "spirit"—whether they are made by stained glass windows and organ music or by drum beats and dancing—will need to be broken to that purpose.

Furthermore, the welcoming of cultural treasures into the assembly of Christians will always need to show forth the dignity of the baptized people of God, redeemed and beloved ones in Christ who have been made to stand whole in him. No practice can be excused as "my culture" if it trivializes or shames members of the body of Christ or any of the "little ones" for whom Christ died. Women and men, young and old, rich and poor, homosexual and heterosexual, members of dominant and of minority groups, locals and foreigners are to be honored alike here and not to be segregated according to some "cultural" way of dividing people. Patterns of ritual purity are to be rejected. The baptized are never made "unclean" by the bodily functions of God's good creation—including menstruation, that ancient objection to women as candidates for "priesthood"—or by contact in love with those whom a culture may regard as unclean. Circumcision of men and mutilation of women are not to be used as divine requirements, and the latter should be resisted altogether. Cultural practices are not to be made grounds for boasting.

Indeed, *every* culture—including any culture of protest—needs to be subverted in order to come to clarity as an economy of symbols held together by God's mercy in Christ. Such a need for subversion may be hardest to see in our own cultural system or systems. That is why we need each other so badly, in conversation across the *oikoumene,* among fellow Christians asking each other questions and calling each other to faithfulness. Especially is it true that cultures that have long been associated with the church and have left their own gifts imprinted on the "palimpsest" of traditional liturgy may seem impervious to such subversion while profoundly needing it. Western patterns of hierarchy, of androcentrism, of the valuing of wealth, of "genuine community" in intimacy, or of musical and artistic standards are not to be identified, without further criticism, as "Christian." Also from the North and the West, "nothing unclean may enter."

There is no one absolutely pure and godly music, for example, commanded by God or required by the church, by which alone we may sing ourselves into heaven. There are only a variety of human musical traditions, some better suited than others to enable the assembly to gather around the word and the sacraments, suggesting harmony and dialogue, diversity and unity, holiness and accessibility in their singing.

A Method of Juxtaposition

The best way of critically associating the good gifts of our cultures with the purpose of the Christian assembly, then, may well be by a method of juxtaposition. It is essentially such a method that Luther's "greatest and most useful art" proposes to us. What is brought into the assembly must be capable, in clarity and harmony, of serving the gathering of this people as they find the word and the sacraments at the center. What is brought in must accord with this center, enhance it, and serve it, not obscure it. Music must be critically juxtaposed to the Word and to the need to gather around the table in praise. Means of entrance and arrangements in the space of assembly must be juxtaposed to baptismal dignity and to the unity of the shared table. Suggestions of "spirit" must meet that Holy Spirit which enlivens the Scripture when it is read and preached as given to us in the crucified Jesus.

Two means will especially serve this method of juxtaposition. The cultural symbols—music, ceremony, environmental arrangement, gestures, vestments, arts—will come to Christian purpose most clearly as they serve the flow of those very simple ancient *patterns* of Baptism and Eucharist which belong to their origin. We teach; we bathe; we welcome to the table; we remember the poor and we constantly remind each other of these things. We gather; we read and interpret the Scriptures; we pray for all the world; we set the table, also taking a collection for the poor; we give thanks and eat and drink; we are sent in mission. These things may be done slowly or rapidly. They may be done in received ancient patterns or in rich local elaborations or in some combination of the two. But it is these things that the Christian assembly does and that will form the clearest framework for the juxtaposition of cultural materials to the gift of Christ.

The cultural symbols will bring their own strongest gifts to voice when they can be set next to a biblical *Word,* full of the power of God's saving grace, and be used to illuminate the continuing strength of that Word. Thus, in ancient baptismal rituals, a cup of milk and honey given to the newly baptized probably arose from the symbolization of the mystery cults. In the church, however, it became the taste of the promised land (Ex. 3:8), now available to all people in Christ, and the sweet taste of God's grace, the pure milk of the Word of Christ (1 Pet. 2:2-3), through the juxtaposition of the Scripture. The cultural practice was reoriented and the biblical Word was given a strong local resonance.

The examples of this juxtaposition of symbol and Scripture could be multiplied. In current practice among the Gbaya people of Cameroon and the Central African Republic, the leaves of the *soré* tree, long of immense symbolic importance in Gbaya culture, may be used in Christian baptismal, reconciliation, or burial rites, since now Jesus Christ is the true *soré* tree; he is the source of the tree of life yielding leaves for the healing of the nations (Rev. 22:2).[49]

It may be, however, that the actual *use* of the cultural symbol may be too strong, too impervious to breaking for the purpose of the gospel, too evocative of the untamed spirits. That is a pastoral judgment which sometimes must be made. Sometimes the juxtaposition of cultural symbols to Christ and their subversion to grace occur first and perhaps best *verbally*: This *communion* cup is our milk and honey, an old preacher might have said; we need no other. This Word of Jesus Christ in your ears, this water poured out on your body, is our *soré* leaf. "Jesus Christ is our *soré*-cool-thing," say the Gbaya Christians. Such juxtapositions serve to enhance the center while evoking God's great love and mercy for the concretely local.

Such reflections may lead us, finally, to sort out five critical principles for the welcoming of cultural symbolization into the Christian assembly and for the evaluation of the current symbolization utilized there.

1. Is this a strong and real symbol or complex of symbols with a deep social resonance? Does it carry hope and human identity in its use?
2. Does this symbol accord with the Christian doctrines of creation, sin, and justification? Or can it be subverted to serve them?
3. Does this symbol accord with the baptismal dignity of the people of God? Is it capable of being genuinely and graciously communal?
4. Set next to a biblical Word, does this symbol illuminate God's gracious, saving purpose? Is it best exercised as a *verbal* symbol?
5. Can this symbol serve and sing around the central signs of Christ, around word and sacrament used especially on Sunday? With its use, are word and sacrament still central, more clearly and locally central?

One other critical principle listed should probably be listed: *love*. To speak about evaluating our current symbolization or introducing local cultural symbols in worship is inevitably to talk about change. Such change cannot be made while despising the people of the assembly. If this happens, then Christ is dishonored, the spirit of the liturgy is violated, and all is lost.

49. See Thomas Christensen, *An African Tree of Life* (Maryknoll: Orbis, 1990).

Ceremonial change cannot be made a matter of a new law. But listening to the actual cultural circumstances of each local community, listening to the questions raised by the international community of churches, loving and teaching, calling people to the importance of the central things, encouraging local gifts to be celebrated around those central things, juxtaposing all of our ceremonial patterns to the gift of Christ in those things—these are methods that can be used.

In fact, juxtaposition has been the method of the liturgy down through all the ages. Word has been set next to sacrament, teaching to bath, texts to preaching, thanksgiving to eating and drinking, praise to lament, presider to assembly, hospitality to reverence, the local to the universal. When the basilica was adopted as the Christian building, it was most faithfully used as long as it still had something of the domestic about its central table and table prayers. When the winter solstice festivities of the Mediterranean world were adopted as a Christian feast, the observance had a double character: waiting (Advent) and celebrating presence (Christmas). When the Lutheran churches encouraged more singing in church, they did so in at least two ways: chant and chorale. Why? Because "here on earth we can never rightly say the truth of God with just one word, but always only with two words."[50] Because Christ only, not some pure or right ceremonial practice, is our way to God, and that will be clearest if each practice is set next to another and the whole is made to bear witness to him. Because even the bath and the meal have needed to be set next to the Word of Christ, to be transformed by it, in order for us to see how great is God's gift of grace on, in, and under materials drawn from human culture.

We all, in each place, need to receive and continue this history of juxtapositions. The whole cultural palimpsest of the liturgy is ours: Jewish washings and meals, Roman festivals, imperial vestments and buildings, North African and Syrian prayers, European hymns, African and Asian instrumentation, North American and Australian inclusivity. We need, however, to sort its treasures, to make sure the gospel of Jesus Christ is really being heard and known in word and sacrament. And we need to make sure that gospel is being heard *here,* in each local place, saving and transforming the concrete cultures which are none other than the *people* whom God loves and welcomes to mercy. As that transformation continues to occur, new gifts will emerge that have more than local meaning—a song will be sung that

50. A. Köberle, *Rechtfertigung und Heligung,* (Leipzig: 1929), 295. See also Lathrop, *Holy Things,* 121.

will spread to all the churches, a gesture be used that many peoples discover they need in order to more profoundly understand God's good earth and God's great, saving, life-giving love.[51]

In the second century, Justin, our earliest recorder of the great patterns of juxtaposition that are the Christian liturgy, wrote an assertion that must continue to be true: "There is not one single human race, whether barbarians or Greeks or whatever they may be called, nomads or vagrants or herders living in tents, among whom prayers and the giving of thanks are not offered through the name of the crucified Jesus."[52]

Like the city of God, of which it is both anticipation and symbol, the liturgical assembly must have a center and permeable boundaries, the Lamb and the open gates.

51. For a survey of the many kinds of relationships that are necessary between Christian worship and culture—worship as transcultural, contextual, countercultural and cross-cultural—see *The Nairobi Statement,* appendix 2 below.

52. Justin, *Dialogue with Trypho* 117.

9

The Practice of Holiness

The liturgical assemblies we have been considering, assemblies constituted through Baptism and continually renewed through the use of the Scriptures and the Eucharist, take place amid the many peoples and cultures of the world. Present in specific localities, in dialogue with local cultures—with all the ways in which groups are formed, time is kept, location is known, wisdom transmitted, communal survival cultivated— these assemblies nonetheless propose an alternate way to see the world itself, in the light of God's great mercy. One way to speak of that vocation to the alternative vision is to say that the assemblies are called to *holiness*.

This may at first seem an odd use of language. We are more used to applying the word "holy" to persons or communities of persons who seem utterly at odds with cultural norms, not engaged in some dialogue with culture. Through Christian history, at least since the time of Constantine, the holy ones have been regarded as those people who withdraw from the local and ordinary means of passing on culture: the silent monks with their own self-sufficient agricultural economy and their own time keeping; the ascetic women who tried to stop eating altogether; the celibate and childless men and women who devoted themselves to making all of the poor their own family; the German Anabaptist groups in America who restricted their commerce with the dominant "English." Withdrawal from speech, meals, economy, child rearing, and familial identity is indeed a kind of withdrawal from culture. Of course such a withdrawal could never be total: monasteries may accumulate great wealth and become economic forces themselves, in interplay with other local economic forces; communities of the withdrawn may become rich workshops of language and art that exercise wide cultural influence; and the subcultures of separated communities may show, if only in negative image, traits of the very cultures they are rejecting. Such experiments of withdrawal may, of course, become crazy and, from a Christian point of view, too deeply marked by a rejection of the reality of God's beloved world. They may also lose their way, turning the biblical "holiness" as separation for the purposes of God in the world[1] into a new idea: personal freedom from all stain of sin, especially personal sexual sins. Then an ascetic community might concentrate only on the personal behavior of its participants and remain, in all other regards, exactly like its surrounding culture. On the other hand, when these experiments have maintained their original sense of cultural resistance while remaining in dialogue with the "great church," with Christianity as it was often marked by compromise and accommodation with local cultures, they have provided an important sign of the vocation of all Christians to live out of an alternate vision of the world and its exchanges. The "holiness" of monasticism and of communitarian movements of all sorts has stood as a summons to the whole Christian movement to avoid an overwhelming and uncritical cultural accommodation.

But in an older Christian use, the term "holy" is applied to the church itself, to the assembly. The vocation to propose an alternate way of understanding the world comes profoundly, basically, not just to certain "athletes for God," but to the liturgical assembly. Since earliest times, the church throughout the world and the assembly in each local place have been called the "*holy* assembly"[2] or the "assembly of the holy people"[3] or, especially in Pauline writing, "all the holy ones."[4] In spite of the tendency, increasing over time, of Christians to apply such language primarily to heroic exemplars of the faith—the "saints"—or to use it only for the dead, this ancient name for the churches has not died out. The regularly repeated ecumenical creeds invite us to confess our faith in the "holy catholic church." In the eastern churches, the assembly hears again and again, in the presider's invitation to communion, an offer of "holy things to the holy people," a phrase which is rightly understood as a warning but also as a description of the

1. In the Hebrew Scriptures, holiness is basically that which is consistent with God and God's character and, negatively, that which is threatened by "impurity," and therefore separated to God's purpose. David P. Wright, "Holiness," *Anchor Bible Dictionary*, 3:237. One way to discuss the crisis introduced into this picture by some of the prophets and parts of the New Testament is to say that "God's character" invades and subverts that which is "impure."

2. *Martyrdom of Polycarp* inscr. Greek text in Kirsopp Lake, ed., *The Apostolic Fathers* (New York: Harvard University Press, 1959), 2:310. See above, chapter 2.

3. 1 Cor. 14:33.

4. For example, 2 Cor. 13:12; *cf.* Rom. 1:7; 1 Cor. 1:2; 2 Cor. 1:1; Eph. 1:1; Phil. 1:1; 4:21-22; Col. 1:2; 1 Tim. 5:10.

communicants.[5] And modern western celebrations of All Saints Day have frequently come to be observed as festivals of the church, of all the baptized, including the local and living community. In Slovakia and in Slavic communities elsewhere, Christians since the seventeenth century have made remarkable, ecumenical use of an extensive collection of hymns, assembled by the Lutheran pastor Jiri Tranovsky and called the *Cithara Sanctorum,* the "cithara of the saints," the "harp of the holy people."[6]

It would be an appropriate extension of Pauline language to call every collection of hymnody the "harp of the holy people," when the hymnal is used to give voice to the assembly and is marked by the many mutual gifts of the assemblies to each other through the ages. Indeed, with Paul, every Christian assembly might be addressed as those called to be "the saints in this place." But if "holiness" involves being set apart for the purposes of God, how is the assembly set apart? And for what purpose?

Holy People

By our reckoning, this ancient name—"the holy people"—is a sort of short-hand for "God's assembly," as that idea is known in the Hebrew Scriptures. The name functions as a typological synecdoche for the whole biblical account of assemblies.[7] As a figure of speech moving through time, the name evokes and stands for the story of God gathering the people of the exodus at Sinai and calling them "a holy nation," God's own "treasured possession out of all the peoples," a people who are set aside—"holy"—in their hearing of God's voice and who live in that holiness by keeping the requirements of the covenant (Ex. 19:5-6). "Holy people," "holy church," "all the saints"—such names then apply that story in faith to the present assembly gathered in the name of Christ, borrowing the language of the

---

5. On the eastern text as both invitation and warning, see Gordon W. Lathrop, *Holy Things: A Liturgical Theology* (Minneapolis: Fortress, 1993), 116–38.

6. Through difficult times, the Bible and the *Cithara Sanctorum,* sometimes called *Tranoscius* after its collector and principal author, functioned as the two pillars of Christian identity for many western Slavs. See A. A. Skodacek, *Slovak Lutheran Liturgy* (1968), 109–17.

7. A *synecdoche* is a figure of speech that uses a part for the whole. Here the part is a name found in a narrative and used to evoke the whole narrative, one name for the "assembly" used to evoke all its meaning. A "typology" can be most usefully understood as a figure of speech that moves through time, so that what happened at the exodus—or what is promised for the end—are applied to the times of Jesus and the gathering around him and, by extension, to the present. See Northrop Frye, *The Great Code: The Bible and Literature* (New York: Harcourt Brace Jovanovich, 1982), 80.

story to speak of Christian eschatology and make sense of the Christian meeting. According to the Christian faith, the God who acted in the exodus, forming a holy nation of witnesses and priests for the world, also promised to assemble all nations at the end of time to hear the life-giving Word. The faith says that this promised assembly of the nations is beginning to occur now in every local Christian meeting and in the great "assembly" which the whole Christian movement throughout the world is becoming. The word "holy" can be applied to Christians, primarily, as they are members of this assembly. So 1 Peter asserts to churches in first-century Asia Minor: "you are a chosen race, a royal priesthood, a holy nation, God's own people, in order that you may proclaim the mighty acts of the one who called you out of darkness into the marvelous light of God" (2:9).

But the same New Testament letter says another thing, deepening the sense of the journey into light: "Once you were not a people, but now you are God's people; once you had not received mercy, but now you have received mercy" (2:10). A Christian assembly is the "holy people" only in the sense that the prophet of the return from the exile used the term: a people that might have been called "no people at all" or "a forsaken people" shall now be called "The Holy People" (Isa. 62:12). The Isaian sense is even further intensified, for the Christian community is made up of people from many different nations, of sinners and outsiders, with no birth claim to the holy inheritance of the Word. They are "called to be the holy ones" (1 Cor. 1:2) with the same "call" that makes them part of the *ekklesia*. Not many of them are wise, powerful, or noble "by human standards" (1 Cor. 1:26). Or at least they easily understand themselves as one with all unholy, unwise, unclean people of world, for whom Christ alone is both wisdom and sanctification, the "holy-making" mercy of God (1 Cor. 1:2, 30). The assembly, as we have seen, can be imaged as the naked ones enfolded by the cloak and pulled from hell, the women on the way to the tomb, the Laodiceans with hands out for garments and salve, a representative group speaking for the needy nations of the world yet rejoicing in the astonishing presence of bread and forgiveness.[8]

The practice of Christian holiness, then, has a two-fold character. It involves the continuous reconstitution of an assembly in communion with all the other assemblies of Christians, a continual rediscovery of the force of the biblical name—"the holy assembly of God"—as applied to this gathering, and a constant extension into daily life of practices learned in the focal

8. See above, chapter 3, "Images of the Church."

practice of the gathering. It involves seriousness about the meeting and what flows from the meeting.

At the same time, the Christian practice of holiness must always involve the subversion of all religious ideas of holiness. If Jesus Christ is our holiness, then holiness is no longer separation and ritual purity and perfect observance. In Christ, holiness is connection with others. It is the unclean cross and life through death and welcome to the outsiders and transformative mercy for the world.[9] If the meeting constitutes just *us* as the insiders, then Christian holiness involves the subversion of the meeting. It involves the transformation of the meeting to be much more than our social conventions of gathering, from any culture, could ever make it. The practice of holiness involves the constant work on the open door, both that all others may come in and that what is seen in the liturgy may flow out. The practice of holiness is the discovery of God's gift to all of us, together.

This assembly, constituted by God's holy voice going out to the nations, discovers that the central content of that voice is the word of God's mercy to the ungodly in Christ. This holy gathering is consecrated by that washing in the cross which does away with ritual purity. This convocation of the holy ones eats that meal which is for the hungry, turning its participants toward their neighbors. So the Christian people do borrow the language of the Sinai assembly, hearing God say: "You have seen . . . how I bore you on eagles' wings and brought you to myself" (Ex. 19:4). Only they understand the "eagles wings" to be the Holy Spirit enlivening the meeting around the word and sacrament of Jesus Christ. And they understand the astonishing intimacy with God, God's powerful *election* of this people, to be an election not to go away with God but to practice this assembly in each place and bear witness and act in loving service in the world.

Such dialectic and reversal are basic characteristics of all Christian liturgy and thus of a liturgical ecclesiology. "Holy things for the holy people," sings out the presider, inviting and warning at the Eucharist, affirming the centrality and the holiness of both the proffered food and the surrounding assembly. "Only one is holy," counters the voice of the assembly, the people evidencing the truth about themselves and the truth of any symbol apart from the mercy of God and yet affirming, because of that mercy, both food and assembly as the very locus of God's presence.

In the oldest form of that assembly response, known from the fourth-century work of Cyril of Jerusalem, the people sing, "One is holy, one is

---

9. For more on "holiness" in the liturgy, see Lathrop, *Holy Things*, 132–38.

Lord, Jesus Christ." The christological center of the liturgy, with its transformed sense of what holiness has become in the cross and resurrection of Jesus, stands forth in clarity. One encounters the presence of Jesus Christ in the word and sacrament at the heart of the meeting and this presence transforms the meeting, pulling its participants to be where Jesus Christ is, with the world in its need. In a later form of the response, known from the much developed Alexandrine Liturgy of St. Mark, but known also already in the early fifth-century work of Theodore of Mopsuestia, the voice of the people sings back: "Only one the holy Father, only one the holy Son, only one the holy Spirit, in the unity of the Holy Spirit." Here the people develop the christological meaning to its trinitarian and ecclesiological implications: the merciful God wraps this needy and sinful assembly, gathered in the very unity of the Holy Spirit, with the life of the triune God. This meeting can only be *ekklesia* as it is in the unity of the Holy Spirit. To be at the heart of the meeting, enlivened by the Spirit, is to be in Jesus Christ and so to be before the Father with all of needy humanity. There are not three "holies" but one Holy One, and yet that Holiness is a flowing life, given here to eat and drink, given here to be sent into the world.

Assembly, like all the central materials of Christian worship, like Baptism and Eucharist themselves, involves the transformation of cultural goods. We have ways to meet, ways to be with each other, ways to enter into such a meeting, and these ways may differ from culture to culture. There are many sorts of meetings in the world, many assemblies,[10] and we need to have them. Probably, we need to have them in ways that are more healthy, productive, beautiful, and communicative—even "sacred" or "holy"—than we usually achieve. Christianity receives our meetings. If anything, Christianity intensifies them, reawakening our need for healthy and beautiful human assembly. Have we forgotten, in the age of "bowling alone" and electronic, "virtual community," the exhilarating possibilities of festival, town meeting, parade, pilgrimage, fair, corroboree? Church may still remember something of that communal meaning, larger than the intimate family. And yet, by the juxtaposition of word and sacraments to our manner of meeting, by the placement of these things at the center of our assembly, the meeting itself may be transformed. Its boundaries are to be broken down, its internal relationships changed, its doors opened, its connections to the world and to other assemblies throughout the world enabled. The meeting

10. As Martin Luther wrote, "*ecclesia* means 'a people,'" quite simply, and "the Turks too are *ecclesia*, 'a people.'" *Luther's Works* (Philadelphia: Fortress, 1966), 41:145; *D. Martin Luthers Werke* (Weimar: 1914), 50:625.

is to become a paradigm of God's intention for the world, a sign of God's own holiness.

So here are the practices of holiness: Establish the meeting. Make it memorable, intense. Strengthen the leadership. Heighten the sense of participation. Exercise its symbols beautifully. Enliven the communal voice. Yet, because of Jesus Christ at the heart of this meeting, because of the enfolding of the assembly in the flowing life of the triune God, discover how the inevitable sense of boundary such a meeting always creates—the "we-ness" of the participating group—is subverted. Rejoice and proclaim that the symbols this meeting celebrates intensely are symbols that turn the meeting inside out, uniting us with those who surround us, not dividing us. Work on the openness of the door. Send word and meal and representatives of the assembly to the absent. The "we" here is the "we" of all the dying and needy earth. And the Word of God, the only true holiness in the heart of this meeting—the alternative "vision" of the world that is here proclaimed, sung, prayed, washed over bodies, and eaten and drunk—is giving life to us all together. The Word of God comes to this meeting, calling it "holy assembly." And the Word does what it says, making the meeting be that assembly indeed.

This double method, this *yes, no, yes*,[11] is the pattern of all liturgy. It is implied in the juxtapositions of the *ordo*, practiced in the transformation of baths and meals to be Baptism and Eucharist, expressed in the biblical pairing of Leviticus and Amos, rooted in the biblical chains of new images that critically restate old ones.[12] The basic process involved in the localization of liturgy reflects this same method, as local symbols, too, are taken seriously, yet broken to the purposes of the gospel. And a liturgical ecclesiology builds on the same basis, as our meeting is called by a biblical name, given a new center and an open door, and continually broken open to the existence of other such meetings. In liturgical practice, *holy things* and *holy people* are set next to the basic Christological and trinitarian assertion of Christian faith, *only one is holy*. The holiness of both things and people is thus radically questioned—if either things or people would subsist on their own—and yet radically established as symbols of holiness for the world.

But why would any local community want to have such a meeting? Are not our local cultural symbols adequate to reinforce in us and pass on to our children what we need to live in a place? Do we really wish for any of our

---

11. Gail Ramshaw, *Christ in Sacred Speech* (Philadelphia: Fortress, 1986), 23–26.
12. See Lathrop, *Holy Things*, 15–36, 79–82, 162–64.

symbols to be relativized or "broken?" For example, Christians eat many other meals, bathe in many other waters, tell many other stories, go to many other meetings. Why do they need Eucharist and Baptism, Scripture and church?

In fact, however, our many cultural symbols are ambiguous in value. Certainly, we cannot live without the most basic of these symbols: words to communicate; patterns of economy and signals of identity; markers to enable work sharing, food distribution, and child rearing; myths and artifacts recording religious interactions. The symbols themselves are living records, sometimes of excruciating beauty, of the interaction between our people and the local earth. One can see this beauty concretely in the food set out for a festival, in any culture.

But beauty is not the only characteristic of our cultural practices. Our cultural symbols are also frequently inadequate to new situations, incapable of welcoming other people, unable to express a relationship to all the earth, and even murderous to their transgressors. Not every person is welcome to that beautiful festival food. The unclean, the outsiders, the women, the ritual transgressors frequently are not. And the ritual of a festival is often scripted in such a way that it obscures the forgotten ones or makes them willing participants in their own demise. In the Hindu festival of lights, for example, the gods that are again ritually defeated are the ancient gods of the Dalit, the now casteless and excluded people of society.[13] In the myth of the American Thanksgiving, the native peoples have become peaceful suppliers of food to the newly arrived Europeans. Both practices obscure the histories of exclusion, death, and loss that have marked the interactions of the dominant culture with an aboriginal people. What is more, in order to live in new global economies, with new global connections, we have sometimes supplanted old, primary, communal cultures with partially elaborated global ones, themselves little able to give us a symbol system capable of holding human life in an orientation toward meaning. The whole world seems to have lined up at McDonald's.

The point of liturgical life is not to urge Christians to eat and drink only the Eucharist. Unlike the medieval women who sought to limit their diet in such a way, proposing a radical holiness of withdrawal and contradiction to the regnant economy,[14] the celebration of the liturgy instead pro-

---

13. Marcus Felde, "The Church Year in the Context of Hindu Culture," in S. Anita Stauffer, ed., *Worship and Culture in Dialogue* (Geneva: Lutheran World Federation, 1994), 210–12.

14. Carolyn Walker Bynum, *Holy Feast and Holy Fast: The Religious Significance of Food to Medieval Women* (Berkeley and Los Angeles: University of California Press, 1987).

poses a holiness in dialogue with both daily meals and cultural festivals. A healthy liturgical practice will strengthen the meal of the assembly, making it beautiful, participative, honest about its sources, and gracious, frequently using specifically treasured cultural idioms to do so and thereby casting a light over all our meals, inviting us to see them as daily occasions for such thanksgiving, such grace, such honesty, such focussed practice. This can be a simple thing: western Christians who have long since ceased to use candles and beautiful linens at their festive tables can still encounter them in the Eucharist. They may well reconsider using the candles and textiles—the focussed table—at home, reclaiming the idiom of their own culture. It can be a more complex matter: many modern Christians, people of East and West, who have forgotten where their food comes from—have forgotten the effort and the death involved in its harvesting—and who have started to take much of their food alone, on the run, can still encounter an honesty about the source of food and a presence of the meal-keeping community in the Eucharist. They may be invited to think again about sources, about the importance of the common preparation of food, about the meal-community at home. A strong eucharistic practice needs to flow into a strong love of meals and strong truth about their practice.

At the same time, because of Jesus Christ the Eucharist is only the fragment of a meal, the beginning and ending of a meal, with the rest of the food given away. It is a meal that constantly presses for the inclusion of the least one, the outsider. It is a meal that cries out for signs of connection to the other assemblies. In the light of the Eucharist, our cultural meals may also become places of hospitality, places to remember connections. The home of the western Christian, for example, may become again not only the place of the lit candle, but also, at least in deep intention, of the open door. In any case, Christians will find the Eucharist calling all of our cultural methods of food distribution to justice, to honor and care for the sources of our food, and to a lively sense that food is given by God that all may eat and live.

The double method of the liturgy, the establishing of the strong symbol and the breaking of that symbol in the gospel of Jesus Christ, can be proposed as a method for sorting and reasserting the symbols of our daily life as well. The very Christian meeting itself, its rhythms and patterns, its use of the biblical Word, its practice and remembrance of Baptism, can thus engage in dialogue with our other assemblies, the other narratives and fictions we live by, our other means of identity. We ought not, thereby, seek a sort of imperialism of the liturgical assembly. It is not that all of our cultural symbols must come into the meeting or undergo Christianization or become bearers of the gospel. But the dialectic of the liturgy can illuminate the many ways in which we live by symbolic practices.

Culture's Times

Take, for example, our time keeping. In an earth of global connections, we have come to realize the ways in which the measurement of time itself reflects local culture, local human interaction with the conditions of the land, and local symbolization. Of course, time keeping originates with real events outside of human culture: the revolution of the earth around its own axis, the orbit of the earth around the sun, the orbit of the moon around the earth, and the response of tides, weather, vegetation, and animal life to these changes. But human beings are part of that animal life, and they have interacted with these recurring events. So the beginning of the day—at evening, at midnight, at dawn—has been culturally determined, with differing results. The number, names, uses, and many meanings of the seasons depend upon local cultural interaction with the local conditions of the earth. And the numbers of the years and the number of years in an age have also been variously calculated. Human beings in ancient Mesopotamia noticed the phases of the moon and counted four, dividing the more or less approximate twenty-eight-day lunar cycle thereby into four periods of seven days each. These same ancient sky-watchers then noticed the correspondence between this number, *seven,* and the number of visible wanderers in the sky, the *planeta*—the sun, the moon, and the five visible planets. So ancient Mesopotamian culture created the week, and Roman (and then Romano-German) culture embellished it, regarding each of the days as under the influence of one of the planets, understood as one of the gods known in the communal stories: Sun-day, Moon-day, Saturn-day, but also Tiu's-day, Woden's-day, Thor's-day, Freia's-day. Along the way, Jewish culture made the seven days into a symbolic reference to the God of Israel: the old Mesopotamian "unlucky day," unwise for any action, being radically reinterpreted into a rest day in memorial of the rest of God at the creation or the rest of the slaves at their exodus from slavery. A similar interaction of observation and narration resulted in the months: the more or less twelve cycles of the moon found in a year were seen to correspond to twelve patterns of stars found in the sky. And surrounding this time keeping, there have been larger cultural tales of origin and of catastrophe: calculations of the beginning of all things and expectations of an end or, at least, a massive change, perhaps at the "millennium," itself determined by a culturally determined count.

Although we probably do not observe the old Jewish new moon, many of us may still occasionally consult the ancient astronomy, now become a modern superstition, by looking up a current horoscope in the newspaper. But there are different horoscopes, based on different patterns of stars discovered in the sky—say, the *Chinese* zodiac—and different cultural narrations. There are different sets of numbers used to calculate the number of hours in a day or years in an age. And there are different ways to speak of the surrounding, mythic time and its crises and changes. The peoples of Mesoamerica, believing in a catastrophic succession of worlds, expected also the end of our world, the "fifth sun." Aboriginal people of Australia understand all things as arising out of the Dreamtime and falling back into it. The landscape itself is marked out with lines and features that originated in the Dreamtime and that still enact the intersection of our days with that dreaming, so that, for the indigenous Australian, it remains difficult to separate "time" and "place."

But in a deep sense, that inseparability of time and place is true for us all. The diverse systems of time are all rich in the meanings of place. In one way or another, they all represent the interplay between our own, human, bodily time—sleeping and waking through the day, experiencing the menstrual cycle in a time period roughly parallel to the cycle of the moon, changing our activities through the year, being born, growing and dying through a series of years—and the conditions of the land in which we live, the nature of the seasons. The time systems all carry for us, as we live *here,* cultural patterns of work and rest as well as occasions for communal expectation, festivity, remembrance, mourning, and hope. They are astonishing, beautiful, cultural creations, encapsulating and expressing a particular human history in relationship to particular places on the earth, in the earth's particular place around the sun, in this galaxy, in this universe.

Of course, our time systems also have their problems. Are the horoscopes right? Are my days determined by my birth date? Is the "child that is born on the Sabbath day" always "bonny and bright and good and gay?" And what if I am sad when the time of the community or the time of the local earth calls for joy? Is the April of the northern hemisphere, for that reason, "the cruellest month?" Or, given the massive, nostalgic pressure for a "perfect Christmas," is December more cruel yet? And what of January's long sense of cold disappointment? But the problems are not simply present in northern and western psychological disharmonies. What if I refuse or cannot join the observance, in whatever culture it takes place? What if I do not have enough money or cannot meet the standards of ritual purity? What if, in the terms of Hasidic Judaism, I have lost the sacred place in the forest, important for any ritual in a time of threat to the people?[15] Or what if, in the terms of the Aboriginal, I do not know the place of my dreaming, the very source of my identity and my insertion into the time of my people? Am I then to be shunned, excluded? Is no festival possible for me? And as a yet deeper and communal question, has the festival calendar revealed or obscured the real events of history in the community?

Adding to these problems is yet another complexity. To a very large degree, the system of time keeping that originated in the Mesopotamian and then the Mediterranean cultures and was further elaborated in Europe has spread throughout the world. The spread has been the result, of course, of a combination of navigation, colonization, trade, and cultural exchange. The dominance of this system has been enhanced by the current need for global communication. In any case, now it is with Japanese-made watches that we calculate our variations from Greenwich time. Other local systems are not gone, they are simply quieter, having withdrawn into local festival observance or folk custom. It is certainly true, for example, that the observance in the temperate zones of the southern hemisphere of festivals that originated in the northern hemisphere out of longing for the light in the dark time, the winter solstice time, or the observance of twenty-four-hour days in the long Arctic or Antarctic night—such transplanted observances can begin to feel like travel in an isolated spaceship, with the "days" calculated according to another place, having little or no reference to the place where we actually are.

Further, the classic western system of time-keeping is itself in trouble. Although this system involved a serious observance of local times of dark and local times of light and a serious awareness of the cycles of the heavenly bodies around us, our electric lights have pushed back the importance of this observance, and we do not have much time to look at the sky. We do not have much *time*, we say, partly because of the commodification of time. "Time is money" or "my time is valuable"; such comments reveal the most serious of our current time-keeping systems, the system of consumer sales in which the past signifies outmoded goods, the future represents "growth opportunities," and "our sales agents are available twenty-four hours a day."

15. Elie Wiesel, *Souls on Fire: Portraits and Legends of Hasidic Masters* (New York: Random House, 1972), 167–68.

There are also related sub-systems of time. In the "leisure time" that is, for many people, the only respite from the time-money equation, the primary times we know may be the times of our favorite programs on television. Or for the adventurous young among us, respite may be found in the relative timelessness of the Internet, "real time" being a "window" through which we are in a simultaneous exchange of messages with others known only by their pseudonyms. The old ritual year is still around, but its festivals have very largely become occasions for individual and familial withdrawal from communal life, for the celebration of private relationships, not public and communal engagement with the surrounding conditions of the earth.[16]

The technologies present underneath all of these developments have remarkable possibilities for good, but their effect upon our experience of time may well remain insufficiently calculated. On the one hand, freedom from the natural cycles of time can be a freedom for life, an end of enslavement to drudgery, fear, and constant need to labor for survival. On the other hand, the general equation of time and money and its other side, the time of leisure, carry along a whole number of time casualties or people with "time on their hands": the unemployed, the retired, the aged, the outmoded, the uninsured, the television addicted, the people with massive, even unconquerable debt, to which they try to respond with time-payments.[17]

The Time of the Assembly—Holy Time

Set in the midst of all of these experiences of time, the Christian liturgy has two major things to do. It must initiate a strong recovery of the symbolization of time, inviting us to see again the ways in which human beings know something of who they are and where they are by knowing what time it is. And characteristically, paradoxically, it must subvert the very symbolization of time which it so strongly supports, doing so by the proclamation and celebration of God's time.

In the first of these tasks, the liturgy has powerful tools. The assembly meets once a week and so underscores the rhythm of the week, with the week's echo of the phases of the moon and the other *planeta* around us. The assembly's Sunday gathering for Eucharist then may be surrounded by other, smaller gatherings for daily morning and evening prayer, marking

16. Ronald Hutton, *The Stations of the Sun: A History of the Ritual Year in Britain* (Oxford: Oxford University Press, 1997), 426–27.

17. Marianne Sawicki, "How Can Christian Worship Be Contemporary?" in G. Lathrop, ed., *What Is "Contemporary" Worship?* (Minneapolis: Augsburg Fortress, 1995), 23–25.

with praise and prayer the cardinal points of the sun as it travels through each day. Or individual members of the assembly may adopt this daily practice, in one or another form, as an echo of their participation in the Christian assembly's interest in time. In any case, Sunday meeting and daily prayer make basic reference to the root categories of time.

The gatherings of the assembly do yet more: they move through the year, taking the seasons seriously in the assembly's own programs of symbolization. In the northern hemisphere, on the background of the dating of Passover, Easter's celebration is set out in the light of the springtime sun—just after the vernal equinox—and in the light of the full moon—the "paschal moon"—like some ancient image of the cross with both sun and moon over either arm. Then the Christmas cycle—*Pascha* in winter—is anchored in the period of the winter solstice. Other festivals and observances fall into place, some more obscurely, but all of them keeping the time: Advent as a quiet, truth-telling alternative to the world's Saturnalia of December; the seven days of the O-Antiphons counting through the actual time of the present winter solstice; the twelve days of Christmas uniting East and West in a full-hearted mid-winter rejoicing; the forty days of Lent, *lente,* as a springtime of the church amid the lengthening of days; the Annunciation at the spring equinox, proclaiming the most astonishing flowering; the fifty days of *Pascha* as a kind of Sunday to the year; the nativity of John the Baptist at mid-summer, remembering the brightest of the world's lights which, nonetheless, must decrease as Jesus Christ increases (John 3:30); All Saints and the remembrance of eschatology in the time of harvest and the time of the dying vegetation. All of these observances need to be seen as ways of preaching the gospel into a concrete time of year in a concrete area of the earth. They are therefore, secondarily, ways in which we know what time it is.

But there is even more. The biblical stories that the assembly reads and sings and the hope for the future that the assembly awakens underscore the awareness that a *past* and a *future* surround our own present day. The churches at Lohja and Hattula in Finland surround the assembly with a history and position the assembly toward the east, as toward a hoped for future.[18] The liturgical narratives from the Bible know how to take particular historical events, the exodus, for example, and the crucifixion of Christ, and invest them with mythological force, since the faith says that these particular events embrace all times.[19] These practices of the liturgy also have

18. See above, chapter 3.
19. On this practice of the liturgy, see Lathrop, *Holy Things,* 16–20, 27–28.

pedagogical force in our lives, showing us the character of keeping time. Human beings do not just live through time's cycles. They also live, with beginnings and endings, on time's line. Like trees, they know cycles, rings of growth; they also know seeds and seedlings and then the tree itself and then felling, falling, rotting. They also know powerful single moments that seem to embrace and let in all times. Past and future; remembrance and hope; days and nights; weeks, months, seasons and years—all of these have a deep, basic integrity in the practice of the assembly when that assembly makes use of its own great heritage.

It is not that the assembly should be our only clock. Nor could it be. It is certainly true that some Christians find refreshment in a temporary retreat to a monastic life regulated by the communal bell and the communal hours of prayer and work, the healthy monastery being a kind of intense, countercultural realization of the assembly's vocation. And it is true that, far from being old-fashioned and romantic, the time of the liturgical year is strikingly realistic to the actual experience of the year—more so, for example, than the year invented by the greeting-card marketers. But we all, rightly, have many other clocks. Other communities to which we belong, besides the assembly, have their own hours of work and rest and festivity: our familial daily schedule, our company work week, our village organization of hunting or harvesting, our school calendar, our neighborhood or tribal or national festivals, our observances and anniversaries with those who are our most beloved ones, our participation in familial rites of passage, and our own personal rhythms of time. These are the true bearers of culture, the ways we gather food and eat and live. These are the ways we reinforce in ourselves and pass on to our children the wisdom needed for living in the particular place that we inhabit.

But the observance of the assembly, its strengthened use of the symbols of time, can cast a light on all of our cultural time keeping. Especially amid the temptations and the amnesia of consumer time, the assembly can invite us to notice again the actual place where we live, to attend to its seasons, its relationship to terrestrial and to celestial events, and by that particular attention to also turn a new awareness toward the good earth itself. Our cultures all have means to exercise this attention, though many of these means have been neglected. The practice of the assembly, its observance of time for its own purposes, can encourage in us their recovery. The assembly can also invite us again to take all of history with great seriousness, on the model of the biblical history which is most narrated in the liturgy, and it can urge us to seek continually revisionist ways to tell more of the truth of history in our cultures. It can also urge us to pay attention to those personal moments of encounter with each other and with the earth that seem to let in all times, embracing us in meaning. And the assembly can help us recover a deep gratitude to those persons—nurses and fire brigades and pilots and radio operators and more—who, for the sake of the community, live against the cycles of time. By the strength of its time-keeping symbols, the assembly can also help us to see how much delusion may be present in the virtual time of electronic entertainment, how much we need to keep time together with a larger circle of other people than those who may join us around the screen of a television monitor. The focussed time practices of the Christian liturgical assembly might encourage its participants, in each cultural setting, to see the dawn again, to realize where we live, to treasure the festival, to know communal rhythms of joy and sorrow, to pay attention to history.

In order to do this well, however, the liturgical assembly needs to keep time in ways that accord with the city or the land that it inhabits, not just with the Mediterranean places of Christian origins.[20] In fact, the assembly needs to know the local time in order to do its own work, its standing on the good earth, before the face of the God who made all the timekeepers— the sun, the moon, the rotating earth, and the people upon the earth. The local culture of time needs to come along with those people who know that culture, as they come into the assembly, and it needs to come there in the ways that all cultural materials come, joining the palimpsest of cultures that makes up the Christian liturgy. Of course, in the giving and sending of gifts between assemblies, the old patterns of keeping Sunday, observing the *Pascha,* and marking the day ought not be lost. Sunday assembly and morning and evening prayer have more-or-less universal applicability. Even in the southern hemisphere, the date of Easter, about which Christians now have new hope of finding agreement, may also be kept at the common time, for the sake of Christian unity and because of the festival's historic reference to events that occurred in Jerusalem at Passover time in the first century. In the tropics and in the southern hemisphere, Christmas and its cycle might be kept in the common place for similar reasons, although the historical anchor

---

20. This insight makes clear not just the ongoing need for liturgical inculturation but also the need to avoid the widespread medieval custom of "anticipating" liturgical observances, as if the liturgy were an unanchored, unearthly law to be kept. In the West, for example, clerics—not the whole assembly—were keeping the Easter Vigil on Saturday *morning* until the middle of the twentieth century. The liturgical movement has been partly about the recovery of the integrity of time symbolization.

of the feast is much more dubious and its direct pastoral response to the natural cycle much more important than is the paschal response to springtime. In the observance of these festivals juxtaposed to different seasons from those of their origin, however, the festivals themselves will be enriched if the local community does not forget what time it is locally. The whole Christian church, north and south, can be helped to see a new thing as, for example, the resurrection is proclaimed in the autumn and the incarnation celebrated in high summer. New hymns, new liturgical texts, new practices arising from these juxtapositions may also spread north, assisting a globalized church to know the gospel more clearly.

But Christians of the tropics and of the southern hemisphere also need to do another new thing. They might be attentive to ways in which the assemblies in those places can proclaim the gospel in relationship to observances of the wet season and the dry, in relationship to summer beginning in December and winter beginning in June. Other agricultural festivals, other "new year's days" from other time systems, other festivals of nomadic peoples born out of a more liquid and local experience of time await the same pastoral wisdom, the same variety of response that marked the Christian attention to the Mediterranean winter solstice. If new Christian festivals thereby arise, they will be born naturally, as all authentic symbols come into being, not designed by committees. They may also spread north, in the mutual gift-giving of the assemblies, as they articulate an insight into the gospel we newly learn to be indispensable. But we need to begin by saying that the strong use of local time symbols is one of the practices of the liturgy.

The other major time practice of the Christian assembly is the subversion of our time symbols. The purpose of the assembly, after all, is not to be a custodian of time systems, but to proclaim and celebrate the life-giving Word of God. It does this in ways that take seriously the time of the world, the time of God's creation. But the assembly engages in this proclamation also as a word to all the time-casualties: to those excluded from festivals, those not able to put in their time at work, not able to find the sacred place in the time of need, but also to those at the limits of their time, to the dying and the dead. Because we all are at the limits of our time, this Word of God is for us all.

In the subversion of time the assembly also has powerful tools. All of the great Christian celebrations are *appointed* to begin just a little late, a little bit off time. The assembly meets after the week is over, after the Sabbath, after the exact day of the equinox and the exact paschal moon, after the solstice. It does so in order to gather around Jesus Christ risen, the one who carries humanity beyond the possibilities of time. And it calls its primary meeting after a day that cannot be, yet *is* because of the resurrection, the "eighth day."[21] The intention of this meeting is not so much to mark the week as to proclaim the resurrection, that event of the first day of the week, to all of our cycles of weeks. At each of the turnings of time—the turn of the week, the evening and morning of the day, the turn of the seasons—the classic Christian liturgy sets out signs, great and small, of the transfiguration of time in the Risen One, and juxtaposes those signs to the actual time. So the Eucharist, the limited meal of unlimited life, marks every Sunday and thus every week. So the light of the risen Christ and the Magnificat, the song of the reversals God works for the overwhelmed and defeated ones, marks every evening, every declining day. So biblical texts are appointed to unfold the hope that lies in any calendar observance: the summer sun is made to point to the greater Light coming into the world, to which John only bears witness; the first day of spring is made to hear the word of the angel's Annunciation. The rolling year will not bring us, by sheer chronology, into these promises. Nonetheless, the promises are given to us in our times. Says the liturgy by its practices of subversion: the mercy of God in Jesus Christ proclaimed in the unity of the Holy Spirit is the sun that does not go down, the creator and holder of the stars, the deepest night of rest, the safe and healing dark, the brightest yet unburning day, the lover of the earth and the life-giver, the festival for the unclean and those who did not prepare, the place in the forest itself, the deepest place of our dreaming.

The point of such practices is subversion of the laws of time, transfiguration of the experience of time. The point is not to take us out of here, away from the times and the limits, the very world in which we live. Nor is it to give us some mastery over time, as if we could use time for our own purposes.[22] Rather, the liturgy—its bath, its Scripture reading and preaching, its Holy Supper, set amid and juxtaposed to all of our times—proclaims the Risen One who holds in his hand all seven of the stars which the world imagines as rulers of the days (Rev. 1:16). The liturgy should welcome the time-hurt ones into the center of all time, where the Holy Spirit is poured out upon the assembly so that it may be gathered into Christ and so be brought, like God's own holy ones, before the Ancient of Days (Dan. 7:13, 18), who made and embraces and transcends all time. In the preaching of

21. See Lathrop, *Holy Things,* 36–43, 68–79.
22. On the transfiguration of time and the refusal of "mastery" in the focal practices of the church, see Richard R. Gaillardetz, "Doing Liturgy in a Technological Age," *Worship* 71 (1997):446.

the liturgy and in its sacraments, the assembly should hear and know the one who stands in all the holy history that surrounds them, as at Lohja and Hattula, and pulls them now out of death and beyond the rule of calendars, of "special days, and months, and seasons, and years" (Gal. 4:10), and yet leaves them right here. Such is the nature of eschatology, as Christian faith knows it in the resurrection of Jesus Christ: the transfiguration of the limits of our time, not their removal; life in the Risen One now, beyond the fear of death, beyond its determinative rule in our days; utter freedom, though all the constraints are still around us; an alternative vision of the world. Through and in the presence of the Holy Trinity, because of the resurrection, the Christian liturgy sings, to all who will hear, a song like that which W. H. Auden expected from the poet:

> Follow, poet, follow right
> To the bottom of the night,
> With your unconstraining voice
> Still persuade us to rejoice;
>
> With the farming of a verse
> Make a vineyard of the curse,
> Sing of human unsuccess
> In a rapture of distress;
>
> In the deserts of the heart
> Let the healing fountain start,
> In the prison of his days
> Teach the free man how to praise.[23]

Christians who participate in this assembly practice of the subversion of time will not expect that all the time-keeping systems of their culture will become preachers of Christ, symbols of the resurrection. But they will experience the relativization of our various systems of time keeping. They will become more humbly aware that none of these systems, not even the dominant western one, is *God* or *God's own time,* but that each system belongs to particular life upon God's beloved earth within God's universe of many times. They will be able to stand beside the many peoples hurt by time. They will have a place from which to engage in an ongoing sociocul-

---

23. "In Memory of W. B. Yeats," in *Selected Poetry of W. H. Auden* (New York: Random House, 1958), 54. Reprinted with permission.

tural dialogue about the uses and abuses of time keeping for human life. And they will have a place where the distortions and tyrannies of time in their own lives may be healed.[24]

Only One Is Holy

This liturgical practice of holiness could be articulated in exactly these same terms in dialogue with many other "languages" of our cultures besides that of time. We have already considered meal keeping. We could also turn to the ways cultures mark *place*—their geographies—and the ways they pass on identity-determining *stories*, though each of these is also interwoven with the cultural practices of time keeping. In both cases, the Christian liturgy is not a full culture but a practice of holiness in dialogue with culture. The liturgy draws on geographies, ancient and modern, and yet it undercuts all geographies. The assembly turns toward the east and it also newly sings of galaxies in its hymnody. Yet Jesus Christ—and our Baptism into the assembly of his name—is our holy place, our temple, the place of our dreaming. This place in God is here, in the land. Its orientations train us to walk new paths in God's beloved earth and give us a place from which to engage in dialogue with all mapping systems. And the liturgy tells a great variety of stories, mostly biblical stories, still learning how to tell them with wider resonance in the many cultures where it dwells. Yet even while the assembly tells stories, it also undercuts the inevitability of narratives, the legalisms they reinforce, by its celebration of the reversals of trinitarian faith: Jesus Christ is always with the outsider or the unspoken ones of our narratives. The practice of the assembly can be a pedagogical force for the recovery of healthy stories and a healthy interest in location. Yet it can also be one force for resistance to the wounding power of cultural narratives, the untruth of boundaries, the massive distortion present when land is regarded only as economic resource.

But the practice of the assembly—the strong use of symbols yet the breaking of symbols; the focussed center yet the open door—does not exist, in the first place, in order to be in dialogue with cultures. It exists in order to tell the truth about God. And the practices of holiness, the acts whereby the assembly bears witness to the truth of God, are like beggars' hands out for mercy, naked bodies presented for the cloak, for only One is holy. But holiness itself, God's holiness as it is known in Jesus Christ, is not purity and arrogant distance but unity with all the needy world. The Christian faith trusts

24. On the liturgy as healing to the distortions of time, see Marianne Sawicki, "How Can Christian Worship Be Contemporary?" 29–30.

that the very signs at the heart of the assembly, the signs of word and meal and bath as these have been transformed in Christ, are gifts of God which communicate that holiness as an alternative vision of the world, a symbolic reorientation in all that is concretely real. The "word" that is proclaimed by these signs, the very Word and voice of God—the presence of the holiness of God[25]—places the "unconstraining voice" in the midst of all cultures, calling these patterns whereby we live our lives to a constant reorientation.

The mission of the church, then, is not to supplant cultures, not to "lord it over" cultures, not to create its own culture. The mission is rather to be the holy assembly in each place, the focussed, open assembly in communion with all the other assemblies, and to set out the life-giving Word in the midst of each culture, in loving and critical dialogue with that culture, with our culture. The religions of the world will not be our "enemies," not any more than any other of the cultural systems of the world. Indeed, the self-critical movements in religion, the movements that use yet call into question their own symbolizations—Zen Buddhism, for example, or the devotions of Saivite Bhakti Hinduism—may even be regarded as our near neighbors. But our business, as their neighbors, will still be to set out the holy things in an assembly of needy beggars.

So come into the assembly. Hear the word of forgiveness that reconciles you to God's purposes with this gathering of people. Help renew the strength of the meeting, participating anew in the power of its symbols. Help make the connection with other Christians in other places. Welcome to the way of Baptism those who wish to join us. Help open the door. And see how, in the heart of the meeting, a mantle is wrapped around all of naked humanity and the jaws of death are opened. With the Crucified Risen One pulling you out, sing along:

> I will declare your name to the community;
> in the midst of the congregation I will praise you. . . .
> My praise is of God in the great assembly; . . .
> The poor shall eat and be satisfied,
> and those who seek the LORD shall give praise:
> "May your heart live forever!"
> All the ends of the earth shall remember and turn to God (Ps. 22:22, 25-27).

---

25. "This is the principal item, and the holiest of holy possessions [das hohe heubtheiligthum], by reason of which the Christian people are called holy; for God's word is holy and sanctifies everything it touches; it is indeed the very holiness of God." Martin Luther, "On the Councils and the Church," LW 41:149; WA 50:629.

Appendix 1
The Ditchingham Report

Excerpts from Part I, "Biblical and Theological Foundations," of "Towards Koinonia in Worship: Report of the Consultation" held in Ditchingham, England, August 1994, and published in Thomas F. Best and Dagmar Heller, *So We Believe, So We Pray: Towards Koinonia in Worship*, Faith and Order Paper 171 (Geneva: World Council of Churches, 1995), 5–8.

1. ... Blessed be God's great love which has already given us the holy koinonia for which we pray through the one baptism into Christ Jesus, which continually founds and forms all the churches. Beyond our expectation, God has given us that koinonia as we all, together, being "buried with Christ by baptism into death," are raised with him day after day "by the glory of the Father, so we too might walk in newness of life" (Rom. 6:4). That koinonia has been given us in the common life of the believing community, which is empowered with many gifts by the Holy Spirit, which eats and drinks the "holy communion" of Christ, and which shows forth a foretaste of the communion of the whole creation with God, a foretaste of all peoples reconciled to God and to each other through the cross and resurrection of Jesus Christ. The gift we have received is our calling and task. The koinonia we seek between and within the churches is a koinonia in and through Jesus Christ. It is a participation in the grace and eternal life of God for the sake of the life and salvation of the world. "God is faithful, by whom you were called into the fellowship of his Son, Jesus Christ our Lord" (1 Cor. 1:9).

2. This crucified and risen Christ, the ground and source and center of our koinonia, is alive today in our midst. Koinonia is found in the scriptures

opened to speak of him to our burning hearts (Luke 24:13-32), in the broken bread and cup of blessing which are a participation in the body and blood of Christ (1 Corinthians 10:16), and in the one Spirit in which "we were all baptized into one body" of Christ (1 Corinthians 12:13). Word and sacraments, signs of the presence of Christ, are set forth in the midst of a participating assembly of people who are gathered by the Spirit, blessed with many different gifts, and sent to bear witness with their lives to the same love and mercy of God for all the world which has been shown forth in their assembly.

3. Through the coming of the Spirit, Christian worship is thus a continual meeting with Christ, so that we might be gathered into the grace and life of God. Many different Christian traditions enrich us as we think of the meaning of this encounter: It is a speaking of the gospel of Christ so that we might come to faith. It is grace flowing from the sacrifice of Christ. It is the beginning of the transfiguration of all things in the Spirit of Christ. It is a gift and call for personal holiness according to the measure of Christ. It is the visible manifestation of the incarnation of Christ so that we might be formed in incarnational living amid the "sacrament of the world." It is beholding Christ in the gathering so that we might be able to behold him and love him among the marginalized, outcast and disfigured ones of the world. It is participation in the Spirit-led meeting as "baptism" and in every shared meal as the "Lord's Supper." It is praise and thanksgiving to the Father through Christ in the unity of the Spirit. But all these understandings depend upon Christian worship being centered in the encounter with God in Jesus Christ through the power of the Spirit enlivening the word and the sacraments. And all these understandings presuppose that this encounter occurs in an assembly which is itself a witness to God's intention with the world and which forms its participants for a life of witness and service. The liturgy of Christians occurs in assembly: it also occurs in the midst of daily life in the world.

4. The pattern of this gathering and sending has come to all the churches as a common and shared inheritance. That received pattern resides in the basic outlines of what may be called the *ordo* of Christian worship, i.e., the undergirding structure which is to be perceived in the ordering and scheduling of the most primary elements of Christian worship. This *ordo*, which is always marked by pairing and by mutually re-interpretive juxtapositions, roots in word and sacrament held together. It is scripture readings and preaching together, yielding intercessions; and, with these, it is *eucharistia* and eating and drinking together, yielding a collection for the poor and

mission in the world. It is formation in faith and baptizing in water together, leading to participation in the life of the community. It is ministers and people, enacting these things, together. It is prayers through the days of the week and the Sunday assembly seen together; it is observances through the year and the annual common celebration of the *Pascha* together. Such is the inheritance of all the churches, founded in the New Testament, locally practiced today, and attested to in the ancient sources of both the Christian East and the Christian West.

5. This pattern of Christian worship, however, is to be spoken of as a gift of God, not as a demand nor as a tool for power over others. Liturgy is deeply malformed, even destroyed, when it occurs by compulsion—either by civil law, by the decisions of governments to impose ritual practice on all people, or by the forceful manipulation of ritual leaders who show little love for the people they are called to serve. At the heart of the worship of Christians stands the crucified Christ, who is one with the little and abused ones of the world. Liturgy done in his name cannot abuse. It must be renewed, rather, by love and invitation and the teaching of its sources and meaning. "And I, when I am lifted up from the earth, will draw all people to myself," says Jesus (John 12:32). The liturgy must *draw* with Christ, not compel.

6. Furthermore, this pattern is to be celebrated as a most profound connection between faith and life, between gospel and creation, between Christ and culture, not as an act of unconnected ritualism nor anxious legalism. Every culture has some form of significant communal assembly, the use of water, speech which is accessible but strongly symbolic, and festive meals. These universal gifts of life, found in every place, have been received as the materials of Christian worship from the beginning. Because of this, we are invited to understand the Christian assembly for worship as a foretaste of the reconciliation of all creation and as a new way to see all the world.

7. But the patterns of word and table, of catechetical formation and baptism, of Sunday and the week, of *Pascha* and the year, and of assembly and ministry around these things—the principal pairs of Christian liturgy—do give us a basis for a mutually encouraging conversation between the churches. Churches may rightly ask each other about the local inculturation of this *ordo*. They may call each other toward a maturation in the use of this pattern or a renewed clarification of its central characteristics or, even, toward a conversion to its use. Stated in their simplest form, these things are the "rule of prayer" in the churches, and we need them for our own faith and life and for a clear witness to Christ in the world. And we need each

other to learn anew of the richness of these things. Churches may learn from each other as they seek for local renewal. One community has treasured preaching, another singing, another silence in the word, another sacramental formation, another the presence of Christ in the transfigured human person and in the witnesses of the faith who surround the assembly, another worship as solidarity with the poor. As churches seek to recover the great pairs of the *ordo,* they will be helped by remembering together with other Christians the particular charisms with which each community has unfolded the patterns of Christian worship, and by a mutual encouragement for each church to explore the particular gifts which it brings to enrich our koinonia in worship.

8. This pattern or *ordo* of Christian worship belongs most properly to each local church, that is, to "all in each place." All the Christians in a given place, gathered in assembly around these great gifts of Christ, are the whole catholic church dwelling in this place. As efforts are made to enable local occasions of ecumenical prayer and as local churches are clarifying the full pattern of Christian worship as the center of their life, a groundwork is being laid for local unity. "Local churches truly united" will be one in faith and witness, and, amid a continuing diversity of expression, one in the practice of the most basic characteristics of the *ordo.* This same pattern or *ordo* of Christian worship is a major basis for the koinonia between local churches, a koinonia spanning both space and time, uniting churches of the New Testament times, of the sweep of Christian history and of the present *oikumene.* Such a koinonia is only enriched by those authentic forms of inculturation which the *ordo* may have taken in each local church, not diminished.

Appendix 2
The Nairobi Statement

E
xcerpts from the "Nairobi Statement on Worship and Culture: Contemporary Challenges and Opportunities," prepared by the third international consultation of the Lutheran World Federation's Study Team on Worship and Culture, held in Nairobi, Kenya, in January 1996, and published in S. Anita Stauffer, ed., *Christian Worship: Unity in Cultural Diversity* (Geneva: Lutheran World Federation, 1996), 23–28.

1. Introduction

1.1 Worship is the heart and pulse of the Christian Church. In worship we celebrate together God's gracious gifts of creation and salvation, and are strengthened to live in response to God's grace. Worship always involves actions, not merely words. To consider worship is to consider music, art, and architecture, as well as liturgy and preaching.

1.2 The reality that Christian worship is always celebrated in a given local cultural setting draws our attention to the dynamics between worship and the world's many local cultures.

1.3 Christian worship relates dynamically to culture in at least four ways. First, it is *transcultural*, the same substance for everyone everywhere, beyond culture. Second, it is *contextual*, varying according to the local situation (both nature and culture). Third, it is *counter-cultural*, challenging what is contrary to the Gospel in a given culture. Fourth, it is *cross-cultural*, making possible sharing between different local cultures. In all four dynamics, there are helpful principles which can be identified.

2. Worship as Transcultural

2.1 The resurrected Christ whom we worship, and through whom by the power of the Holy Spirit we know the grace of the Triune God, transcends and indeed is beyond all cultures. In the mystery of his resurrection is the source of the transcultural nature of Christian worship. Baptism and Eucharist, the sacraments of Christ's death and resurrection, were given by God for all the world. There is one Bible, translated into many tongues, and biblical preaching of Christ's death and resurrection has been sent into all the world. The fundamental shape of the principal Sunday act of Christian worship, the Eucharist or Holy Communion, is shared across cultures: the people gather, the Word of God is proclaimed, the people intercede for the needs of the Church and the world, the eucharistic meal is shared, and the people are sent out into the world for mission. The great narratives of Christ's birth, death, resurrection, and sending of the Spirit, and our Baptism into him, provide the central meanings of the transcultural times of the church's year: especially Lent/Easter/Pentecost, and, to a lesser extent, Advent/Christmas/Epiphany. The ways in which the shapes of the Sunday Eucharist and the church year are expressed vary by culture, but their meanings and fundamental structure are shared around the globe. There is one Lord, one faith, one Baptism, one Eucharist.

2.2 Several specific elements of Christian liturgy are also transcultural, e.g., readings from the bible (although of course the translations vary), the ecumenical creeds and the Our Father, and Baptism in water in the Triune Name.

2.3 The use of this shared core liturgical structure and these shared liturgical elements in local congregational worship—as well as the shared act of people assembling together, and the shared provision of diverse leadership in that assembly (although the space for the assembly and the manner of the leadership vary)—are expressions of Christian unity across time, space, culture, and confession. The recovery in each congregation of the clear centrality of these transcultural and ecumenical elements renews the sense of this Christian unity and gives all churches a solid basis for authentic contextualization.

3. Worship as Contextual

3.1 Jesus whom we worship was born into a specific culture of the world. In the mystery of his incarnation are the model and mandate for the contextualization of Christian worship. God can be and is encountered in the local cultures of our world. A given culture's values and patterns, insofar as they are consonant with the values of the Gospel, can be used to express the meaning and purpose of Christian worship. Contextualization is a necessary task for the Church's mission in the world, so that the Gospel can be ever more deeply rooted in diverse local cultures.

3.2 Among the various methods of contextualization, that of dynamic equivalence is particularly useful. It involves re-expressing components of Christian worship with something from a local culture that has an equal meaning, value, and function. Dynamic equivalence goes far beyond mere translation; it involves understanding the fundamental meanings both of elements of worship and of the local culture, and enabling the meanings and actions of worship to be "encoded" and re-expressed in the language of local culture. . . .

3.4 Local churches might also consider the method of creative assimilation. This consists of adding pertinent components of local culture to the liturgical *ordo* in order to enrich its original core. The baptismal *ordo* of "washing with water and the Word," for example, was gradually elaborated by the assimilation of such cultural practices as the giving of white vestments and lighted candles to the neophytes of ancient mystery religions. Unlike dynamic equivalence, creative assimilation enriches the liturgical *ordo*—not by culturally re-expressing its elements, but by adding to it new elements from local culture.

3.5 In contextualization the fundamental values and meanings of both Christianity and of local cultures must be respected. . . .

4. Worship as Counter-cultural

4.1 Jesus Christ came to transform all people and all cultures, and calls us not to conform to the world, but to be transformed with it (Rom. 12:2). In the mystery of his passage from death to eternal life is the model for transformation, and thus for the counter-cultural nature of Christian worship. Some components of every culture in the world are sinful, dehumanizing, and contradictory to the values of the Gospel. From the perspective of the Gospel, they need critique and transformation. Contextualization of Christian faith and worship necessarily involves challenging all types of oppression and social injustice wherever they exist in earthly cultures.

4.2 It also involves the transformation of cultural patterns which idolize the self or the local group at the expense of a wider humanity, or which give central place to the acquisition of wealth at the expense of the care of the earth and its poor. The tools of the counter-cultural in Christian worship may also include the deliberate maintenance or recovery of patterns of action which differ intentionally from prevailing cultural models. These patterns may arise from a recovered sense of Christian history, or from the wisdom of other cultures.

5. Worship as Cross-cultural

5.1 Jesus came to be the Savior of all people. He welcomes the treasures of earthly cultures into the city of God. By virtue of Baptism, there is one Church; and one means of living in faithful response to Baptism is to manifest ever more deeply the unity of the Church. The sharing of hymns and art and other elements of worship across cultural barriers helps enrich the whole Church and strengthen the sense of the *communio* of the Church. This sharing can be ecumenical as well as cross-cultural, as a witness to the unity of the Church and the oneness of Baptism. Cross-cultural sharing is possible for every church, but is especially needed in multicultural congregations . . .

5.2 Care should be taken that the music, art, architecture, gestures and postures, and other elements of different cultures are understood and respected when they are used by churches elsewhere in the world. The criteria for contextualization should be observed.

6. Challenge to the Churches

6.1 . . . We call on all member churches to recover the centrality of Baptism, Scripture with preaching, and the every-Sunday celebration of the Lord's Supper—the principal transcultural elements of Christian worship and the signs of Christian unity—as the strong center of all congregational life and mission, and as the authentic basis for contextualization. We call on all churches to give serious attention to exploring the local or contextual elements of liturgy, language, posture and gesture, hymnody and other music and musical instruments, and art and architecture for Christian worship—so that their worship may be more truly rooted in the local culture.

Indexes

Biblical Texts

237

Classical Texts and Sources

Modern Authors

Subjects